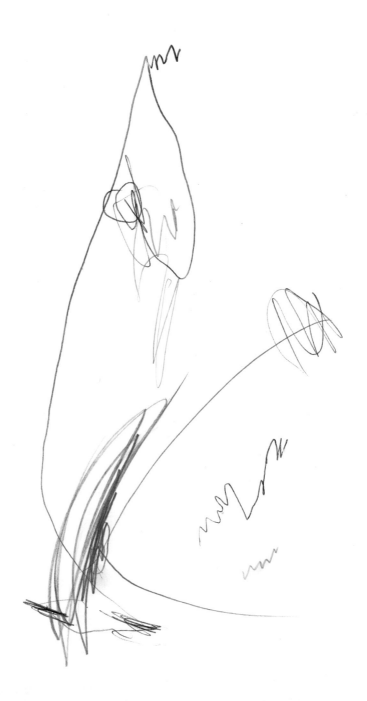

Systems Design in a Database Environment

Dr. Kenneth S. Brathwaite
AKI Group, Inc.

Intertext Publications
McGraw-Hill Book Company

New York St. Louis San Francisco Auckland Bogotá
Hamburg London Madrid Mexico Milan Montreal
New Delhi Panama Paris São Paulo
Singapore Sidney Tokyo Toronto

Library of Congress Catalog Card Number 89-83767

10 9 8 7 6 5 4 3 2 1

ISBN 0-07-007250-7

Intertext Publications/Multiscience Press, Inc.
One Lincoln Plaza
New York, NY 10023

McGraw-Hill Book Company
1221 Avenue of the Americas
New York, NY 10020

Composed in Ventura Publisher by Context, Inc.

To my dear wife, March,
whose love and encouragement
were a constant source of
strength throughout the writing
of this volume.

Contents

Preface

The work reported in this book is the result of research conducted in systems design in the database environment since 1979 and active participation in designing systems for several large corporations since 1984.

The main objective of the book is to provide readers with definitive information on topics that are crucial to the understanding of what is required to develop a system from its conceptual stage through analysis, design, testing, implementation, and performance monitoring. In this volume, I provide readers with information on traditional topics such as data analysis, user requirement analysis and user survey development, design methodologies, logical database design, and development of security controls.

It addresses topics of interest to data administrators, database administrators, systems programmers, systems analysts, application programmers, information processing managers, data processing managers, and database users. The book can be used effectively by practitioners in business as well as in government, and also for an introductory course in a business or technical school. The readers need no preparation beyond the application programmer's level, but would benefit more if some experience were obtained in database environments, VSAM and IMS in particular.

As the title suggests, the volume provides information on topics that are interrelated and interdependent. Thus the chapter on data analysis techniques includes information on data analysis, logical database design, physical database design, and development of controls. This chapter is meant to be a synopsis of the whole book with each subsequent chapter giving increasingly more detailed coverage of the various phases of systems design.

Chapter 1 introduces various data analysis techniques and shows how these techniques are used in the development of database systems. Chapter 2 discusses the place of user requirements in system design and outlines the survey method of collecting and analyzing the user requirements. Chapter 3 outlines a database design methodology that was developed, tested, and implemented by a major public utility.

Chapter 4, on data models and entity-relationship diagrams, discusses the role these play in database design and shows how they are integral parts of data analysis and are the major input to the physical design phase. Chapter 5, on the normalization process, discusses normalization in a mathematically rigorous way and may be omitted by most readers. Chapter 6 discusses logical and physical database design. It is during these phases that the user requirements are first developed into physical models and stored in database files. The chapter on design of specific systems and databases shows how one can apply the techniques of database design developed in previous chapters to database management systems (DBMS) such as IMS and DB2.

Chapters 8, 9, 10, and 11 of the volume discuss topics that, although not part of the design process, very often determine the success or failure of database design. Chapter 8 discusses the role of data dictionaries in system design. Chapter 9 discusses the use of CASE tools as an aid to systems design. Chapter 10 is on data security in a database environment. Chapter 11 indicates how security controls can be built into database systems.

The case studies discussed in Part Two are illustrated for the express purpose of strengthening the discussion on user requirement analysis and the selection of CASE tools.

Finally, as with any large undertaking, errors may remain in this volume. I have worked diligently to maintain the accuracy of this work. However, if errors remain, I solicit your assistance in bringing them to my attention. I, in turn, will do my utmost to ensure that they are corrected.

ACKNOWLEDGMENTS

I am grateful for the comments and suggestions I received from Vic Howard, Stanley Locbe, Francis Chin, and Jay Louise Weldon. The initial draft of this manuscript was ably typed by Jane Cuffy and Andrea Drayton. Their efforts are appreciated.

Ken S. Brathwaite
Plainfield, New Jersey
January, 1989

Database Design

1

Data Analysis Techniques

1.1 INTRODUCTORY REMARKS

This chapter discusses a structured method of conducting the data analysis phase of database design: data analysis development life cycle. It is during this phase that formulations of the user requirements are developed.

The user requirements form the basis of the system design. Therefore, the success or failure in obtaining adequate information about the user requirements determines the success or failure of the entire system.

The structured methodology discussed in this chapter begins by defining data as a corporate resource which must be planned for like any other corporate resource. It details how the users' needs for processing that data are collected, analyzed, and formulated into data models, showing the relationship among the various entities or collections of data elements.

The Chapter concludes by discussing the normalization of these data models and the translation of these models into physical databases.

1.2 DEFINITIONS OF SOME DATA ANALYSIS TERMS

Some of the terms used in data analysis are transplanted from the old approaches of system analysis. Other terms, like attribute, entity, and relationship, are new and resulted from efforts to adopt structured methods of designing systems with the data as the driving force rather than the processing of that data. The following table gives some definitions of these new terms.

Table 1.1   Definitions and Terminologies

ITEM	DEFINITION
DATA ITEM	The smallest unit of named data. A data item is often referred to as a field or data element.
DATA	The values taken by various data items are called data. For example, the value of the data element, Customer Name, is data.
INFORMATION	Data that is processed, accessed, and assimilated or used in the decision-making process. Information results from the analysis and synthesis of data.
ENTITY (OR ENTITY CLASS OR ENTITY TYPE)	A fundamental thing of interest to an organization. An entity may be a person, place, thing, concept, or event, that is real or abstract; it should have a unique identifier.
ATTRIBUTE	A descriptive value of property associated with an individual entity.
RELATIONSHIP	An association between two or more entities.
ENTITY MODEL (SNAPSHOT)	A diagrammatical representation of the relationships between the entity classes. The representation allows us to include only those entities that are required to solve the user's data processing problem. It depends on the relationships you are concerned with.
LOGICAL SCHEMA (EXTERNAL STRUCTURE/SCHEMA)	The mapping of the entity model into the constructs or constraints of the database management system (DBMS). In general, the logical schema indicates how the model will be stored and accessed.
DATA ANALYSIS	The determination of the fundamental data resources of an organization. It deals with the collection of the basic entities and the relationships between those entities.

1.3 DATA AS A RESOURCE

Data must be seen as a resource in much the same way as employees, products, natural resources, finances, and other material products or resources. As a resource, it must be recognized to have cost and value. In order to exploit the data resource, it must be understood, conserved, employed, and integrated. It is necessary to learn about its nature and characteristics, how it is used, what it is used for, where it resides, and where it comes from.

Information Resource Management (IRM) deals with planning for, allocating, maintaining and conserving, prudently exploiting, effectively employing, and integrating the data resource. To manage this resource effectively, it is necessary to obtain as much data about it as possible. This data about the data is often referred to as "metadeta." There must be stringent procedures for collecting, maintaining, and using the resource.

1.4 MANAGEMENT CONTROL OF THE DATA RESOURCE

Management control of data includes the following:

- Common procedures for access to the data
- Establishing lines of authority and responsibility for the data
- Common procedures for collecting, updating, and maintaining the data
- Common formats and procedures for data definition
- Identifying entities that are important to the enterprise
- Evaluating, mediating, and reconciling the conflicting needs and prerogatives of functional departments
- Ensuring the auditability of the data and all transactions against the data
- Controlling the data in order to measure and evaluate the corporation and predict its reaction to changes in its environment and in its own internal organization

1.5 DATA OWNERSHIP PHILOSOPHIES

The introduction of the database era not only meant a change in traditional data processing, but also in traditional definitions of "data ownership." In traditional data processing, total control over creation, maintenance, and processing of data meant ownership of that data. In a database environment, however, data sharing and data integration have lessened total control and now imply loss of ownership.

In data analysis, the establishing of data owners is important to

• Control access to the data
• Allow data sharing
• Establish relationships and interfaces between entities
• Establish common definitions for data
• Resolve discrepancies and conflicts over standards and conventions

1.6 DIFFERENT VIEWS OF DATA

Data about an enterprise is not singularly determined. Different people perceive and describe an enterprise differently, and hence have different starting points concerning what is to be modeled.

It's not merely a matter of scope, of including more or less in the view. People looking at the same thing see it differently. For example:

• The secretary of a department may be, in someone else's view, the secretary of the manager of the department.
• A manufacturing operation might be performed by a certain department, or we might rather view it as performed by a person assigned to that department.
• A social security number is generally considered to identify a person, but it really identifies an account which belongs to that person.

1.7 DATA ANALYSIS

The primary purpose of data analysis is to determine the fundamental nature of an organization's data resources and to organize and document all relevant facts concerning this data. Data analysis has been used to

• Determine the fundamental data resources of an organization
• Provide a disciplined approach toward cataloging existing data in terms of the entities and relationships it represents
• Prove an effective means of communicating with non-data processing users as it deals only with things that the users are familiar with and not with such objects as files and records

- Analyze the inherent structure of that data independently from the details of the applications
- Form a basis for data control, security, and auditing systems
- Organize all relevant facts concerning the organization's data
- Produce a point of reference (the Entity Model) against which a logical database structure for each of the database management systems can be designed
- Prove a sound basis for database design

The components of data analysis are:

1. Entity analysis — which provides a means of understanding and documenting a complex environment in terms of its entities and their attributes and relationships.
2. Functional analysis — which is concerned with understanding and documenting the basic business activities of the organization. (See Figure 1.1.)

In Figure 1.1, the two components of data analysis are clearly illustrated. These two components, although interrelated, are traditionally done independently of each other and very often by independent project teams.

The vertical arrows indicate that the deliverable, or output, of entity analysis is an entity model, which is a real-world view of the data relationships. The model is then mapped into a logical database by superimposing the constructs of a particular database management system (DBMS). From this logical database we get a physical database by adding the accessing and storage requirements of the DBMS. The boxes on the right-hand side and at similar levels to those on the left indicate that functional analysis has similar outputs to those of entity analysis at each stage. The horizontal arrows indicate that the left-hand boxes are the data inputs to the right-hand boxes.

The second figure (Figure 1.2) illustrates data analysis activities similar to the first. Here, logical design includes entity modeling and design of logical databases, while physical design includes design of stored database and schema, as shown in Figure 1.1.

In Figure 1.2, requirements analysis includes

- Establishment of organizational objectives
- Derivation of specific database requirements from those objectives or directly from management personnel

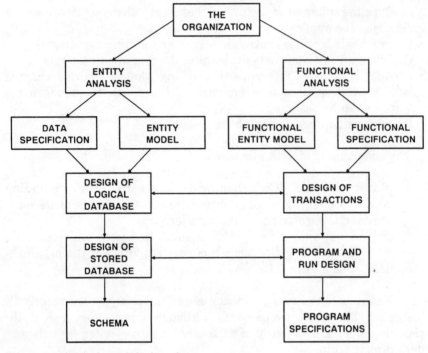

Figure 1.1 Analysis and design phases or steps.

• Documentation of those requirements in a form that is agreeable to management and database designers

The data collected during the requirements analysis step falls into the following categories:

• Personal interviews with various levels of management and key employees involved in the processing of goods, services, and data in the organization
• Diagramming of the flow process with which each employee is involved
• Identifying the data elements associated with that process and the interfaces between processes
• Verifying that both interviewer and employee agree on the flow model-sign off phase

User views are the direct results of formulating the user requirements. They represent both the data requirements and the processing against the data as indicated by the users.

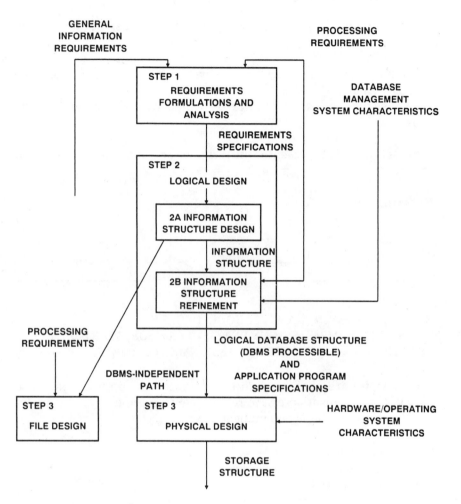

Figure 1.2 Basic database design steps.

User view modeling is defined as the modeling of the usage and information structure perspectives of the real world from the point of view of different users and/or applications. View modeling involves at least the following two components:

- Extracting from the users, or from persons in charge of application development, the relevant parts of real-world information
- Abstracting this information into a form which completely represents the user view so that it can be subsequently used in database design

There are two aspects of user views which must be modeled in order to adequately represent them. These are

• The information structure perspective or non-process oriented view (Entity Analysis)
• The usage perspective or process-oriented view (Functional Analysis)

A user view is represented in terms of entities, associations, and attributes in a view diagram.

Examples of User Views

EMPLOYEE = (EMP#, NAME, SCHOOL, DEGREE)
WORKS ON = (EMP#, ASSIGNMENT#, SUPERVISOR, START-DATE)
ASSIGNMENT = (ASSIGNMENT#, ASSIGNMENT-NAME)

User views are often merged or integrated to obtain a composite view of the organization or the requirements specified by data analysis. View integration is accomplished by:

• Merging of simple associations
• Merging of identifier associations
• Merging of entities

1.7.1 Analysis Using Different Models

Data analysis is essentially the process of producing a mental framework which will allow the viewer to describe his view of the organization's view of data. Different people will produce different mental frameworks. There are several mental frameworks, including

• Data-structure diagrams (See Figure 1.3, A-D)
• Entity-Relationship (E-R) model

Analysis using data-structure diagrams involves record types and data structure sets, which are relationships between record types. In

Figure 1.3A, there are two types of conceptual records, COMPANY and PERSON, and a data-structure set representing the fact that each person is associated with exactly one company and that each company has a set of personnel.

Analysis may indicate that the personnel of the Company are persons in their own right. It may be discovered at the merger of several companies that some of the personnel held two jobs and were personnel to two of the merged companies (Figure 1.3B). Basically, the old personnel-type record has been split into two record types, PERSONNEL and PERSON.

Further analysis may indicate that the address of residence should not be in the person's record. This requires the creation of a PLACE conceptual record type and a new data-structure-set type (Figure 1.3C). It must be assumed that each person has a unique address.

It is then recognized that people move from place to place and that it is desirable to know current address as well as past addresses. Another reason may be: it is discovered that a person may have more than one address. In either case, a new conceptual record type ADDRESS is added to the structure (Figure 1.3D).

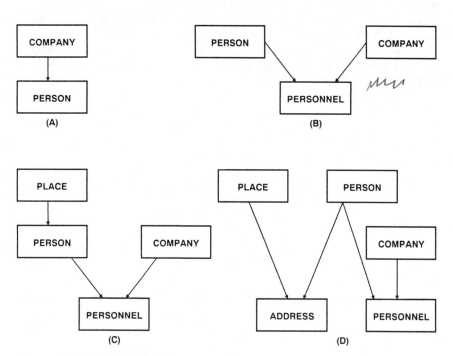

Figure 1.3 Analysis using data structures.

We will demonstrate analysis using Entity-Relationship diagrams by using the same example that demonstrated analysis using data-structures. (See Figure 1.4.)

The E-R diagram (Figure 1.4A) corresponds to the data-structure diagram in Figure 1.3A. There are two types of entities, PERSON and COMPANY, in the user view. The data-structure set is replaced by the relationship set WORKS FOR.

Analysis shows that a new entity, PLACE, should be introduced into the schema. Since many persons can have the same address, a new entity is introduced called ADDRESS. The final E-R diagram is detailed in Figure 1.4B.

In general, the E-R diagram is easier to use to analyze the changes in the user view than data-structure diagrams.

It should be noted that the relationship WORKS FOR can be materialized into an entity called PERSONNEL. Similarly, the relationship LIVES AT can be materialized into an entity called ADDRESS.

1.8 FUNCTIONAL ANALYSIS

Functional analysis is concerned with an understanding and documentation of the basic business activities with which the organization is concerned. Functional analysis has the following objectives:
- To determine how entities are used so as to increase understanding of the entity model

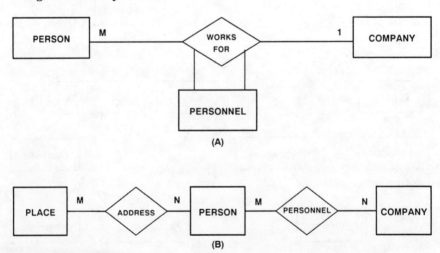

Figure 1.4 Analysis using entity–relationship diagram.

- To provide a firm basis for transaction design
- To gather estimates of data usage for database design

Functional analysis may reveal that entities have attribute types which had not been detected during entity analysis. Similarly, relationships between entities which had not been considered meaningful may be found to be required by certain functions. The basic functions identified in functional analysis would be expected to be translated into transaction types in the data processing system. Estimates of data usage will provide a means of determining which access paths should be made most efficient.

Functional analysis can be divided into the following phases:

- Preliminary
- Framework Development
- Access Path Analysis

In function analysis, the application area which is to be analyzed must be defined. The application area may coincide with the data area examined in data analysis, or it may cross several data areas. Here, data area may be defined as the data utilized in areas determined by the organization structure, e.g., Accounting, Personnel, Manufacturing, Marketing, and Purchasing.

In the process of developing a framework, the analyst identifies the events and functions. Typically, there is a hierarchy of functions, but the basic activities at the foot of the hierarchy are initiated by events recurring in the organization. An event may be defined as a stimulus to the organization and functions may be defined as tasks that must be carried out as a direct result of the event. For example, an order is placed is an event, whereas record the order or produce the invoice are functions.

1.8.1 Functional Analysis Example

One of the functions identified as being carried out in the order processing area is order entry. An order is received from a delivery point. The depot that will make the delivery is selected depending on whether the goods are bulk or packaged. The order is recorded and related to the delivery point and the depot. The goods specified in each order line are validated and the stocks of the goods on hand are amended. Where stocks are insufficient to meet the quantities in one or more lines on the order, a back order is created.

The order lines are recorded and linked to the goods and to the order, or back order as appropriate. The functional entity model resulting from the above description is shown in Figure 1.5.

1.9 DATA ANALYSIS DOCUMENTATION

An essential outcome of data analysis is the documentation for entity types, relationship types, attribute types, functions, and events.

This documentation is in addition to the entity model and functional entity model. Where the volumes and complexity are low, a clerical system has been found to be adequate; but in the longer term and in a dynamic environment, the use of a good data dictionary is advisable.

1.9.1 Data Analysis Documentation Examples

An example of a data dictionary which makes the distribution between the constructs of the entity model and those of the logical database and between the functions of the organization and the transaction which handle them will be discussed in another section.

Examples of the types of forms that could be employed for a clerical system of documentation for data analysis are shown in Figures 1.6-1.10. The forms are used to document an entity, an attribute, and a relationship.

For functional analysis, the access path is documented. In addition, while no information concerning attributes is included in the functional entity model, the grouping of attributes as needed by different functions is normally shown in an attribute usage matrix, where for each entity the attributes are matched against the functions which retrieve, modify, store, or delete their values.

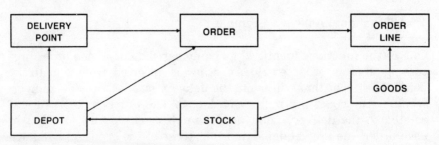

Figure 1.5 Functional entity model for order entry.

Similarly, the entity usage matrix summarizes overall functions the way a particular entity is accessed, whether by value of a particular attribute or by means of relationships.

1.10 THE ENTITY MODEL

The major output of the data analysis phase of database design is the entity model. The entity model is a diagrammatical representation of the relationships between the entities. The representation allows us to include only those entities that are required to solve the particular data processing problem.

The entity model is essentially a real-world view of the data in terms of entities, attributes, and relationships. The model is used by the data analysis team to:

• Reduce redundancy in the relationships

DATA ANALYSIS DOCUMENTATION			ANALYST:	K. Brathwaite
ENTITY TYPE			DATE:	22.11.86
NAME: Order			VERSION:	1
			STATUS:	Preliminary
SYNONYMS:				(final)
DEFINITION: Request for delivery of a stated number of different goods				
IDENTIFIERS Order Number				
OCCURRENCES:				
MINIMUM AVERAGE 240,000 PER YEAR MAXIMUM				
SPECIAL VARIATIONS: GROWTH: 10% per year				
AUTHORIZED TO				
CREATE: Order Processing Department	DELETE: Order Processing Department		COUNT: Marketing Research	
CONFIDENTIALITY: Types 3	SECURITY:			
ENTITY SUBTYPES:	IDENTIFIERS:			
Filled Order	F			
Back Order	B			
DEFAULT FOR ATTRIBUTE DETAILS: AVAILABILITY TIMELINESS STORAGE				

Figure 1.6 Data analysis documentation: entity type.

DATA ANALYSIS DOCUMENTATION	ANALYST: K. Brathwaite
ATTRIBUTE TYPE	DATE: 22.11.86
NAME: Credit Limit	VERSION: 1
SYNONYMS:	STATUS: Preliminary

DEFINITION: If the customer's balance exceeds this value no further orders will be accepted unless paid in advance.
ENTITY DESCRIBED: Customer

AUTHORIZED TO
CREATE: Accounts Receivable   MODIFY: Finance   RETRIEVE: Salesman
PERMITTED VALUES: $10,000 to   MEANING:
FORMAT: 5 numeric digits   RANGE: $25,000
CONSISTENCY: Only for customers with over 3   AVAILABILITY On-line
previous orders

Figure 1.7 Data analysis documentation: attribute type.

DATA ANALYSIS DOCUMENTATION	ANALYST: K. Brathwaite
RELATIONSHIP TYPE	DATE: 22.11.86
NAME: Places	VERSION: 1
SYNONYMS:	STATUS: Preliminary

DEFINITION: The customer has indicated by phone or by mail that he wishes to buy a product
RELATED TO
ENTITY: Order   ENTITY: Delivery Point

AUTHORIZED TO
CONNECT: Order Processing   DISCONNECT: Order Processing
Department   Department
CONFIDENTIALITY: Type 3
CONSISTENCY: AVAILABILITY
On-line

Figure 1.8 Data analysis documentation: relationship type.

FUNCTIONAL ANALYSIS DOCUMENTATION						
ACCESS PATH						
FUNCTION Order NAME: Entry		RESPONSE 5 sec REQUIRED 10 sec			ANALYST: KSB DATE: 22.11.86	
FREQUENCY ASSUMPTIONS: Per Day Avg: 4000 Max: 400 Growth: 10% per year						
ENTITY (E) RELATIONSHIP (R) ACCESSED	E/R	SELECTION CRITERIA		ACTION	VOLUME	
					AVG	MAX
Delivery Point	E	Delivery Point Name		R	1	1
Bulk/Package	R	Bulk/Packaged		R	1	1
Depot	E	Via Relationship		R	1	1
Order	E			S	1	1
Order/Delivery Point	R	Order No. Delivery Point Name		Con	1	1
Order/Depot	R	Order No. Depot Name		Con	1	1
Goods	E	Goods Code		R	10	30
Goods/Stock	R	Goods Code		R	10	30
Depot/Stock	R	Depot Name		R	10	30
Stock	E	Depot/Goods		M	9.5	28.5
Back Order	E	Back Order No.		S	0.5	1.5
Order/Delivery Point	R	Back Order No. Delivery Pt. Name		Con	0.5	1.5
Order/Depot	E	Back Order No. Depot Name		Con	0.5	1.5
Order Line	E	Order No. Goods Name		S	10	30

ACTION (ENTITY) RETRIEVE, MODIFY, STORE, DELETE ACTION (RELATIONSHIP)
RETRIEVE, CREATE, CONNECT, DISCONNECT

Figure 1.9 Data analysis documentation: access path.

• Determine which entities are significant to the model and the requirement of the problem

Once the entity model is produced, the analysis team sets about the task of making revisions to the model. This is done in order to:

• Produce the optimum model
• Normalize the entities
• Synthesize the relationships

The entity model can be produced using either a bottom-up or top-down approach. The bottom-up approach produces a composite or

FUNCTIONAL ANALYSIS DOCUMENTATION								
SUMMARY OF ACCESS TO AN ENTITY TYPE								
ENTIY NAME: Goods TIME PERIOD: Per Day ANALYST: KSB DATE: 22.11.86								
DIRECT ACCESS		FREQUENCY OF ACCESS						
ATTRIBUTES	SELECTION CRITERIA	RETRIEVE		STORE		DELETE		
		AVG	MAX	AVG	MAX	AVG	MAX	
DESCRIPTION	GOODS CODE	8×10^4	10^5	50	100			
UNIT OF ISSUE	GOODS CODE			10	15			
COST PRICE	GOODS CODE	260	300	50	80			
SALES PRICES	GOODS CODE	8×10^4	10^5	50	100			
VIA RELATIONSHIP	ACTION PERFORMED							
RELATIONSHIP	SELECTION CRITERIA	RETRIEVE		TRANSFER		CONNECT		
		AVG	MAX	AVG	MAX	AVG	MAX	
Stock/Goods	Goods delivered	4×10^4	5×10^4	20	30			
Order Line/Goods	Goods of			80	100			
Order Line/Goods	amended order							
	Goods of							
	cancelled order							

Figure 1.10 Data analysis documentation: summary of access.

global view of the organization's data based on the integration of several user views of the immediate problems requirements and not on the inherent structure of the data. The resulting model is limited to the immediate problem and cannot reflect the entire business activities of the corporation.

The top-down approach produces a global, corporate, or organizational view of the data first before the application views are identified. The entities and relationships that are of interest to the organization are identified from the business activities of the total organization and are independent of any particular application.

The bottom-up approach is the one most often used in data analysis. This approach produces a model with more clearly defined boundaries than the top-down approach. The processing requirements can be used by the data analysis team to precisely determine what entities are required and the composition of those entities. The clustering of attributes into their respective entities or the splitting of entities can be done with more precision. It is easier with this approach to determine whether an attribute is indeed an attribute of an existing entity or is itself an entity with relationships to other entities.

1.10.1 Translation of User View to an Entity Model

A significant difficulty in defining the relationships and representing them in the entity model is determining which relationships are directly significant and which are redundant. This can be done only with a detailed understanding of the environment, as there are no mathematical rules that can be applied but merely patterns in entity models which prompt further investigation.

To determine the existence of relationships, the following procedure can be employed:

- Take each attribute type and determine which entity type it describes, whether it could describe any other entity type, and whether these entity types are related.
- Take each entity type and pair it with another to determine if a meaningful question can be asked.
- Determine if the relationship is relevant.

No less difficult is the decision concerning each element, as to whether it should be treated as an attribute type or an entity type or as a second entity type related to the first. As a guideline, it has been found that an attribute of an entity-1 is best treated instead as entity-2 related to entity-1 if:

- The attribute itself is found to have further relevant attributes.
- The resulting entity-2 is itself of significance to the organization.
- The attribute in fact identifies entity-2.
- Entity-2 could be related to several occurrences of entity-1.
- Entity-2 is seen to be related to entity types other than entity-1.

Thus in Figure 1.11 customer location is seen not to be an attribute of customer, as a customer may have several locations and as each location has its own attributes, such as postal code.

During the translation of the user view to the entity model, the most significant entity types and relationship types are defined. But inevitably a model will be extended or modified during the detailed analysis phase as a result of reexamining the attributes.

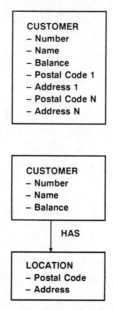

Figure 1.11 Replacing attributes by entities and relationships.

1.10.2 Selection and Identification of Entities

Data analysis permits the selection and identification of entities in the following three ways:

• By one or more attributes
• By the combination of a relationship with one or more attributes
• By two or more relationships

The simplest case of entity identification is where each occurrence of the attribute has a unique value which is used to identify the entity. Combinations of attributes may also be used, such as when employees are identified by their name, together with the date they joined the company.

The members of the relationship are often uniquely identified within that relationship by the values of the attribute type, but for uniqueness within the system the owner of the relationship needs also to be known. In effect, it is the relationship occurrence as identified by its owner that is contributing to the unique identification of its members. Entity identification by relationships and attributes is illustrated in Figure 1.12.

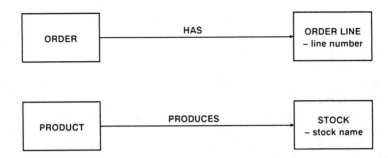

Figure 1.12 Entity identification by relationships.

A problem arises when different functions wish to use clearly identifiable subsets of the total population of attributes of an entity type.
The question then arises as to whether the entity type, as defined, is
taking too global a view and is better considered as being several
entity types. In general, it may be preferable to treat entities as
being of different types if they have either:

• Significant differences in their attributes
• Different means of identification
• Participation in different types of relationships

Examples of entity subtypes are (a) regular employees, (b) casual
employees, (c) manager, and (d) pensioner. These are all categories of
the entity type EMPLOYEE.

1.11 DATABASE DESIGN — SCHEMA DEVELOPMENT

The process of developing a database structure from user requirements is called database design. The database design process consists of two phases:

• Design of a logical database structure (schema development) that
  is processable by the database management system (DBMS) and
  describes the user's view of the data
• Selection of a physical structure (physical database design) that is
  available within the DBMS

Four basic components are necessary to achieve a database design
methodology:

- A structured design process that consists of a series of design steps where one alternative among many is chosen
- Design techniques to perform the required selection and evaluation of alternatives at each step
- Information requirements for input to the design process as a whole unit to each step
- A descriptive mechanism to represent the information input and the results at each design step

The result of the logical design step is a database definition or schema.

1.11.1 Formulating the DBMS Specific Logical Database Schema

Using the entity-relationship diagrams developed during the user view modeling phase of database design, a processing matrix which links specific applications and entities identified in the processing requirements, and allowable DBMS characteristics, a logical database schema can be formulated.

In the simplest case, entities become record types and attributes become item types, or entities become logical databases. In the more complex cases, entities can split or merge to form record types. This step begins the phase where consideration of the DBMS-specific rules and constraints must be given.

The logical database schema can now be revised on the basis of quantitative information and performance measures. Processing volume is defined as the combination of two parameters:

- Processing frequency
- Data volume

Processing frequency is the frequency at which an individual application is required to be run. Data volume is the number of occurrences of each record type currently stored or to be stored in the database.

Performance measures at the logical design step are limited to:

- Logical record access counts
- Total bytes transferred to satisfying an application
- Total bytes in the database

These measures attempt to predict physical database performance in terms of elapsed time and physical storage space, as closely as possible.

1.12 DOCUMENTING THE DATABASE DESIGN

Documentation is the recording of facts about objects or events of concern to facilitate communication and to provide a permanent record. In a database environment, documentation is based on giving information about the database itself, its contents and its structure. The documentation focuses primarily on data-related components, such as:

• Data elements
• Data groups (records or segments)
• Data structures
• Databases

Database documentation covers several types of information and is intended to support the needs of several classes of users. Seven types of documentation can be compiled for the database environment:

• Naming/Meaning — a unique identifier and descriptive information that conveys the full meaning of the component. The name is used for reference and retrieval purposes, while the description is valuable to managers' purposes.
• Physical Description — the physical characteristics of the components, such as the size of a data element or the length of a data record.
• Edit/Authorization Criteria — criteria to be used to test the validity of instances of the component, such as acceptable range of values for data elements or passwords for update of a database.
• Usage — information on where and by whom or by what a component is used, such as the programs within the system that reference a given data element.
• Logical Description — the characteristics and structure of each user view of the database, such as logical relationship among data records.
• Procedures — guidelines for human interaction with the database, such as for back-up, recovery, and system restart.

• Responsibility — a record of the individual or organizational unit responsible for the generation and maintenance of the database component.

1.13 THE ROLE OF DATA DICTIONARY/DIRECTORY SYSTEMS

Data Dictionary/Directory Systems (DD/DS) are valuable tools for assisting generally in the collection and management of data about the database. This data about the database is called metadata.

The major objective of a DD/D system is to support the integration of metadata in much the same way that a DBMS supports the integration of an organization's data. The benefits achieved are as follows:

• Minimum redundancy
• Consistency
• Standardization
• Data sharing
• Monitoring of database content
• Effectively enforcing security and integrity policies

1.13.1 Features and Functions of DD/D Systems

All data dictionary/directory systems provide the basic functions necessary to capture and maintain metadata and to generate reports from that store of metadata. Data capture implies the initial loading of the data dictionary with metadata of entry types. The capability may be provided through fixed, or free, format transactions in either batch or on-line mode. Very often, all or part of a data dictionary entry may be generated directly from a source program data description.

Reporting is a primary function of any DD/DS system. Basically, two types of reports are provided:

• A list of dictionary entries, either alphabetically or by entry type
• A cross-reference report

In a cross-reference report, entries in the dictionary are associated by the relationships in which they participate. Since these relationships are bidirectional, the cross reference may be either top-down listing of entries associated with a particular application or might ask for a trace of all entries with which a particular element is associated, a bottom-up view.

Other DD/D system features may include:

- Selectivity — entries associated with a particular element
- Query languages — for users to formulate reports of their own choosing
- Program Code generation
- Directory — indicating the physical location of data in the database
- Maintenance of archival definitions

1.14 THE NORMALIZATION PROCESS

During the data analysis, the relevant attributes are recorded and defined for each entity type. This may lead to identification of new entity types or to the subdivision of existing entities. It also enables the boundaries of the data area to be defined more precisely. Once the entity model is reasonably complete, explicit checks need to be made to detect redundant relationships. These checks may include the process called normalization.

1.15 NORMALIZATION

Normalization requires three actions to be performed on the attributes of an entity. These are as follows:

- First Normal Form — repeating groups are removed
- Second Normal Form — attributes are removed which are dependent on only some of the identifying attributes
- Third Normal Form — any attributes are removed which are not directly dependent on the identifying attributes

The normalization process will be discussed at greater length in Chapter 5.

QUESTIONS

1. Define the terms entity, attribute, data, information, and relationship. What are some relationships among them? Give examples.
2. Discuss the difference between data and information.
3. In an enterprise with which you are familiar, identify several entities, their attributes, candidate key data elements, and data values. Construct a sample data record and sample data file.
4. What are the two components of data analysis? Discuss the major phases of each.
5. What is functional analysis? List the objectives of this analysis.
6. A company has several employees, some of whom fulfill the role of managers. Discuss some criteria for differentiating between the employee and manager entities. List some probable attributes of each entity.

2

User Requirement Analysis

2.1 INTRODUCTORY REMARKS

This chapter discusses various techniques used in collecting, analyzing and defining the data used in the user requirement phase of database design.

The user requirement phase of database design is the most important phase of the Systems Development Life Cycle (SDLC). It is during this phase that information on the feasibility and scope of the project, the constraints and controls, the operating requirements and security, the data requirements, and the processing requirements is obtained.

The success or failure of a project depends largely on the quality of data collected during this phase. The duration of the project may be adversely affected if the analysts have missed significant portions of the requirements or the user has failed in giving detailed responses to the analysts.

The chapter begins with a discussion of different methods used to collect the data for the phase. It highlights the survey method, which is preferred and promoted by the author, and ends by discussing various reports that can be produced during this phase.

2.2 DATA COLLECTION METHODS

There are currently two methods in general use that allow the analysts to collect data for this phase. These are:

- Workshop
- Survey

In the workshop method, the analyst assembles all the relevant users in a room and proceeds to get the users to indicate what their requirements are while the interviewer or another assistant takes notes.

This method has several disadvantages. It is time-consuming since the sessions are very often unstructured and rambling, with users giving very little specifics of their requirements; and sometimes it is uncontrollable. Very often, several meetings are required before enough detail is gotten.

In the SURVEY method, the analyst prepares a detailed questionnaire covering all aspects of the project and gets the users to respond to the questions. This method has the following advantages:

- It is less time-consuming.
- The responses are more detailed and structured.
- The analysts can control the granularity of the questions and hence of the responses.

This method will be discussed in greater detail in the following sections.

2.3 THE SURVEY METHOD

The survey method allows the analyst to structure questions in any area for which requirements are needed. Data can be collected for:

- Programming specifications
- Data security
- Volume statistics
- Scope of project
- Content of operator's instructions
- Formats of files, screens, or reports
- Standards and conventions

Once the analyst has received the detailed responses to the survey, he or she can analyze those responses to obtain input to any phase of the database design process.

The major disadvantage of this method is that the analyst must have a good knowledge of the various areas in which the questionnaire must be structured.

2.4 AN EXAMPLE OF USER SURVEY

Exhibits 2.1 and 2.2 illustrate a survey that was sent out to determine the user requirements for an on-line marketing system and the responses to that survey.

Exhibit 2.1   Example of a User Survey

A SURVEY INSTRUMENT — DEVELOPED FOR THE ON-LINE SCREEN DESIGN PROJECT
(Determination of User Requirements)

QUES. 1:   What *Help* or *Menu Selection* screens do you require for the project?

QUES. 2:   Should screen processing allow for multiple updates? For example, multiple trade class and territories.

QUES. 3:   If multiple updates are allowed, please list the updatable fields and their upper limits. For example, screen should allow for a minimum of five ship points.

QUES. 4:   List physical characteristics of each screen. For example, number of characters per line, number of lines per screen, color for detail heading and updatable fields.

QUES. 5:   List any daily reports to be generated from processing of screens.

QUES. 6:   What requirements do you have for input operator's instructions?

QUES. 7:   Outline some contents of the above documentation.

QUES. 8:   Re: A pageable screen — Identify a key data item to be used as a "next starting point" rather than going to the next prior page.

QUES. 9:   What interactive messages would you want displayed when transaction codes are processed?

QUES. 10:   What limitations do you want placed on scrolling of the screen to locate needed information?

QUES. 11:   What standards do you require in the following areas:
• Naming convention
• Use of colors to highlight data

• Use of flashing colors (red)
• Interactive feedback when data is *deleted* or *changed*

QUES. 12:   What are the editing requirements for processing each transaction code? Also, what tables are needed for validation?

QUES. 13:   What security controls are required for processing of screens? For example, what data items are subject to delete, change, or addition?

QUES. 14:   What are some consistency checks that must be built into the screens? For example, what field must be present before a change can be made to another, but dependent, field?

QUES. 15:   What security controls are required for input operators? For example, which operators can change certain data items, which operators can access certain screens?

QUES. 16:   Are there any main headings or titles that should be present on all screens?

QUES. 17:   List any data items that are not entered by transmittal sheets that can be derived from stored data and not be included in screen formats?

QUES. 18:   What interactive feedback do you require when data items are to be deleted? For example, would you require a confirmation that the item was deleted or a re-affirmation that the stated item is to be deleted as requested?

QUES. 19:   For each transaction code or combination of transaction codes, list the combination or data items that must at best be on the same screen. For example, calls address and supplementary information must be on the same screen.

QUES. 20:   For each transaction, what are the required data items as opposed to those that may or may not be entered at that time.

Exhibit 2.2   Example of Responses to User Survey

1. Menu selection screens that will be required for the on-line development.
    A. Customer, possibly involving two (2) screens
    B. Product, including the table maintenance
    C. Major, Hierarchy System
    D. Zip Master

All of the above should have the capabilities of on-line updating techniques designed for users.

2. A. Multiple updates for each customer should include the following information by business segment.
   1. Multiple trade class
   2. Current and future territory members
   3. Target indicator both for current and future file
   4. Shipping points (at the present time, all business segments use the same codes)

   B. For the Product Information File (which included currently the tables for territories, destination codes, etc...) there should also be multiple updates permitted.

   A new product that is being entered into the system should allow at least ten (10) report line codes to be assigned to that product.

   C. Zip Master updates should allow at least ten (10) Master updates of ethical territories, and at least four (4) for the other business segments.

3. Multiple updating on the Customer File should include the following screens:
   A. **CUSTOMER** — Multiple updatable fields to be permitted on this screen would include trade classes, territory numbers, and target indicators allocated by business segment sales force. The upper limits for each of the above should be four (4) occurrences.

   B. **PRODUCT** — For any given product package member within the system, the updating of the file should include multiple report lines associated with each individual product. The upper limit for this portion would be ten updates (the business sales force segment is contained within these ten updates). The current system that we now have contains eight updates per product package style, with several distinct PIF's.

   C. **ZIP CODES** — Multiple territory fields by business segment should be five (5) with the exception of the ethical business, which should contain eight (8) occurrences.

4. Each line should contain, at maximum limit, 72 characters (designed on a TSO screen without scrolling to the left). Twenty (20) lines should be the maximum lines before paging to the second screen. The color for all screens should show the detail heading in turquoise with updatable fields in amber — with a flashing red highlight if certain fields do not validate against a

maintenance table. The remaining color on the screen should be white.

As far as can be determined, the Customer Master File will probably be the one to contain two screens, since it carries a large amount of information. A copy of the physical customer file is attached for your perusal.

The Product File should contain a maximum of 70 characters in length and a maximum of 20 lines. Again, attached is a copy of the physical file layout.

Major Code, Super Code Hierarchy System, as well as PC & MGroup updating, screens should be able to have multiple updating capabilities. For this screen, since the customers can belong to more than one group, the upper limit of customers assigned should be ten (10) occurrences.

5. For each screen that is to be designed, there should be reports generated whenever that particular file is updated. Some of these reports are as follows:
   A. Customer Update — Daily basis for those that were either added or changed.
   B. PIF (Product Information File, which at present time contains the tables that use transactions Type 21 and 30 to 40). This should be produced at the time when the file is updated (report generated at night). In addition, a complete report should be generated on request.
   C. MGroup Update Report — to be generated in the evening when the files have been updated.
   D. Zip Updates Report — should also be generated whenever the file has been updated.

6. Input operator's instructions should contain the following data pertaining to on-line updating:
   A. The dotted amber lines represent the fields that can be updated.
   B. Certain fields are validated against a maintenance table. If the field entered is not accepted, then that particular field will be highlighted in flashing red, indicating an error that must be corrected.
   C. Explanation of multiple fields by business segment; and updating of some fields.
   D. Table maintenance online should be thoroughly explained, since at the present time all updates are processed through the product (PIF) updating.

7. Some answers given in Response #6.

8. Since there is no physical report layout for Page One of the Customer Master File, I am making an assumption that the Key Data item might be the supplementary information category, starting with status indicator.

9. If the update has been accepted without field-defined error validation, the message should display either "File Update" or "New Data Added to File."

   However, if there is an error due to validation process, a message should be displayed: "Error in Field — Correction Required."

10. If the data can adequately be shown on one screen without too much traffic, then we should limit scrolling to the second page. The exception to this would be the Customer File.

11. Standards for following areas are:
    A. Naming Convention
        1. For Customer On-Line Updating, it should be noted as "Customer Master File."
        2. Zip Updating — To be known as "Zip Master File."
        3. Product Updating — To be known as "Product Information File." (At this time, I am not sure whether this file will contain the Table Maintenance Files, such as territory, destination codes, etc...)
        4. Major Code, MGroup, or Super Code Hierarchy updating—appropriate naming convention for this area should be "Customer Group Information."
    B. The use of colors to highlight data has been discussed previously, but for convention purposes they are listed below.
        1. Detail heading on all screens should be turquoise.
        2. Updatable areas should be indicated by underlines, and data entered should appear as amber.
        3. The other color to be shown on the screen should be white, in which the naming convention should be, and also white at the bottom of the screen for the program.
    C. If a selected field does not validate against the Master File, that particular field should make use of flashing red to indicate that an error is existing and must be corrected.
    D. Interactive feedback for all updates should indicate on the screen that the file has been updated accordingly.

12. The editing requirements for the processing of each transaction code is to contain the following information:
    A. Fields that are designated as numeric fields should contain numeric data. Also, certain specific numeric and/or alpha

fields will be validated against tables that will be listed in 12B.
- B. Table Files that will be used for validation purposes:
    1. Territory numbers per business segment.
    2. Trade class associated with each business segment.
    3. Zip Codes validated against the Master Zip File.
    4. MGroup, Major Code, and Superhierarchy system—the group code should be validated against a table of valid group codes.
    5. An Alpha State listing to ensure that the correct state is being entered into the system.
13. The security controls for processing of the different screens are listed below.
- A. Customer Master
    1. The SIS number cannot be deleted from the file. Related information can be changed for that SIS number, however.
    2. Territory number changes for the Business Segment Sales Force cannot be readily updated. Some type of signaling device should predicate the user into obtaining additional information before processing the transaction. Especially true where the non-Ethical Business Sales Forces territories may be updated.
- B. Zip Master
    1. Again, we allow no deletions from a Master File. All data items can be added or changed as warranted.
- C. Product Information File (P.I.F.)
    1. No deletions allowed (as yet).
    2. Changes that involve the product file include the report groups that the product is associated with, activity code of the product (1 or 2), and additional related items.
- D. MGroup, Major Code, Super Code Hierarchy System
    1. This is about the only file where we would allow deletions to occur. In a manner of speaking, the deletions are actually treated as changes where customers are changed from one group code to another, added to multiple group codes, etc.
    2. Group names and their appropriate group number can be deleted from the file.
14. For the Customer File, you must have an SIS number present before a change or an add can be implemented. On an add, the Type 11 card is required as well as the Type 13 card. The lat-

ter card contains the supplementary information such as territory, shipping point, trade class, etc., for each customer.

Also, an add may require other fields that are designated by the Business Segment Sales Force. For example, if the customer is both an OTC and an Ethical account, then both Type 13 and Type 15 input as well as the Type 11 transactions are required. The same could also apply if the account is an Ethical and Oncology account. Then, the Type 11, 13, and 14 transactions are required.

On a change, the ability to update any field can be accomplished.

For Product Updating, the product code and the report group codes are required when adding a new product to the file. For a change, only the product number is required, and one other related data field.

For Zip Master Updates, new adds require a zip code and all three card inputs at the current time, which includes territory fields by Business Segment Sales Force.

MGroup, Major Code requires a group code before adding customers associated with that code. Also required are the name and address of the group code.

15. The input operators (in Sales Services listed on a supplemental sheet) can update all fields on the Customer Master, Zip Master, Product Files and the Major Group files with the exception of group codes less than the 11XXX Series. Under no circumstances does any other department have the authority to update the Customer, Zip, Product (PIF — all inclusive) and the Major Code File (11XXX Major Code Series).

16. Headings for the screens will be required as follows:
    A. Customer File — Customer Master File
    B. Zip Master — Zip Master File
    C. Product — PIF — Product Information File (which may include all maintenance tables)
    D. MGroup — Major Grouping File

17. For all changes to the Major Code Super Hierarchy System that encompasses major codes in the 11XXX Series, the updating of the Type 44 transactions could be taken from the Customer Master File. However, those that are used by PC & A Department may have to be continued through updating processes. (I am not sure of the PC & A techniques).

For Major Group, MGroup updates, for Transactions 37 and 43, the group code number, name and address, trade class and region identification should be taken from one file instead of the user completing two similar transactions to update two separate files. One transmittal should update both files (need to check with PC & A on this).

18. If a physical deletion was permitted on the file, it would require at least a re-affirmation before the request was allowed. However, all updates made in the Sales Services Department are considered as adds or changes.

19. Customer Master File requires that, for changes or adds, the following should be on the same screen: calls address data, supplementary data, territory information by business segment (if applicable), the date added to file, and last date of change fields. The mailing address, the DDD SRA# (DDD Sales Reporting Area) and other related items pertaining to the particular customer should appear on the second screen. (Need to see a physical format to determine other data fields to be shown.)

The Zip Master Updates should show all the pertinent data that is now on the file. For example: zip code, city name and state code, county code, shipping point, prime territory, all secondary territories, and territories by business segment (current, old, and future territory assignment).

Product File Updates are to include all information required on the current Type 21 transaction. Type 40 transactions as well as the Type 30-36 transactions should, as far as I can foresee, probably fit all on one screen entitled Table Updates. May have to pursue this idea further.

MGroup, Major Group updating requirements are as follows: for a Type 43 or Type 37 transaction, the screen should allow at the most 18 updates at one time. The Type 44 transactions could appear on the screen for most parts as a split screen (left and right), where 36 transactions could update the file. (This would also apply to the Type 45 transactions as well.)

20. Customer File and required data items, for an add, consist of the SIS number, calls address, the supplementary data items as activity status, shipping point, territory number (as per business segment, trade class, and sample invoice fields).

On a change to the Customer File, the SIS# is required, and any one field data item.

For the Zip Master File, for an add, the zip code, city name and state, shipping point, territory number (business segment), county name and code are required. (Currently, all three (3) input transactions to update file with business segments are required). For a change, zip code is required and any other related data item on the Master File.

For Product Updating, the product number, as well as the product name, the report line group codes, department indicator, activity status, and unit of use indicator are required. For a change, the update must require a product number and any other related data item on the product file.

For Major Group, MGroup updates, for Transactions 37 and 43, the group code number, name and address, trade class, region identification are required. For Type 44 and 45 transactions, the group number is required, and customer number(s) start and end dates.

2.5 ANALYSIS OF USER RESPONSES

A preliminary analysis of the user responses in Exhibit 2.2 indicates that the main intent of the project was to allow the users to do online maintenance of the following four master files (databases):

• Customer Master File
• Zip Master File
• Buying Group File
• Product Information File

In the case of the Customer Master File, on-line updating should include all the fields that are currently being done in batch from input-coded on the Customer Master File Maintenance Input-Transmittal form.

In addition, the user wanted the ability to include updates to the Sales Reporting Area (SRA), multiple trade classes, and territories on the same screen.

In the case of the Zip Master File, the user wanted to update all the fields that are not being done by Transaction Codes 40, 43, 44 and 45.

For the Product Information File, the user wanted the ability to update all the fields now shown on the Product Master Maintenance Input-Transmittal form. In addition, the program must maintain all tables including territory numbers, destination codes, shipping points, regions, districts, report group, and product line.

EXHIBIT 2.3 covers, in some detail, the scope of the project, the user requirements, the expected deliverables from the study, and any requirements for the users to sign off the project results.

Exhibit 2.3   Analysis of User Responses

A. SCOPE OF THE PROJECT
   The scope of the project includes the development of on-line
   screens which allow the user to update and maintain the following files:
   • Customer File
   • Zip Master
   • Buying Group
   • Product Information
   The scope is limited to the system design for the screens,
   which includes development of a logical model, the formatting
   of the screens for all updating transactions, and development of
   some programming specifications. It does not include development of maps or dialogs and codes for transaction processing.
   The project calls for development of all on-line processing
   using IDMS with ADSO as the development tool for the screen
   design.

B. USER REQUIREMENT
   The user requirements for the project were obtained by analy-
   sis of the responses to the user survey that was sent to the
   Marketing Department. The requirements for the project will
   be collected during the following phases:
   • General
   • Detailed
   • Signed-off
   In the General phase, the requirements are stated in terms of
   types of screens, transactions, and reports that are needed.
   Limits are given to number of characters per line and number
   of lines per screen, the occurrences of required data elements,
   the frequency of reports, and headings of each screen.
   In the Detailed phase, the requirements are documented in
   terms of their ability to be used as input to detailed screen
   formats, data element characteristics, security requirements,
   and programming specifications.
   In the Signed-off phase, the requirements are documented in
   terms of their accuracy and adequacy in meeting the needs of
   the users and in ways to cause general satisfaction with the
   users in terms of contents. The users complete this phase by
   actually signing off the documents.
   B.1 GENERAL USER REQUIREMENTS
      The following sections discuss the general user require-
      ments as obtained from the user survey.

B.2 MENU SELECTION SCREENS

There will be at least four menu-selection screens which will direct the user to the other transaction processing screens. These are
• Customer
• Product
• Major Code (Hierarchy System)
• Zip Master

B.3 MULTIPLE UPDATES TO MAJOR FILES

The user requirements call for the ability to do multiple updates to each of the four major files.

For the Customer File, the multiple updatable fields include Trade Class, Territory Number, Shipping Points, and Target Indicator. The number of occurrences for each field will be limited to four.

For the Product File, the system should allow for multiple updatable fields including the tables for Territories, Declination Codes, etc. The system should also support multiple report lines associated with each individual product. The upper limit for this screen(s) would be 10 updates.

For the Zip File, there should be multiple updates to fields such as the Territory. The upper limit of occurrences are 10 for Ethical territories, and at least 4 for other business segments.

For the Major Code File, the updatable fields should have a maximum occurrence of 10.

B.4 REPORTS GENERATED BY SYSTEM

As changes are made to the file, the system should generate reports of those changes. The following reports should be generated:

1. Customer Update — report of addition or changes (daily report)
2. Product Update — one report to be produced when file is updated (daily report) and a more detailed report to be produced on request
3. Major Code Update — report to be produced when file is updated (daily report)
4. Zip Code Update — report to be produced when file is updated (daily report)

B.5 INPUT OPERATOR'S INSTRUCTIONS

The user requirements call for an operator's instruction document, which will indicate to the terminal operator the fields that can be updated, fields that must be validated against maintenance tables, some explanation of multiple updatable fields by Business Segment and what maintenance should be carried out on the various tables.

B.6 SCREEN MESSAGES

The user requirements call for messages to be displayed at the bottom of each transaction screen to indicate whether an update was successful or not. The format and content of these messages will be given in the detail requirements.

B.7 SCROLLING OF SCREENS

The user requirements indicate that, wherever possible, "page scrolling" should be limited to the second page of a screen.

B.8 STANDARDS AND CONVENTIONS

The user requirements call for standards to be established in the following areas:

- Naming Conventions — name of file or screen updating customer data should be known as "Customer Master File."
- Use of Colors — turquoise for headings, amber for updatable fields, and white for other parts of screen.
- Flashing Red — when fields selected for update cannot be validated against the Master File, the flashing red will indicate an error.
- Interactive Feedback — messages must appear to indicate success or failure in updating fields.

B.9 EDITING REQUIREMENTS

The editing requirements for the project will be discussed in more detail in the Detail Requirements. The editing requirements obtained so far are in the areas of numeric checks or data fields and validation rules for table maintenance.

B.10 SECURITY REQUIREMENTS

Some security requirements obtained from the responses are:

- SIS Number cannot be deleted from the file
- Territory number changes for the Business Segment Sales Force cannot be updated before the user is prompted into getting additional information.
- No deletions from a Zip Master File.
- Input operators cannot update group codes less than the 11XXX Series.

B.11 SCREEN CHARACTERISTICS

For the Customer File, there must be an SIS number before a change or an add can be implemented. For an add, Type 11 and 13 cards are required. If the customer is both an OTC and an Ethical account, then Type 11, 13 and 15 cards are required. If the customer is an Oncology account and an Ethical, then Type 11, 13 and 14 transactions are required.

For the Product File, before updating can take place there must be a product code and the report group codes present.

For the Zip File, new adds require a zip code and all three card types now being entered.

Major code updates require a group code and the name and address of the group code before an ADD can be done.

B.12 SCREEN HEADINGS

The major headings for the transaction screens will be as follows:

- Customer Master File
- Zip Master File
- Product Information File
- Major Grouping File

B.13 DERIVABLE FIELDS

The derivable fields for the project are defined as fields that can be updated by the system, rather than from input from the operators.

The user requirements indicate that changes to the Major Code Super Hierarchy System, which encompasses major codes in the 11XXX Series, are done by Transaction 44 and could be taken from the Customer Master File. However, those that are used by PC & A Department may still be required to be done by the input operators.

B.14 DATA ITEMS ON THE SAME SCREEN

The user requirements call for the following data items to be on the same screen:

- Calls address, supplementary data, territory information, data added, and last date of change
- Mailing address and DDD Sales Reporting Area
- All data on Transaction 21
- All data on Transaction 40, and possibly 30-36
- All data on Transactions 43 or 37

2.6 DELIVERABLES FROM ANALYSIS

The analyst will produce several deliverables from the analysis of the user responses to the survey. These will include:

• Entity-Relationship diagrams
• Logical data models
• Entries for the Corporate Data Dictionary
• Volume statistics
• Report format
• Process definitions
• Data Dictionary Analysis Reports
• Attribute vs. Report Analysis
• Attribute vs. Entity Analysis

2.7 DISCUSSION OF SOME DELIVERABLES

In this section, I will discuss two deliverables that the analyst should produce. These are:

• Attribute vs. Report Analysis
• Attribute vs. Entity Analysis

Figures 2.1 and 2.2 illustrate the content and format of these reports. The usefulness of them is demonstrated as follows:
   Let's say a user gives the analyst all the report types, entity types, and attributes required for processing. The analyst can, from these two reports, determine if any attributes or entities are missing. In Figure 2.1, we notice that reports R1, R3, R5, and R8 require some attributes that are as yet undefined. In Figure 2.2, we notice that attributes A10, A11, A12, and UND do not belong to any of the nine entities that the user indicated were relevant to his or her business. This situation indicates that the analyst must do some further interrogating of the user.

2.8 REMARKS IN CONCLUSION

This chapter attempted to cover a topic in database design that is only mentioned in some texts on the subject and treated in a cursory fashion by others. This in-depth coverage should serve the readers

	R_1	R2	R3	R4	R5	R6	R7	R8
A_1	X			X		X	X	X
A_2		X	X	X	X	X	X	X
A_3	X	X						
A_4	X	X	X		X	X	X	
A_5	X	X				X		X
A_6	X	X	X	X	X			
A_7	X					X	X	X
A_8		X	X		X			
A_9		X			X	X	X	X
A_{10}		X	X	X				
A_{11}		X			X	X	X	X
A_{12}			X					
UND	X		X		X			X

Figure 2.1 Attributes vs. reports.

	E_1	E2	E3	E4	E5	E6	E7	E8	E9
A_1	X								
A_2		X							
A_3			X						
A_4				X					
A_5					X				
A_6						X			
A_7							X		
A_8								X	
A_9									X
A_{10}									
A_{11}									
A_{12}									
UND									

Figure 2.2 Attributes vs. entities.

well and assist them in designing surveys to determine user requirements.

The complete analysis of the survey used in this chapter can be seen in Part II of this text, under Case Histories.

QUESTIONS

1. Name the two methods of collecting user requirements data. Discuss the advantages and disadvantages of each.
2. A user wants to collect information on employee performance on certain projects and report to management on this performance. Develop a survey that would collect data about the employee, performance, projects, and reports. (Hint: The report formats and reporting media are very important in the CASE study).
3. Create attribute vs. report and attribute vs. entities matrices for the problem given in question 2.
4. What are the deliverables from the user requirements phase of database design?
5. Discuss the role of data analysis in determining user requirements.

3

Database Design Methodology

This chapter presents an overview of database design and development methodologies and a detailed discussion of one of these methodologies — the entity-relationship (E-R) approach.

Database design refers to the process of arranging the data fields needed by one or more applications into an organized structure. That structure must foster the required relationships among the fields while conforming to the physical constraints of the particular database management system in use. There are really two parts to the process. There is logical database design, which is then followed by physical database design.

Logical database design is an implementation-independent exercise that is performed on the fields and relationships needed for one or more applications.

Physical database design is an implementation-dependent exercise that takes the results of logical database design and further refines them according to the characteristics of the particular database management system in use.

A variety of reasons make careful database design essential. These include data redundancy, application performance, data independence, data security, and ease of programming. All are important factors in the data processing environment, and all can be adversely affected by a poor database design.

3.1 REVIEW OF EXISTING METHODOLOGIES

This section will present two of the most common database design methodologies. In the case of the first methodology we will give only a brief introduction, whereas for the second we will give a more detailed discussion.

The first method, data normalization and data structuring, is representative of the class of methods that take as input a list of fields and the associations among those fields. The second method, the entity-relationship method, is representative of the class of methods that take entities and relationships as input.

Database design using the entity-relationship model begins with a list of the entity types involved and the relationships among them. The philosophy of assuming that the designer knows what the entity types are at the outset is significantly different from the philosophy behind the normalization-based approach.

The entity-relationship approach uses entity-relationship diagrams as illustrated in Figure 3.1. The rectangular boxes represent entity types, the diamond-shaped box represents a relationship between entities, and the circular figures represent attributes.

A more detailed discussion of the entity-relationship method is given in the following sections.

3.2 DETAILED DISCUSSION OF DATABASE DESIGN

Developing a database structure from user requirements is called database design. Most practitioners agree that there are two separate phases to the database design process: the design of a logical database structure that is processable by the database management system (DBMS) and describes the user's view of data, and the selection of a physical structure such as the indexed sequential or direct-access method of the intended DBMS. Other than the logical/physical delineation, the overall structure of the design is not well-defined.

Novak defined four basic components that are necessary to achieve a database design methodology:

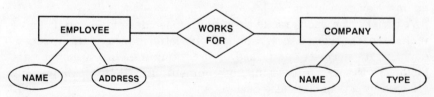

Figure 3.1 The entity-relationship diagram.

- A structured design process that consists of a series of steps where one alternative among many is chosen
- Design techniques to perform the enumeration required as stated previously and evaluation criteria to select an alternative at each step
- Information requirements for input to the design process as a whole and to each step of the design process
- A descriptive mechanism to represent the information input and the results at each design step

Current database design technology shows many residual effects of its outgrowth from single-record file design methods. File design is primarily application-program dependent since the data has been defined and structured in terms of individual applications that use them. The advent of DBMS revised the emphasis in data and program design approaches. The concept of the integrated database spanning multiple users was a direct result of the complex data structuring capabilities which the DBMS afforded. Data can now be viewed as a corporate resource instead of as adjunct to a program and, consequently, should have an integrated requirements orientation instead of a single-program orientation.

Achieving a design which results in an acceptable level of database performance for all users has become a complex task. The database designer must be ever conscious of the cost/performance trade-offs associated with multiple users of a single integrated database. Potential savings of storage space and expanded applicability of databases into corporate decision making should be accompanied by a critical analysis of potential degradation of service to some users. Such degradation is to be avoided if possible. Acceptable performance for all users should be the goal.

Another aspect of database design is flexibility. Databases that are too tightly bound to current applications may have too limited a scope for many corporate enterprises.

Rapidly changing requirements and new data elements may result in costly program maintenance, a proliferation of temporary files, and increasingly poor performance. A meaningful overall database design process should account for both integration and flexibility.

3.2.1 Inputs to Design Process

The major classes of inputs to and results from the database design process are:

Inputs
- General information requirements
- Processing requirements
- DBMS specifications
- Operating system/hardware configuration
- Application program specifications

Results
- Logical database structure (user view)
- Storage structure (physical design)

The general information requirements represent various users' descriptions of the organization for which data are to be collected, the objectives of the database, and the users' views of which data should be collected and stored in the database. These requirements are considered to be process-independent because they are not tied to any specific database management system or application. Database design based on these requirements is considered to be advantageous for long-term databases that must be adaptable to changing processing requirements.

Processing requirements consists of three distinguishable components: specific data items required for each application, the data volume and expected growth, and processing frequencies in terms of the number of times each application must be run per unit time. Each of these components is very important to a particular stage or step of the database design process.

Performance measures and performance constraints are also imposed on the database design. Typical constraints include upper bounds on response times to queries, recovery times from system crashes, or specific data needed to support certain security or integrity requirements.

Specific performances measures used to evaluate the final structure might include update, storage, and reorganization costs in addition to response requirements.

The three major outputs of the database design process are the logical database structure, the physical storage structure, and specifications for application programs based on these database structures and processing requirements. As a whole, these results may be considered the specification for the final database implementation.

3.2.2 The Entity-Relationship (E-R) Approach

As more and more organizations implement systems employing database technology, the need arises for better methodologies to design these databases. The methodology described here provides a means of mapping the entity model produced from the data analysis phase to the database management system-supported structure.

The E-R approach requires several steps to produce a structure that is acceptable by the particular DBMS. These steps are:

- Data analysis
- Producing and optimizing the entity model
- Logical schema development
- Physical database design process

3.2.3 Definitions and Terminologies

The following definitions and terminologies are frequently used in E-R theory and are basic to an understanding of the methodology. A more complete description of the process is available in existing literature.

1. An ENTITY is a fundamental thing of interest to an organization. An entity may be a person, place, thing, concept, or event that is real or abstract.

   Entity and entity class are used interchangeably in some of the literature, whereas some researchers define an entity as an occurrence of an entity class. For example, EMPLOYEE is an entity class, whereas S.T. LOCKE, an occurrence of the entity class EMPLOYEE, is an entity.

2. An ATTRIBUTE is a descriptive value or property associated with an individual entity. Attributes can be classified by one or more rules as follows:
   - Describe an entity
   - Uniquely identify an entity
   - Describe relationships between entities
   - Use to derive other attributes

3. A RELATIONSHIP is an association between two or more entities. For example, EMPLOYED BY, is a relationship between an employee and his employer.

4. An ACCESS GROUP is a physical clustering of attributes based on common usage, access requirements, and same data security or privacy requirements.

   In a database environment using the Information Management System (IMS) database management system, an access group could be attributes from one or more IMS segments. For example, a user may form an access group consisting of Employee name and Employment history taken from two segments, Employee and Position, respectively.

   The concept of access groups in an IMS environment which uses the current retrieval language (DL/1) to retrieve segments is not readily accepted. However, many organizations are using user-written routines to retrieve access groups.

5. ACCESS STATISTICS may be defined as data collected about the frequency of retrieval of a particular stored attribute over a given period of time. These statistics provide a means of making performance-oriented judgments when designing physical databases.

   In particular, these statistics assist in the choice of physical and logical parents and the left-to-right ordering of segments. They are useful in the selection of secondary indices, since attributes that are updated frequently make poor target fields.

   Access statistics can have a major effect on the placing of dependent segments in relation to their root and on the decision to combine segments in preference to decreasing data independence.

3.3 THE DATA ANALYSIS PHASE

A fundamental part of the E-R methodology is the data analysis phase. This phase is concerned with identifying the data resources of an organization. Although methodologies for data analysis have stemmed from the need for a new approach to system design in a database environment, experience has shown that the concept of data analysis has a wider applicability, whether or not database software is involved. The approach to data analysis, the same scale involved, and the emphasis placed on the various tasks that must be done, depend very much on the objectives of the project.

Davenport indicates that data analysis is used to:

• Determine the fundamental data resources of an organization

- Permit the design of flexible file structures capable of supporting a number of related applications
- Aid application development or conversion by providing a fundamental understanding of the data involved
- Form a basis for data control, security and auditing of the resulting applications and systems
- Organize all relevant facts concerning the organization's data
- Aid the unification of an organization by indicating the commonality between its departments and data requirements
- Provide a basis for evaluating the structuring capability of competing database management systems

Further uses of data analysis are to:

- Identify the entities that are relevant to solve the existing data processing problem
- Determine the relationships among those entities
- Establish data and process definitions in a data dictionary
- Produce the entity model

The primary interest in data analysis tends to be in providing a sound basis for database design. It provides a disciplined approach toward cataloging the existing data in terms of the entities and relationships it represents. Without such an understanding of that part of the organization being analyzed, it is more difficult to establish whether and where a database could be efficiently installed. Data analysis provides a very effective means of communicating with non-data processing users as it deals only with things that the users are familiar with and not with objects such as files and records.

The data analysis phase is sometimes referred to as requirements formulation and analysis, which involve the establishment of organization objectives, derivation of specific database requirements from these objectives or directly from management personnel, and documentation of these requirements in a form that is agreeable to management and database designers.

3.4 CONDUCTING THE DATA ANALYSIS PHASE

Data analysis is best conducted by a team of individuals drawn from the user community, the systems development department, data administration group, and corporate standards department.

The data analysis team may not be involved in the requirement analysis phase of the project if that phase is limited to personal interviews with various levels of management and key employees involved in the processing of goods, services, and data in the organization. The result of such interviews should be flow diagrams of the process; e.g., illustrations of steps required to process an invoice and where in the organization these steps are undertaken, with which step each employee is involved, an identification of the data elements associated with each process, interfaces between processes, and a verification that both the interviewer and employee agree on the flow model semantics. Specific objectives and database requirements should be obtained at the highest possible level in the organization.

The data analysis team first identifies the entities that are needed to solve the problem defined by the users. During the initial stages of data analysis, all of the attributes of each entity may not be known. However, as each attribute is determined, the team should document the attribute definition and role in an appropriate data dictionary.

3.5 THE ENTITY MODEL

During the data analysis phase the major entities and their relationships are determined. These entities and their relationships are represented by models called Entity Models. The model is a diagrammatical representation of the relationship between the entity classes.

The representation allows us to include only those entities that are required to solve the particular data processing problem. The entity model is essentially a real-world view of the organizational data in terms of the entities, attributes, and relationships.

During the entity modeling phase the most significant entity classes and relationships are defined. But inevitably a model will be revised, modified, or extended as a result of new knowledge about the entities being discovered. The model is used by the analysis team to:

• Reduce redundancy in the relationships
• Determine which entities are significant to the model and user requirement
• Resolve non-binary relationships between entities

3.6 APPROACHES TO ENTITY MODEL

There are two main approaches to entity modeling. These are:

• Top-down approach
• Bottom-up approach

The top-down approach produces a global, corporate, or organizational view of the data before the application or user views are identified. The entities and relationships which are of interest to the organization are identified from the point of view of the organization and independent of any particular application.

The bottom-up approach produces a composite or global view of the data based on the integration of several application views of the immediate problem requirements. The resulting model is limited to the immediate problem and cannot reflect the entire business activity of the corporation.

The bottom-up approach is the one most often used in entity modeling. This approach produces a model with more clearly defined boundaries than the top-down approach. The processing requirements can be used by the analysis team to precisely determine what entities are required and the composition of those entities. The clustering of attributes into their respective entities, or the splitting of entities, can now be done with more precision. It is also easier to determine whether an attribute is indeed an attribute of an existing entity or is itself an entity with relationships to other entities when using this approach.

The bottom-up approach produces entity models for each data area analyzed, but these models can be merged together to produce an integrated model which will satisfy all data areas or the whole corporation. This integration phase initially involves some editing to remove inconsistencies in the type of attributes, entities or relationships. These inconsistencies may be in the form of one name referring to different components of the same model (homonyms) or different names referring to the same component (synonyms).

3.7 STAGES OF INTEGRATION OF ENTITY MODELS

The stages required to integrate entity models are as follows:

• Identify any synonyms or homonyms in the different models. This task is made easier if a data dictionary is used. Components with

homonyms will have to be renamed. Components with synonyms will have to be referred to by a single name.
- Entity models for two data areas are integrated by superimposing the identical or similar entity types in the different entity models. This may increase the total number of attributes in the entity type, as identical entity types in each model have been concerned with different subsets of the total group of properties.
- As a result of the integration, the composite entity model may contain redundant relationships. This redundant relationship may be eliminated. However, determining which relationships are directly significant and which are redundant can present difficulties that can only be solved by an understanding of the environment.

3.8 ENTITY MODELING CASE STUDY

The following case study will serve to illustrate the use of entity modeling in database design. The database application is a general payroll system. The relevant department consists of a number of employees for whom paychecks must be processed. The employees' pensions can be paid in a lump sum or by installments on retirement, death of employee, or resignation. The department also wishes to make enquiries about projects a particular employee has worked on.

The entities and relationships from the above case study are represented in the entity model (Figure 3.2).

The model shown in Figure 3.2 will require several revisions as the data analysis phases continues and the requirements are more clearly identified. Some researchers indicate that anywhere from 4 to 20 revisions to the model may be required. Revisions to the model may be required for any of the following reasons:

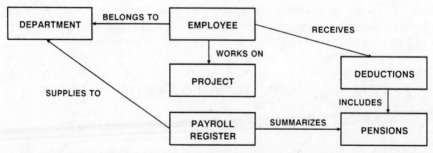

Figure 3.2 Entity model for paycheck processing.

* One entity class may be shown to be a subset of another entity; i.e., merging of entities.
* An entity class may be best represented as a relationship between two entity classes.
* Some attributes of an existing entity may better describe a new entity; i.e., splitting of entities.
* The role of the attribute has changed during analysis.
* More attributes are discovered during analysis.

3.9 APPLICATION OF REVISIONS TO ENTITY MODEL

This section applies some of the above revision rules to Figure 3.2. Let us examine three of the entity classes of that model.

ENTITY	TYPICAL ATTRIBUTES
DEPARTMENT	Department number, name, head, description
EMPLOYEE	Employee social insurance number, name, address, status, supervisor
PENSIONS	Pensions identifier, type, description, amount

In the department and employee entity classes the attributes Head and Supervisor best describe another entity class. We can now create a new entity class, Manager, for example and replace the two attributes with pointers or relationship codes to the original entity classes. We can also add new attributes to the entity class, Manager. Some typical attributes are as follows:

ENTITY	TYPICAL ATTRIBUTES
MANAGER	Manager identifier, description, authority

This revision to the model will also require that we establish two more relationships, i.e.,

Manager/Department and Manager/Employee relationships

In the pensions entity class the attribute Type indicates that pensions can be paid on retirement, death of employee, resignation of employee, in a lump sum, annually, or by deferred payment.

Because of the queries the users want to make one may decide to split the pension's entity class into one or more entities. For example, we may have one entity class for natural retirements and another for all lump sum payments. In this case the entities are application views of the entity class pensions. We will discuss application views in a later section.

In summarizing revisions to the entity model we may list a few rules in determining when an attribute of an entity is best treated as an entity in its own right related to the first entity. The rules are:

• Determine if the attribute itself has any other related attributes.
• Determine if the new entity is required in order to solve the data processing problem.
• Determine if the attribute in fact identifies the second entity.
• Determine if the new entity is related to the original entity.
• Determine if the new entity is related to any other entities in the model.

3.10 DERIVING ENTITY MODELS FROM TRADITIONAL OR FLAT FILES

This section discusses some approaches for deriving entity models from flat files or databases that were not designed using E-R methodology. There are no hard and fast rules for this derivation. One would have liked to say that there is a one-to-one correspondence between the entity classes in a model and the number of file descriptions (FD) in a program.

However, the clustering of data items from which the logical files were constructed may not be the same clustering required for the respective entity classes. Nevertheless, the following simple rules can be followed when converting from flat files to the entity model of that application.

• List all the file types in the relevant programs.
• List all the logical records in the files.
• List all the data items in the records.
• Eliminate redundancies and inconsistencies in the data items and logical records.
• List all possible combinations of entity classes from the logical records. The record name is an indicator of the entity class.
• List all codes in the records which can give the relationships of the entity model.

- Conduct a preliminary data analysis of the data items.
- Cluster the attributes into their respective entity classes.

This procedure will result in a baseline entity model which will serve as a framework for making further revisions, which will become necessary due to more detailed data analysis.

The procedure to follow for old databases created by methods other than E-R methodology will depend largely on how the data was physically clustered for data retrieval. Very often if the physical clustering was performance-oriented, the logical clustering into entity classes becomes a very complex, if not impossible, task.

It is my experience that the most productive method is still to obtain data definitions for all the data items in the databases, take the applications that use those data items, and cluster the data items into entity classes using any known data analysis techniques. The entity model for the particular user area can then be obtained by an integration or superimposition of the individual program-oriented models.

3.11 SUPERIMPOSITION OF ENTITY MODELS

In the conversion of existing physical databases back to their entity model equivalents, the designer may arrive at several different models depending on the programs or applications from which the models were derived. He or she should then attempt to remove redundancies and inconsistencies by superimposing the models from several programs to arrive at one integrated model.

The superimposition of entity models would allow the designer to determine:

- What are the common entity classes and attributes. These can be recognized on the basis of names only.
- The inconsistencies in the naming and use of attributes. These inconsistencies exist when two entities with different names are clearly shown to be one and the same entity.
- The adequacy of the model in terms of meeting the needs of the user.
- Whether attributes clustered into an entity class are indeed members of another entity class or new entity classes themselves.
- The existence of inconsistencies in the relationships.

The superimposed entity model can now be used as a framework for further revisions to arrive at an integrated entity model that will serve a larger data area than several smaller application-oriented models.

3.12 CLUSTERING OF ENTITY CLASSES

Clustering of entity classes in database design may occur in the logical or physical design stage. In the physical design stage, the clustering of the entity classes may be done solely on the basis of performance considerations. The entity classes may be merged or split into different physical databases depending on the access requirements.

The logical clustering of entity classes is dependent on the inherent nature of the data and data structure, whereas physical clustering is not. It is a necessary, but not sufficient, rule to say that attributes are clustered within an entity class because they best identify and describe that entity class, and entity classes are clustered into an entity model to satisfy a user's data processing requirement.

The logical clustering of entity classes is done to satisfy the following:

- the area served by the data or from which the data originated
- the inherent data structure
- the local view of the user
- the usage of the data
- the queries against the data
- the data processing needs of the user

The clustering of entity classes on the basis of data area means essentially that all data for which the accounting department has a functional responsibility will be clustered as accounting data. Similarly, all data for which the personnel department has that responsibility will be clustered as personnel data. The data areas are usually determined by the same methods that were used to create the organizational structure or boundaries.

The inherent data structure of an organization would indicate that employees are assigned to departments, assigned to projects; customers place orders; and orders are for products. Thus in clustering of entity classes the cluster must reflect that inherent data structure. The inherent data structure now reflects the business practices of the organizations and the clustering would also reflect those practices.

The clustering of entity classes on the basis of the local view of the user can be translated to mean that only those entities in which the user has some interest are assembled. The cluster may be part of a larger cluster or an amalgamation of several clusters. Thus, if the user wanted to determine the projects an employee worked on, his local views would consist of the cluster of the employee and project entity classes.

The attributes within an entity class and the clustering of the entity classes must satisfy the queries made against them. For example, one could not satisfy a query about employees' skill and education if these attributes were not in the entity class. Similarly, a query about the percentage of an employee's time spent on a project could not be answered if there was not a clustering of employee and project entity classes.

As in entity modeling, so in clustering of entity classes; the object of the exercise is to satisfy the data processing need of the user. The adequacy of the model is measured in relation to how well those needs are met. The entity classes will be clustered in accordance with those needs.

3.13 APPLICATION VIEW AND LOGICAL SCHEMA DESIGN

An application view may be defined as the set of data which is required by that particular application to fulfill a specific data processing need. For example, one application may be interested in materializing employee name and social security number as its employee entity class while another may materialize employee name, social security number, and salary as its employee entity class. In turn these two entity classes may be just a subset of a larger set of attributes which make up a corporate or global entity class called employee entity class.

We may have application views of:

• An entity class
• Cluster of entity classes
• Cluster of entity classes and physical databases
• Cluster of physical databases

The logical schema may be defined as the mapping of the entity model into the constructs provided by the database management system (DBMS) — for example, the mapping of the entity model into an IMS construct. In general, the logical schema indicates how the model will be stored and accessed. In the design of the logical schema some restructuring of the model and changes to conform to the DBMS may be necessary.

The entity model is not the logical schema. The entity model is:

- A representation of real-world view of the data
- The building blocks used for further data analysis and database design
- Not restricted to any database management systems (DBMS)
- Not directly implementable
- A stable framework or frame of reference into which new entities, attributes, and relationships can fit as more organizational database needs evolve

3.14 LOGICAL SCHEMA — CASE STUDY

In this section, I will endeavor to construct a logical schema from the entity model shown in Figure 3.1. Due to space limitations, I will not do the schema for the entire model as shown. A partial logical schema for Figure 3.1 is shown in Figure 3.3.

In the logical schema of Figure 3.3 we should note that the hierarchical data structure of IMS is now applied to the entity model. We also see that the pointers and unique keys are imposed on the entity model.

If other relationships than those shown in the logical schema are required, they are shown including all materialized attributes of relationships and their pointers. The logical schema should also show the occurrences of major groups of data or segments.

It should be noted that the logical schema for RELATIONAL and NETWORK databases will exhibit the constructs provided by their respective database management system.

3.15 TRANSLATION OF THE LOGICAL SCHEMA INTO PHYSICAL DATABASES

The details of this phase depend very much on the characteristics of the database management system (DBMS) chosen for the database design.

In an IMS environment the translation from the logical schema to physical databases requires the following selections:

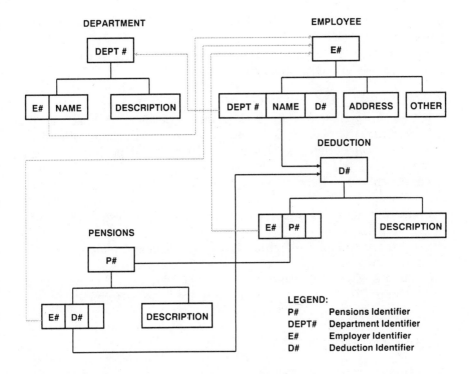

Figure 3.3 Logical schema for paycheck entity model.

- Physical databases and types of logical relationships, whether unidirectional or bidirectional, physically paired
- Access methods, whether HISAM, HIDAM, OR HDAM
- Segments and hierarchical structures and data representation, including type and size
- Secondary indices
- Types of pointers in relationship

In addition to the selections mentioned above, the implementation of the physical databases includes

- Allocation to storage devices
- Loading and organization of the databases

The logical schema should be so developed by the logical database designers that the only selection requirements left to be done by the physical designers would be the selection of access methods and secondary indices. The translation of logical schemas into physical

databases is dealt with at considerable length in the current literature.

Finally, Hubbard indicates that the following rules should be followed during the physical design process:

• Each entity class should be treated as a physical database.
• If two entity classes share a relationship between at least one attribute and the primary key, then the structures should consist of
  two physical databases with physical or virtual pairing between
  them.
• Parent-child relationship should be defined in a single physical
  database.
• Frequently accessed segments should be kept as close to their root
  as possible.
• Reduce the time for searching large data groups by using secondary indexing
• Segments of varying sizes should not be placed in the same data
  set group if frequent inserts or deletes are to be performed.

3.16 SUMMARY

This chapter has served to discuss database design methodologies in
general and the Entity-Relationship Approach (E-R) methodology in
particular.

The chapter started off with a review of the existing methodologies
and highlighted two methodologies. These were (a) data normalization and data structuring and (b) entity-relationship.

The chapter gave a step-by-step approach to design using the E-R
method and cited a case study using a payroll application.

QUESTIONS

1. What is logical database design? Discuss the deliverables from
   this exercise.
2. What are the two most common database design methodologies? Discuss the relative merits of each.
3. List the four basic components that are necessary to achieve a
   database design methodology.
4. What are the major classes of inputs to the database design
   process? Discuss the role of each input into the process.

5. List the two main approaches to entity modeling. Discuss the advantages and disadvantages of each approach.
6. What is an entity model? Discuss its role in database design.
7. Discuss the relative merits of entity-relationship diagramming as a database design tool.

4

Data Models and Entity Relationship Diagrams

4.1 INTRODUCTORY REMARKS

This chapter discusses data models and entity-relationship (E-R) diagrams and the role they play in database design.

Data models are the basic building blocks for all database design. They provide the underlying structure for the three dominant data structures of today's database management systems (DBMS). In addition, data models are used by many large corporations in business systems planning, strategic systems planning, and corporate data modeling.

Entity-relationship diagrams or entity models, as they are also called, are used to define a conceptual view or real-world view of data and the data requirements of an organization. E-R diagrams were popularized by P. Chen in 1976 and have since revolutionized the world of structured design.

4.2 SOME DEFINING TERMS

Data model is defined as a logical representation of a collection of data elements and the association among these data elements.

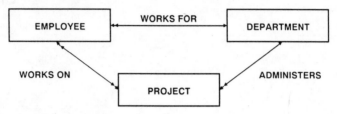

Figure 4.1 Example of a data model.

A data model can be used to represent data usage throughout an organization, or can represent a single database structure. A data model is to data what a logical data flow diagram is to a process.

There are three types of data models: (a) conceptual, (b) logical, and (c) internal or physical.

The entity diagram is a representation of the relationship between entity classes. The representation allows us to include only those entities that are required to solve the particular data processing problem.

The entity diagram is essentially a real-world view of the organization data in terms of the entities, attributes, and relationships.

The entity diagram (model) is an example of a conceptual data model.

4.3 ENTITY AND ENTITY CLASSES

Entity and entity class are used interchangeably in some of the literature, whereas some researchers define the entity as an occurrence of an entity class. For example, EMPLOYEE is an entity class whereas P. CAREY, an occurrence of the entity class EMPLOYEE, is an entity.

4.4 SUPER ENTITIES AND ENTITY SUBTYPES

An entity may be broken down into smaller sub groups on the basis of the function of each sub-group. This sub-group is often called an entity subtype. The original entity is often referred to as a super entity.

The representation of entity subtypes and super entities is as shown in Figure 4.2.

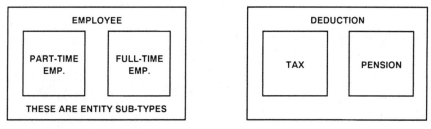

Figure 4.2 Representation of entity subtype.

4.5 TYPES OF RELATIONSHIPS

A relationship was defined earlier as an association between two or more entities. In this section, we will discuss the types of relationships and how they are represented diagrammatically.

4.5.1 One-to-One Relationship

At a given time, one EMPLOYEE may be assigned to one DEPARTMENT. The relationship between EMPLOYEE and DEPARTMENT is termed one-to-one. This relationship is represented diagrammatically as shown in Figure 4.3.

In Figure 4.3, the single-headed arrows denote the one-to-one relationship.

4.5.2 One-to-Many Relationship

At a given time many EMPLOYEES may be assigned to one DEPARTMENT. The relationship between DEPARTMENT and EMPLOYEES is termed one-to-many. This is represented diagrammatically in Figure 4.4.

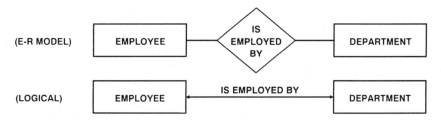

Figure 4.3 Representation of one-to-one relationship.

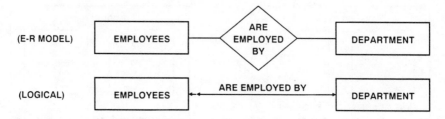

Figure 4.4 Representation of one-to-many relationship.

4.5.3 Many-to-Many Relationship

At a given time many EMPLOYEES may be assigned to many DE-PARTMENTS. The relationship between EMPLOYEES and DE-PARTMENTS is termed many-to-many. This is represented diagrammatically in Figure 4.5.

4.5.4 Mutually Exclusive Relationship

At a given time an EMPLOYEE may be assigned to either DEPART-MENT A or B, but not to both. The relationship between EM-PLOYEE and either DEPARTMENT is termed mutually exclusive. This is represented diagrammatically in Figure 4.6.

In Figure 4.6, the vertical bar in the direction of DEPARTMENT A indicates that DEPARTMENT A must always exist in the relationship. The O indicates that DEPARTMENT B is optional. We obtain exclusivity by switching the O and I around in the relationship.

4.5.5 Mutually Inclusive Relationship

At a given time an EMPLOYEE may be assigned to both DEPART-MENT A and B. The relationship between EMPLOYEE and both DEPARTMENTS is termed mutually inclusive. This is represented diagrammatically in Figure 4.7.

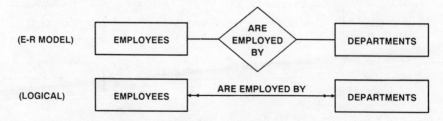

Figure 4.5 Representation of many-to-many relationship.

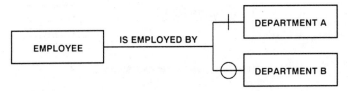

Figure 4.6 Representation of mutually exclusive relationship.

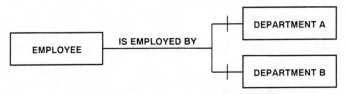

Figure 4.7 Representation of mutually inclusive relationship.

In Figure 4.7, the presence of vertical bars in the direction of both departments indicate that both must coexist for the relationship to be completed.

4.5.6 Mandatory Relationship

Sometimes an employer may rule that a DEPARTMENT must exist before the EMPLOYEE is hired. The relationship between EMPLOYEE and DEPARTMENT is termed mandatory. This is represented diagrammatically in Figure 4.8.

In Figure 4.8, the presence of a vertical bar in the direction of DEPARTMENT indicates that it must exist in the relationship.

4.5.7 Optional Relationship

Sometimes an EMPLOYEE may be hired but not assigned to a DEPARTMENT. The relationship between the EMPLOYEE and DEPARTMENT is termed optional. This is represented diagrammatically in Figure 4.9.

Figure 4.8 Representation of a mandatory relationship.

Figure 4.9 Representation of an optional relationship.

In Figure 4.9, the presence of the O in the direction of DEPART-MENT indicates that DEPARTMENT is not required to exist in the relationship.

4.6 TRANSLATION OF E-R DIAGRAMS TO LOGICAL MODELS

E-R diagrams (models) are sometimes called Business Entity models, since they reflect the business practices of an organization independently of any requirement for the underlying structure of a database management system (DBMS). However, in order for these diagrams to be processed by a computer, they must take on the constructs of the chosen DBMS. This section discusses the translation of E-R diagrams to logical data models.

Let us consider the following problem: A company is heavily project-oriented. Each project has one or more employees assigned to it full-time, perhaps from different departments.

Office space is assigned from time to time. Employees are assigned to an office in the department where they work. Several may share an office. Each department has one employee who is a manager.

The Company needs better information on projects, project costs, utilization of office space, and of employee's time.

4.6.1 Identification of Business Entities

When business entities are identified, careful consideration should be given to:

• A generally acceptable *name* for the entity
• A complete definition which makes clear what is included and what is excluded from the members of the entity
• A *business-oriented* entity identifier which can be agreed upon across the enterprise

The business entities with their name, abbreviation, identifier, and description are shown in Table 4.1.

Table 4.1   Business Entities — Illustrative Example

ENTITY NAME	ABBREVIATION	IDENTIFIER	DESCRIPTION
Department	Dept	Unique ID of DEPT	An organizational unit in the company
Project	Proj	Unique ID of PROJ	A budgeted project now in progress
Employee	Emp	Unique ID of EMP	An active employee of the department. He/she may be full- or part-time
Office	Office	Unique ID of OFFICE	A room allocated to a department

4.6.2 Determination of E-R Diagram for Problems

The determination of the E-R diagram for the problem may be carried out in a variety of ways. The simplest of these is to take all the nouns in the problem statement and declare them to be entities and the significant verbs as relationships.

The diagram resulting from the problem is as shown in Figure 4.10.

In Figure 4.10, the degree of the relationships between the entities may be denoted by using 1, M, single-headed or double-headed arrows.

4.6.3 Conversion of the E-R Diagram to a Logical Data Model

The following steps are taken to convert E-R diagrams to logical data models:

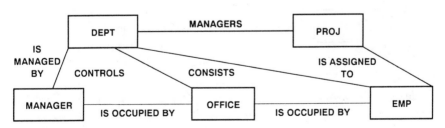

Figure 4.10 E-R diagram for illustrative problem.

- Convert business entities to data entities
- Represent the degree of the relationship between entities
- Convert many-to-many relationships to associations
- Look for conditional relationships
- Convert repeating groups to characteristic entities

If we apply the above steps, we can convert the E-R diagram of Figure 4.10 to a logical data model, as depicted in Figure 4.11.

In Figure 4.11, the single-headed arrow in the direction of DEPT and the double-headed arrow in the direction of PROJ indicate that one DEPT may administer many PROJs. The double-headed arrows in the two directions PROJ and EMP indicate that many employees may work on many projects. The "O" in the direction of PROJ indicates that there is an optional relationship between PROJ and EMP. In other words, an employee does not have to be assigned to a project in order to become an employee.

4.6.4 Conversion of Many-to-Many Relationship

Many-to-many relationships are common among business entities, but awkward to represent in a logical data model by just two entities, since completeness would require much of the same attribute data appearing in each data entity. However, there is often a need to associate two business entities, and, further to store data about that association. Hence, for each many-to-many relationship, we create a new data entity with the following characteristics:

- The new data entity is called an ASSOCIATION data entity
- It has a many-to-one relationship with each of the original data entities
- It is a *child* of each of the original data entities

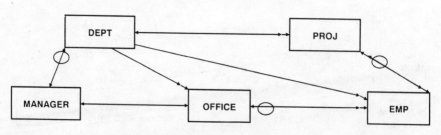

Figure 4.11 Logical data model for problem.

• The unique identifier of the new data entity will contain the unique identifier of both original data entities

The new data entities form an association with the two original entities, as shown in Figure 4.12.

4.6.5 Handling of Repeating Groups

A repeating group is a group of one or more attributes of a data entity which may have multiple values for a given value of the unique identifier.

Repeating groups are undesirable because:

• There is no way to pick a single occurrence within the group.
• They either impose limitations or cause more complex processing of the physical structure.

In order to remove repeating groups from the logical model, we must:

• Create a new entity called a CHARACTERISTIC data entity.
• Create a one-to-many relationship between the original entity and the new entity.
• Use the unique identifier of the original entity as part of the identifier of the new entity.

Figure 4.13 illustrates the handling of repeating groups found in the entity PROJ. Let's say that PROJ has the following attributes:

PROJ (Proj ID, name, address, cost, type)

where cost, address and type have several values. We can now create a one-to-many relationship with PROJ and a new entity PROJ-TYPE whose attributes are: proj-type ID, type name, cost, and address. The relationship is now as shown in Figure 4.13.

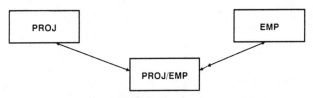

Figure 4.12 Representation of association entity.

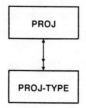

Figure 4.13 Representation of repeating groups.

4.6.6 Translataion of Data Models to Logical Schemas

Logical schemas are defined as data models with the underlying structures of particular database management systems superimposed on them. At the present time, there are three main underlying structures for database management systems. These are:

- RELATIONAL
- HIERARCHICAL
- NETWORK

The next several sections discuss these structures in more detail.

4.7 OVERVIEW OF DBMS STRUCTURES

The hierarchical and network structures have been used for database management systems since the 1960s. The relational structure was introduced in the early 1970s.

In the relational model, the entities and their relationships are represented by two-dimensional tables. Every table represents an entity and is made up of rows and columns. Relationships between entities are represented by common columns containing identical values from a domain or range of possible values. Some of the commercially available relational database management systems are:

VENDOR	DBMS
IBM	SQL/DS, DB2
TYMSHARE	MAGMUM
CINCOM	SUPRA
RELATIONAL TECHNOLOGY	INGRES

The hierarchical model is made up of a hierarchy of entity types involving a parent entity type at the higher level and one or more dependent entity types at the lower levels. The relationship established between a parent and a child entity type is one-to-many. At the same time, for a given parent entity occurrence, there can be many occurrences of the child entity type. Some examples of the hierarchical model are:

VENDOR	DBMS
IBM	IMS
SAS	SYSTEM 2000

In the network model, the concept of parent and child is expanded in that any child can be subordinate to many different parent entities or owners. In addition, an entity can function as an owner and/or member at the same time. There are several commercially available DBMS based on the network model. Some are as follows:

VENDOR	DBMS
CULLINET	IDMS
HONEYWELL	IDS
UNIVAC	DMS 1100

4.8 THE RELATIONAL DATA MODEL

We shall use the example discussed in earlier sections of this chapter to illustrate the various relationships between the entities of an organization. The example will also serve to illustrate the various approaches to creating a relational database.

Consider the example shown in Table 4.2. This data is represented in a two-dimensional table, which is called a relational model of the data. The data represented is called a relation. Each column in the table is an attribute. The values in the columns are drawn from a domain or set of all possible values. The rows of the table are called tuples.

Table 4.2 Representation of Data in a Relational Model

DEPARTMENT TABLE		
DEPARTMENT ID	DEPARTMENT NAME	DEPARTMENT ADDRESS
101	Engineering	Building A
102	Computer Science	Building B
103	Biology	Building C
104	Medical Technology	Building D

In Table 4.2, the DEPARTMENT ID, 101, is the value of the key that uniquely identifies the first row. This key is called the PRIMARY key.

We can now show how the relationship between DEPT and MANAGER in Figure 4.11 can be represented in the relational model. Let us say that the MANAGER relation is shown as (MGR.ID, TITLE, NAME) where MGR.ID is the PRIMARY key of the relation. We can now represent the relationship as shown in Table 4.3.

Table 4.3   Representation of a Relationship in a Relational Model

		MANAGER TABLE	
MANAGER ID	DEPARTMENT ID	TITLE	NAME
MG101	101	Chief Scientist	Mr. Brown
MG102	102	Systems Designer	Mr. Charles
MG103	103	Sr. Biologist	Dr. Green
MG104	104	Sr. Technologist	Mr. Cave

In Table 4.3, column MANAGER ID is called the PRIMARY key and DEPARTMENT ID is called the FOREIGN key. We can also have a column or set of columns identifying the rows of the table. This column is called a CANDIDATE key.

The creation of a table to represent the many-to-many relationship is done as follows:

- Create the ASSOCIATION entity as outlined earlier.
- Create the ASSOCIATION entity table in a manner similar to the MANAGER Table 4.3.

4.8.1 Advantages of a Relational Data Model

The end user is presented with a simple data model. His or her requests are formulated in terms of the information content and do not reflect any complexities due to system-oriented aspects. A relational data model is what the user sees, but it is not necessarily what will be implemented physically.

Nonprocedural Requests   Because there is no positional dependency between the relations, requests do not have to reflect any preferred structure and therefore can be nonprocedural.

Data Independence This should be one of the major objectives of any DBMS. The relational data model removes the details of storage structure and access strategy from the user interface. The model provides a relatively higher degree of data independence than do the next two models to be discussed. To be able to make use of this property of the relational data model, however, the design of the relations must be complete and accurate.

4.8.2 Disadvantages of a Relational Data Model

Although some database management systems based on the relational data model are commercially available today, the performance of a relational DBMS has not been comparable with the performance of a DBMS based on a hierarchical data model or a network data model. As a result, the major question yet to be answered concerns performance. Can a relational data model be used for a DBMS that can provide a complete set of operational capabilities with required efficiency on a large scale? It appears today that technological improvements in providing faster and more reliable hardware may answer the question positively.

4.9 THE HIERARCHICAL DATA MODEL

The hierarchical data model is based on a tree-like structure made up of nodes and branches. A node is a collection of data attributes describing the entity at that point. The highest node of the hierarchical tree structure is called a root. The nodes at succeeding lower levels are called children.

A hierarchical tree structure must satisfy the following conditions:

- A hierarchical data model always starts with a root node.
- Every node consists of one or more attributes describing the entity at that node.
- Dependent nodes can follow the succeeding levels. The node in the preceding level becomes the parent node of the new dependent nodes.
- Every node occurring at level 2 has to be connected with one and only one node occurring at level 1.
- A parent node can have one child node as a dependent or many children nodes.
- Every node except, of course, the root has to be accessed through its parent node.
- There can be a number of occurrences of each node at each level.

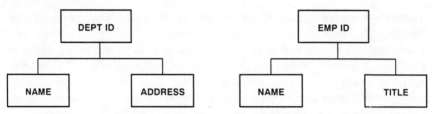

Figure 4.14 Representation of entities in the hierarchical data model.

Consider the two data entities discussed earlier in the chapter, DEPT and EMP. The data model for these two entities are shown in Figure 4.14.

In Figure 4.14, DEPT ID is the root node, and NAME and AD-DRESS are the dependent or child nodes. In the hierarchical data model DEPT ID and all occurrences of NAME and ADDRESS will constitute a database record.

4.9.1 Representation of Relationships

As in the relational data model, the representation of relationships in the hierarchical data model is accomplished by making the unique identifier of one entity in the relationship part of the unique identifier of the other entity. For the relationship between DEPT and EMP, we will have the following, as shown in Figure 4.15.

4.9.2 Storage Operations with a Hierarchical Data Model

In the hierarchical data model, insertion and deletion of nodes are carried out as follows

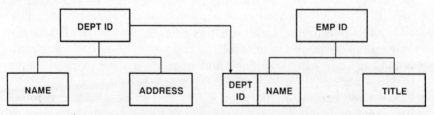

Figure 4.15 Representation of relationships in the hierarchical data model.

- Insertion — a child node occurrence cannot exist without a parent node occurrence.
- Deletion — when a parent node is deleted, the child occurrence is deleted, too.

4.9.3 Advantages of a Hierarchical Data Model

- The major advantage of the hierarchical data model is the existence of proven database management systems that use the hierarchical data model as the basic structure.
- The relative simplicity and ease of use of the hierarchical data model and the familiarity of data processing users with a hierarchy are major advantages.
- There is a reduction of data dependency.
- Performance prediction is simplified through predefined relationships.

4.9.4 Disadvantages of a Hierarchical Data Model

- The many-to-many relationship can be implemented only in a clumsy way. This often results in a redundancy in stored data.
- As a result of strict hierarchical ordering, the operations of insertion and deletion become very complex.
- Deletion of parent results in the deletion of children.
- Any child node is accessible only through its parent node.

4.10 THE NETWORK DATA MODEL

The components of a database with a network data model as the underlying structure are shown in Figure 4.16.

The network data model interconnects the entities of an enterprise into a network.

In Figure 4.16, the blocks represent the entity types. It should be noted that the entity EMPLOYEE is owned by two entities, DEPARTMENT and PROJECT. It is this fact that distinguishes the network data model from the hierarchical data model, where the dependent entity has one and only one owner.

In the network data model, a database consists of a number of areas. An area contains records. In turn, a record may consist of fields. A set, which is a grouping of records, may reside in an area or span a number of areas.

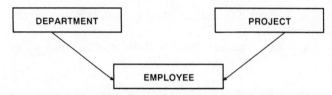

Figure 4.16 Representation of the network data model.

A set type is based on the owner record type and the member record type. For example, if the entity DEPARTMENT had an attribute ADDRESS with several values, we may want to create a new entity ADDRESS. In turn, this new entity ADDRESS may have a relationship with the entity EMPLOYEE, hence we will have a set made up of the DEPARTMENT and ADDRESS relationship and another set made up of the EMPLOYEE and ADDRESS relationship. These two sets are shown in Figure 4.17.

4.10.1 Advantages of the Network Data Model

- The major advantage of the network data model is that there are successful database management systems that use the network data model as the basic structure.
- The many-to-many relationship, which occurs quite frequently in real life, can be implemented easily.

4.10.2 Disadvantages of the Network Data Model

- The main disadvantage of the network data model is its complexity.
- The application programmer must be familiar with the logical structure of the database.
- The programmer has to know his or her position in set occurrences when moving through the database.

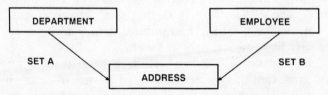

Figure 4.17 Representation of sets in the network data model.

4.11 CONCLUDING REMARKS

This chapter dealt in great detail with the three major data models RELATIONAL, HIERARCHICAL, and NETWORK. It was shown how those three form the underlying structure for the three major database management systems bearing their names.

We developed some ideas about normalization, logical database design, and physical database design. These ideas will be further cemented in the next two chapters.

QUESTIONS

1. Give a definition for a data model. Discuss its merit in representing data usage in an organization.
2. What are the three types of data models? Discuss the role of each type in the database design process.
3. List the major types of relationships between entities. Give examples of each type.
4. Is there any difference between an entity-relationship diagram and a logical data model? If so, please discuss the differences.
5. What are the steps involved in translating data models to logical schemas?
6. List the three major data models. Discuss the advantage and disadvantage of each.
7. On what basis would you recommend any of the three data models to a prospective user?

5

The Normalization Process

5.1 INTRODUCTORY REMARKS

During data analysis, the relevant attributes are recorded and defined for each entity type. This may lead to identification of new
entity types or to the subdivisions of existing entities. It also enables
the boundaries of the data area to be defined more precisely. Once
the entity model is reasonably complete, explicit checks need to be
made to detect redundant relationships. These checks may include
the process called NORMALIZATION.

5.2 NORMALIZATION

Normalization requires three actions to be performed on the attributes of an entity. These are as follows:

- First Normal Form — repeating groups are removed.
- Second Normal Form — attributes are removed which are dependent on only some of the identifying attributes.
- Third Normal Form — any attributes are removed which are not
directly dependent on the identifying attributes.

5.3 FIRST NORMAL FORM

During data analysis *man* was identified as one of the entity types of
interest to the organization and *address* was identified as one of the
attributes of *man*. During the First Normalization process it will be

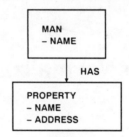

Figure 5.1 First normal form.

shown that there are hidden relationships inside the entity type since several men may reside at the same address or a man may have several addresses.

First Normal Form normalization would produce a new entity type *property* (say). (See Figure 5.1.)

5.4 SECOND NORMAL FORM

A normalized relation (entity) is said to be in SECOND NORMAL FORM if all its nonprime attributes (attributes which do not serve to identify the relation) are fully functionally dependent on each candidate key (attributes which uniquely identify the relation).

SECOND NORMAL FORM EXAMPLE

CUSTOMER (ORDER #	CUSTOMER #	CUSTOMER NAME)
1	241	H. Pratt
2	250	M. Hall
3	241	H. Pratt

In the above example, the nonprime attribute CUSTOMER NAME is fully dependent on the candidate key, ORDER #. That is, for each value of ORDER # there is one and only one value of CUSTOMER NAME.

UNNORMALIZED RELATION EXAMPLE

CUSTOMER (ORDER #	ITEM CODE	UNIT PRICE	QUANTITY)
1	A10	5	10
1	C13	3	20
2	A10	5	15
2	B16	12	2
3	B16	12	11

In the above unnormalized relation the attribute UNIT PRICE is not fully dependent on the candidate key ORDER #/ITEM CODE.

A removal of partial dependence in the unnormalized relation CUSTOMER will produce two relations, ORDER and PRICE, which are in SECOND NORMAL FORM.

SECOND NORMAL FORM EXAMPLE

ORDER (ORDER #	ITEM CODE	QUANTITY)
1	A10	10
1	C13	20
2	A10	15
2	B16	2
3	B16	11

PRICE (ITEM CODE	UNIT PRICE)
A10	5
C13	3
B16	12

5.5 UPDATE PROBLEMS WITH UNNORMALIZED RELATIONS

The following update problems are experienced in unnormalized relations:

- Insertion — if we wish to introduce a new item in the CUSTOMER relation with a specific UNIT PRICE, we cannot do so unless a customer places an order, since we need an ORDER #.
- Deletion — if the information about a customer order is deleted, the information about the item, e.g., UNIT PRICE, is also deleted.
- Modification — since the information about an item appears as many times as there are orders for it, modifications on the item information would be very difficult.

5.6 THIRD NORMAL FORM

A normalized relation is said to be in third normal form if all its
nonprime attributes are fully functionally and directly dependent on
each candidate key.

UNNORMALIZED RELATION EXAMPLE

STOCK (BIN#	PART #	QUANTITY	LEAD TIME	REORDER LEVEL)
210	30	5	10	5
211	30	10	10	5
225	50	7	7	6
231	81	3	15	10
232	81	12	15	10

In the above relation we assume that a bin cannot hold stock of
more than one part number (PART #). If BIN # is the candidate key,
then the relation is not in THIRD NORMAL FORM, since the nonprime attributes LEAD TIME and RECORDER LEVEL are not directly dependent on BIN #.

THIRD NORMAL FORM EXAMPLE

STOCK	(BIN#	PART #	QUANTITY)
	210	30	5
	211	30	10
	225	50	7
	231	81	3
	232	81	12

STOCK B	(PART #	LEAD TIME	REORDER LEVEL)
	30	10	5
	50	7	6
	81	15	10

5.7 NORMALIZATION IN THE RELATIONAL DATA MODEL

Objectives of the relational model:

• Description of data understandable by humans
• Query language with easily understood operations

- Based on solid mathematical foundation

Objectives of normalization:

- Choice of representation of data with low redundancy
- Elimination of anomalies

5.7.1 Basic Concepts of the Relational Model

VALUES

> Integers (e.g., 245)
> Strings of characters (e.g., "J. Smith & Co.")
> Dates (e.g., 83-11-23)

DOMAINS

> Sets of values of the same type, e.g., all integers, all dates, all character strings not more than 30 characters long, all integers in the range 00000-99999.

ATTRIBUTES

> Names to which values from a certain domain can be assigned, e.g., 'EMP-NUM' could be an attribute taking on values in the domain of integers in the range 00000-99999, 'HEIGHT' could take on values in the range 0-300 cm.

RELATION SCHEME

> A relation name together with one or more attributes, all different, e.g.,

> SUPPLIES (SUPPLIER, PART)

> is a relation scheme with relation name SUPPLIES and attributes SUPPLIER and PART.

> Similarly,

> Employee (NAME, HIRE-DATE, DIPLOMA, SALARY)

has relation name EMPLOYEE and attributes NAME (char 30), HIRE-DATE (date), DIPLOMA (a set of possible diplomas), and SALARY (from 1 to 200000).

The domains, attributes, and relation schemes supply a framework or format for describing information. The following concept carries the actual information, like a "record occurrence" in a file:

TUPLE (formatted according to a certain relation scheme)

A sequence of values, one for each attribute in a relation scheme, taken from the domain of that attribute; e.g., the scheme supplies (SUPPLIER, PART). PART has domain the set of integers from 00000-99999.

N-TUPLE

A tuple having values for N attributes

RELATION (FILE)

A set of tuples according to a given relation scheme; e.g., writing the scheme as a first line:

Supplies (Supplier,\ \Part)

J. Smith & Co.	23456
J. Doe & Co.	23456
XYZ Co.	12987
Honest Ed's	76543

RELATION INSTANCE

Same thing as a relation, but emphasizes we don't mean the relation scheme or even just the relation name.

CONSTRAINT

A restriction placed on allowable values for an attribute or on allowable tuples in a relation scheme, e.g., SALARY LT $150000 is a constraint on the value of attribute SALARY. In

Employee (NAME, HIRE-DATE, DIPLOMA, SALARY)

we only allow tuples such that two tuples with the same hire date and diploma have the same salary value (Functional dependency constraint).

DATABASE SCHEME

A set of relation schemes, e.g.,

Employee (NAME, HIRE-DATE, DIPLOMA, SALARY)
Inventory (PART, QUANTITY, LOCATION)
Supplies (SUPPLIER, PART)

DATABASE

A set of relations, one for each relation scheme in a database scheme

EXAMPLE

Employee	(NAME,	HIRE-DATE	DIPLOMA,	SALARY)
	J. HENRY	AUG.1,82	LIBRARIAN	18000
	P. JONES	APR.15,82	H.S. LEAVING	12000
	C. CLARK	JUL.1,54	ELECTRI-CIAN	45000
Inventory	(PART,	QUANTITY,	LOCATION	
	23456	15	EDMONTON	
	23457	23	CALGARY	
	14345	1	RED DEER	
Supplies	(SUPPLIER,	PART)		
	J. SMITH & CO.	23456		
	J. DOE & CO.	76543		

5.7.2 First Normal Form (1NF)

Attributes take on simple values, not values with component parts; e.g., HEIGHT takes on integer values, PART takes on part numbers in the range 00000-99999 as values.

Sets are also not allowed as values in 1NF: the attribute children could have as value {JOHN, DAVID, CASEY} but not in a 1NF relation.

Questionable case: DATE has a value of the form YEAR.MONTH.DAY; e.g., 83-11-26. DATE can be an attribute of a 1NF relation; however, the component parts of a date cannot be extracted separately by relational database query languages.

Alternative: Use three attributes: YEAR, MONTH, DAY

PUTTING A RELATION INTO 1NF (EXAMPLE)

Supplies	(SUPPLIER,	PART)
	J. SMITH & CO.	{12345,76543,23145}
	J. DOE & CO.	{34345,98987}

becomes

SUPPLIES	(SUPPLIER,	PART)
	J. SMITH & CO.	12345
	J. SMITH & CO.	76543
	J. SMITH & CO.	23145
	J. DOE & CO.	34345
	J. DOE & CO.	98987

ADVANTAGES OF 1NF

• We can answer queries based on any values, using the relational operators provided in relational systems.
• The size of storage for a tuple can be fixed.

DISADVANTAGES OF 1NF

• Repetitions of values are apparent, e.g., the supplier name is repeated for each part above.
• We may find it easier to think of values as an aggregate or set; e.g., CHILDREN.

IMPLEMENTATION There is no reason why relations have to be stored in 1NF form. That form is mainly useful for users of the system, so that they can understand the data in the database system and can formulate queries which are independent of the storage format.

PHYSICAL DATA INDEPENDENCE The way in which data is stored can be changed without any changes to the conceptual model of the data, or to the application programs.

LOGICAL DATA INDEPENDENCE Even the conceptual model of the data can be changed due to growth or restructuring, without having to change the application programs or compromise user familiarity.

5.7.3 Functional Dependency (FD)

Functional dependency is a property of data (e.g., tuples) in a relation whereby, given the value for each one of a set of attributes A1,...An, then, no matter how many tuples contain that combination of values, the values of the attributes B1,...,Bm are always the same in all those tuples.

EXAMPLE

Employee	(NAME, HIRE-DATE, DIPLOMA, SALARY)		
J.S.	NOV.1,76	B.SC.	20000
J.D.	MAY 1,77	PH.D.	40000
H.S.	NOV.1,76	B.SC.	20000
A.A.	MAY 1,77	M.SC.	30000
M.B.	MAR.1,80	M.SC.	20000
Q.K.	NOV.1,76	B.SC.	20000
N.N.	MAY.1,77	PH.D.	40000

A1=HIRE-DATE and A2=DIPLOMA together determine

B1=SALARY

NOTATION FOR FDs

A1,...,AN--B1,...,Bm

e.g., +

HIRE-DATE, DIPLOMA--SALARY

Spoken: "HIRE-DATE, DIPLOMA DETERMINE SALARY"

NOTE: In the above example, adding one tuple

H.D.\ \NOV.1,76\ \B.SC.\ \22000

would completely destroy the FD. An FD which holds all the time is called an FD constraint. Other FDs may hold only some of the time. (e.g., MANAGER--DEPARTMENT holds only until a manager has to take on more than one department; EMPLOYEE--SPOUSE holds only in certain countries where monogamy is practiced).

MORE EXAMPLES OF FDs

ONE ATTRIBUTE ON LEFT, ONE ON RIGHT

in the relation

Manages (DEPARTMENT, MANAGER)

DEPARTMENT->MANAGER

ONE ATTRIBUTE ON LEFT, SEVERAL ON RIGHT

in hierarchy (ADMIN-UNIT, SUB-UNIT, MGR-SUB-UNIT)

SUB-UNIT--ADMIN-UNIT, MGR-SUB-UNIT

SEVERAL ATTRIBUTES ON LEFT, ONE ON RIGHT

HIRE-DATE, DIPLOMA--SALARY

SPECIAL CASE OF AN FD: THE CANDIDATE KEY (OR SUPER KEY)   Suppose the left side and the right side of an FD contain between them all attributes in the relation scheme. Then, given values for the attributes on the left, there is at most one tuple in the relation which can have those values. The attributes on the left form what is called a super key or candidate key.

EXAMPLE

In Employee (NAME, HIRE-DATE, DIPLOMA, SALARY, BENEFITS)

NAME, HIRE-DATE, DIPLOMA--SALARY, BENEFITS

so NAME, HIRE-DATE, DIPLOMA for a super key.

SEVERAL ATTRIBUTES ON LEFT, SEVERAL ON RIGHT

In Employee (NAME, HIRE-DATE, DIPLOMA, SALARY, BENEFITS)

HIRE-DATE, DIPLOMA--SALARY, BENEFITS

NONE ON LEFT OR NONE ON RIGHT

Uninteresting cases

GENERAL SITUATION IN DESIGNING A DATABASE   Think of every relation scheme as having associated with it a family of FD constraints (as well as perhaps other constraints). The properties of the data embodied in these constraints are used to replace the original relations with other relations that are more appropriate.

KEYS   These are minimal super keys:

If an FD whose left side is a super key cannot have any attributes removed from it without destroying the property that the remaining set of attributes on the left determines all other attributes in the relation, then the left side of the FD is called a key.

EXAMPLE

In Employee (NAME, HIRE-DATE, DIPLOMA, SALARY, BENEFITS)

NAME--HIRE-DATE, DIPLOMA, SALARY, BENEFITS

So NAME is a key (as well as being a super key).

However NAME, HIRE-DATE, DIPLOMA is a super key but not a key, since the set is not a minimal super key.

5.8 PARTIAL DEPENDENCY

A nontrivial functional dependency of an attribute or attributes on some, but not all, of a set of attributes forming a key is called partial dependency.

EXAMPLE

Consider the relation

Supplies

(SUPPLIER	ADDRESS	ITEM	PRICE)
S1	A1	I1	P1
S1	A1	I2	P2
S1	A1	I3	P3
S2	A2	I1	P4
S2	A2	I2	P5

Here   SUPPLIER->ADDRESS

SUPPLIER, ITEM->PRICE

Key: SUPPLIER, ITEM

SUPPLIER alone is not a key, hence

SUPPLIER->ADDRESS is a partial dependency.

5.8.1 Second Normal Form (2NF)

A relation is in 2NF if it is 1NF and there are no partial dependencies.

PUTTING INTO 2NF   The attributes on the right of a partial dependency are taken out of the relation and put into another one along with the other attributes of the partial dependency.

EXAMPLE

In the above, ADDRESS is taken out of the original relation leaving

Supplies (SUPPLIER ITEM PRICE)

and a second relation is created.

Location (SUPPLIER ADDRESS)

This eliminates the partial dependency of ADDRESS on SUPPLIER.

5.8.2 Another Harmful FD Type

In the relation scheme

Employee (NAME, HIRE-DATE, DIPLOMA, SALARY)

there is an FD: HIRE-DATE, DIPLOMA--SALARY; however, HIRE-DATE and DIPLOMA together do not form a super key (NAME is a key). So there may be several tuples with the same HIRE-DATE, DIPLOMA, and consequently the same SALARY information.

5.8.3 Transitive Dependencies

The redundancy in the above example is due to what is called a transitive dependency: A set of attributes which is not a super key forms the left side of a nontrivial FD; the right-hand side is an attribute, not part of any key (a nonprime attribute).

5.9 RELATIONAL DATA MODEL (3NF)

Transitive dependencies can still occur even for 2NF relations. In order to eliminate them, CODD introduced Third Normal Form (3NF):

3NF
                    The relation is in 2NF
                    and
                    there are no transitive dependencies

Putting into 3ND — Bernstein's Algorithm:
                    Input: A relation scheme plus
                              a collection of FD for it

                    Output: Several relation schemes
                            in 3NF, equivalent to
                            the original scheme

5.10 BOYCE-CODD NORMAL FORM (BCNF)

A relation is in BCNF if for any nontrivial FD holding in it, say A1, A2,..., An--B, with B not one of the A's the left side is a super key of the relation.

NOTE:

A partial dependency violates BCNF since its left side isn't a super key.

A transitive dependency violates BCNF since its left side isn't a super key.

Hence BCNF is a stronger condition to impose than 2NF or 3NF.

5.10.1 Redundancy Reduction Due to BCNF

In any relation in BCNF, an FD A1, A2,...An--B never gives rise to more than one tuple having specific A1, A2,...An values, since the left side is a super key.

5.10.2 Decomposing a Relation into a Collection of BCNF Relations

1. Find an FD A1,...,An--B1,...,Bm whose left side is not a super key and whose right side is as large as possible.

2. Replace the original relation with two relations: the first one obtained by removing B1,...,Bm from the original relation, and the second one having only A1,..., An, B1,...,Bm as attributes.
3. Keep doing this until all relations are BCNF.

5.10.3 Natural Joins

Sometimes a relation has a meaning that involves "AND"-ing two statements; e.g., Supplier X has address Y and supplies item Z. In this case obvious redundancy arises if the relation is stored as a flat file:

ADDRESS & SUPPLIES	(SUPPLIER, ADDRESS, ITEM)		
	J. SMITH & CO.	EDMONTON	12345
	J. SMITH & CO.	CALGARY	76543
	J. SMITH & CO.	RED DEER	45634
	J. SMITH & CO.	EDMONTON	76543

etc. Get all combinations of EDMONTON, CALGARY, RED DEER with
12345, 76543, 45634
then
GO ON TO J. DOE & CO.

5.10.4 A Better Way to Represent the Information

Break the relation up into two relations:

Location	(SUPPLIER,	ADDRESS)
	J. SMITH & CO.	EDMONTON
	J. SMITH & CO.	CALGARY
	J. SMITH & CO.	RED DEER
	J. DOE & CO.	ETC.
Supplies	(SUPPLIER,	ITEM)
	J. SMITH & CO.	12345
	J. SMITH & CO.	76543
	J. SMITH & CO.	45634
	J. DOE & CO.	ETC.

SAVINGS   There are six tuples for J.SMITH & CO. here, but there were nine before. If J. SMITH & CO. has 3 locations and manufactures 100 items, there would be 300 tuples for J. SMITH & CO. in the relation with the three attributes, but only 103 tuples if we decompose into two relations!

5.11 FOURTH NORMAL FORM (4NF)

A relation is in 4NF if it is in BCNF and if it is not a natural join as above.

The existence of a natural join is sometimes referred to as a multi-valued dependency; e.g., above SUPPLIER->->ADDRESS AND SUPPLIER-->->ITEM (SUPPLIER multidetermines ITEM, etc)

Putting into 4NF: Whenever an MVD is detected, decompose the relation into two; whenever a nontrivial FD is detected, decompose if the left side is not a super key. (There are some details of this which we skip over.)

5.12 NETWORK — RELATIONAL COMPARISON

In a network database, the links between the owner records and the member records in a set allow the information in the owner to be available when processing the members; e.g.,

    OWNER = SUPPLIER, ADDRESS
    MEMBERS = PARTS,

J. SMITH & CO., EDMONTON as owner can have members 12345, 76543, 45634

In the relational approach, there are no information-bearing links! To link the parts to their owner in a relational model, we need to include a key for the owner record in the member record; e.g.,

    J. SMITH & CO.   12345
    J. SMITH & CO.   76543
    J. SMITH & CO.   45634

5.12.1 Using Relational Design Methods for Network Databases

If we have a relational model and we want to express it as a network, we can find the FDs and MVDs and use them to design a network structure, modifying it as required for efficiency.

5.12.2 Multiple Data Model Implementations

The relational model can actually be implemented on top of a network database. There are attempts to create multiple data model databases, so that some users can access data relationally and others via a network. This is a very active area of current research!

5.13 SUMMARY

This chapter dealt with the normalization process in a mathematically rigorous manner. The intent here was to appeal to those readers who treat normalization in a very theoretical way.

To those whose mathematics is somewhat suspect, I have devoted the first few sections of this chapter.

QUESTIONS

1. Define the term normalization. What actions are required to be performed on the attributes of an entity during this process?
2. What are the criteria for first normal form, second normal form, and third normal form?
3. Construct a set of unnormalized relations. Normalize these relations to first, second, and third normal forms.
4. Define the terms domain, relation schema, tuple, relation instance, and functional dependency.
5. What is partial dependency? Give an example.
6. What is transitive dependency? Give an example.

6

Logical and Physical Database Design

6.1 INTRODUCTION

This chapter discusses the two major phases of database development. In the first phase, logical database design, we take the user requirements as represented by a data model, superimpose the constructs of the database management system, and obtain input to the second phase, physical database design. In the second phase, we are primarily concerned with storing the data as defined in the logical data model and defining access paths to the stored data.

6.2 THE SYSTEMS DEVELOPMENT LIFE CYCLE

In Chapter 1, we discussed two development life cycles for the development of databases. In both cycles, we placed a lot of emphasis on the processes and functions that were required to satisfy the user requirements. We want to move away somewhat from that approach and adopt an approach where the data is the driving force behind the database development activities. The phases of this approach are shown in Table 6.1.

Table 6.1 The Phases of a Data-Driven SDLC

TRADITIONAL	DATA-DRIVEN
1. Identification Phase	1. User Requirement
• Initiation	• Initial Survey
• Initial Survey	• Data Definitions
	• Feasibility Study
	• Project Scope
	• Security Plans
2. Systems Study Phase	2. Logical Design
• Feasibility Study	• Data Model
• General Systems Study	• Dictionary Population
	• Process Definitions
	• Program Specifications
	• Systems Test Plans
	• Normalization
3. Systems Development Phase	3. Physical Design
• Detail Systems Design	• Program Development
• Data Conversion Plan	• Physical DB Design
• Program Specification	• Database Loading
• System Test Plan	• Testing
• Manual Practices	• Training
4. Systems Implementation	4. Evaluation
• Program Development	• Monitoring
• Data Conversion	• Performance Tuning
• Systems Testing	• Reorganization
• Training	• Auditing
• Parallel Operations	
5. Evaluation	

6.2.1 The User Requirement Phase

The User Requirement phase was discussed at some length in Chapter 2. However, in this section we will concentrate on those areas that are more data-related.

During the Initial Survey subphase, the analyst seeks to determine the entities and relationships that are of interest to the users.

In the Data Definition subphase, the analyst obtains descriptions, functions, data characteristics, and editing rules about the entities and all known attributes.

In the Project Scope subphase, the analyst obtains metadata about the boundaries of the data model, the common usage of items in the user views, and information on what should not be included in the project.

In the Security Plans subphase, the analyst obtains information on the security, privacy, and integrity requirements of the data that will be processed by the system. He begins to formulate plans and policies for the protection of that data.

6.2.2 The Logical Design Phase

In the Data Model subphase of logical database design, the analyst creates a data model of the entities and relationships that were described to him or her in the User Requirement phase. The model is superimposed with the constructs of the relevant database management system. It is during this phase that some attention is paid to key selections and access methods.

In the Usage Statistics subphase, the analyst collects information about the volume of data to be processed, the processing frequencies, the variations in volumes, the volatility of the data, and plans for alternate access to the data rather than by unique keys.

In the Normalization subphase, the analyst seeks to ensure that all attributes clearly belong to the entities they best describe. He ensures that existing entities cannot be further collapsed into other entities and that attributes cannot be further grouped into other entities.

In the Data Dictionary Population subphase, the analyst begins to enter all collected metadata about the entities, attributes, relationships, data models, and processes into the corporate data dictionary. This process is usually started in the Data Definitions subphase but must be emphasized in the subphase.

6.2.3 The Physical Design Phase

In the Physical Design phase, the analyst takes as input the data model from the Logical Design phase, selects the best storage and accessing methods, and produces the physical data model. It is during this phase that storage and time estimates for the chosen database management system are calculated.

The analyst may split existing entities in the logical data model or collapse entities in order to improve performance, reduce redundancy in storage, or to adhere to access methods requirements. The resulting physical model may differ greatly from the input logical model.

In the Database Loading subphase, the analyst uses a database specific utility to load data into storage areas on the relevant storage devices.

6.2.4 The Evaluation Phase

During the Evaluation phase, the performance of the database management system is mentioned to determine if it meets the user's expectation in response time and throughput. The database is stress-tested for large volumes of data. The pointers and chains are tested for their ability to return data items from the lowest levels of the hierarchy.

In the Performance Tuning subphase, utilities are run against the database to repair broken pointers and chains. Transaction rates, mixes, and processing regions are examined to ensure that the job is being performed adequately. The analyst must reexamine main storage space, DASD space, channels, and teleprocessing lines to ensure that the database is doing the work required of it.

In the Reorganization subphase, the analyst reorganizes or re-structures the database in order to recapture all unused space between the valid records as a result of deletion of some records. He also reorganized the database to prevent fragmentation of space, the creation of long chains and excessive fetch times. He may also want to rearrange the records so that, for most of them, their physical sequence is the same as their logical sequence. He may also want to reorganize the database so that the frequently accessed records may be stored on a high-speed medium, whereas the rarely accessed records are stored on a slower-speed medium.

In the case of a sequentially organized database, reorganization may take the form of combining the old database records with the transaction log file to form a new database. In an indexed, sequentially organized database, reorganization means taking all the database records from the prime and overflow areas and reloading the database without any records going into the overflow area.

In the Auditing subphase, the Internal Auditors examine the audit trails, the transaction log file, the backup and recovery procedures, and all relevant standards and procedures that are developed during the database development period to determine their adequacy and their ability to ensure the security, privacy, and integrity of the stored data.

6.2.5 Data-Related Activities During the SDLC

In a data-driven systems development life cycle the analyst, data administrator, database administrator, and system designer carry out some activities and produce some deliverables that are distinctly data-related. These activities and deliverables differ greatly from those that are strictly process-driven or process-related. I have summarized these activities and deliverables in Table 6.2.

6.3 LOGICAL DESIGN OF DATABASES

Logical design of databases is mainly concerned with superimposing the constructs of the database management system on the logical data model. As mentioned earlier, these constructs fall into three categories: hierarchical, relational, and network.

In this section of the chapter, we will develop various logical models of the database using the three structures mentioned above.

6.3.1 Mapping to a Hierarchical Data Model

The steps to follow in deriving a logical hierarchical database from the logical data model are as follows:

- Derive a hierarchical data model, including the constructs of the database management system (DBMS).
- Refine the data model according to performance requirements.
- Select key names.
- Add relationships, association and characteristic entities as required by the particular DBMS.

In deriving a hierarchical data model that includes the constructs of the DBMS, we may want to:

- Eliminate superfluous relationships.
- Derive some parent-child relationships.
- Resolve multiple parentage.

Table 6.2 Data-Related Activities and Deliverables

TRADITIONAL	DATA ACTIVITIES	DATA DELIVERABLES
1. IDENTIFICATION	1. USER REQUIREMENT	• Data Dictionary containing data items, validation rules and other definitions
• Initiation	• Define the entities that will be included in project scope	
• Initial Survey		
2. SYSTEMS STUDY	2. LOGICAL DESIGN	• Logical database and data model
• Feasibility Study	• Identify relationships among data items	
• Data Conversion Plan		
• Program Specifications	• Normalize user views	
• Systems Test Plan	• Produce logical data model	
• Manual Practices	• Logical database and data model	
3. SYSTEMS DEVELOPMENT	3. PHYSICAL DESIGN	• Data Dictionary with all physical flows
• Detail Systems	• Develop physical database from logical model	
• Design		
• Data Conversion Plan	• Verify adequacy of physical design	
• Program Specification	• Data Dictionary with all physical data flows	
• Systems Test Plan		
• Manual Practices		
4. SYSTEMS IMPLEMENTATION	4. EVALUATION	
• Program Development	• Assist DBA in setting procedures for monitoring the database	
• Data Conversion	• Assist auditors in setting procedures for auditing the database	
• Systems Testing		
• Training		
• Parallel Operations		
5. EVALUATION		

Let us examine the relationships represented in Figures 6.1 and 6.2. The relationship between DEPARTMENT and EMPLOYEE is superfluous since it can be derived from the relationship shown in Figure 6.2.

In deriving relationships, we may want to derive a parent-child relationship from a given relationship. Let us examine the relationships represented in Figures 6.3 and 6.4.

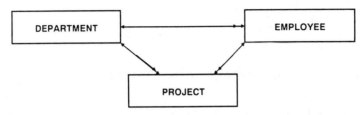

Figure 6.1 Superflous relationships.

We can derive a new relationship where either DEPARTMENT or EMPLOYEE is the parent.

The significance of creating the parent-child relationship is illustrated as follows. Let us, say, store some information on the date the employee joined the department, the results of performance reviews, promotions within the department, and job functions. We can see that all of these attributes that have stored do not identify either DEPARTMENT or EMPLOYEE entity, but identify the relationship between DEPARTMENT and EMPLOYEE. When this situation occurs, the key of the new entity is a combination of the keys of the two original entities.

The resolution of multiple parentage depends on whether some parents are their normal form relations or created one. Very often, created entities are needed mainly for the physical implementation of the data model. When this is the case and no data is lost by eliminating the created entity or combining it with another entity, we can very safely opt for eliminating the created entity and not the one in third normal form.

Very often, the data model must be modified to conform with the constraints of the DBMS. For example, if the DBMS was Information Management System (IMS), we would have the following constraints:

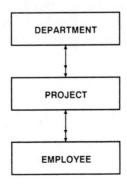

Figure 6.2 Modify relationships.

Figure 6.3 Relationship between department and employee.

- There can be no more than 255 node types or segment types.
- There can be no more than 15 hierarchical levels.
- A child segment type can have no more than two parents, a "physical" parent and a "logical" parent.
- A logical child cannot have a logical child.

Very often, we may want to add some relationships to the data model. The reason may be to add entities that may better support the data needs of the organization in the future. This should not be done in a way that would degrade the performance of the system.

6.3.2 Mapping to a Relational Data Model

As we have discussed before, the relational model consists of a number of relations or tables. In mapping the data model onto the constructs of the relational DBMS, we would produce a table for each entity in the model. The relationships between entities would show up as foreign keys in one of the related entities.

The mapping into a relational DBMS is a relatively easy process.

6.3.3 Mapping to a Network Data Model

In mapping a data model onto the constructs of the network DBMS, we derive owner-member relationships within set types. We may collapse some of the set types by combining entities or eliminating after the normalization process.

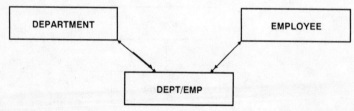

Figure 6.4 Representation of parent-child relationship.

The logical database designers will have to pay more attention to performance considerations during this phase than during similar phases of hierarchical or relational database design.

6.4 PHYSICAL DESIGN OF DATABASES

The physical model is a framework of the database to be stored on physical devices. The model must be constructed with every regard given to the performance of the resulting database. One should carry out an analysis of the physical model with average frequencies of occurrences of the groupings of the data elements, with expected space estimates, and with respect to time estimates for retrieving and maintaining the data.

The database designer may find it necessary to have multiple entry points into a database, or to access a particular segment type with more than one key. To provide this type of access, it may be necessary to invert the segment on the keys, thereby posing some overhead on space and/or time. This is very often the price that must be paid to satisfy this particular business requirement.

The physical designer must have expertise in at least three areas:

• Knowledge of the DBMS functions
• Understanding of the characteristics of direct access devices
• Knowledge of the applications

The physical designer must know how the DBMS performs its specific functions. For example, in IBM's Information Management System (IMS) the designer must know the following:

1. Access to all segments, except when using secondary indexing, is through the root segment. Hence, remote segments should be confined to few levels and less spread out from left to right.
2. Retrieval from the database is by segments. This means that a programmer may be presented with more data than is necessary. This often poses security problems for the installation. In this case, the trade-off is between too few and too many segments.
3. Frequently accessed segments should be kept to the top of the hierarchy, since all access is through the root of the hierarchy.
4. One physical database is based on one root segment. Hence, if one physical database is expected to become too big, the designer should consider splitting it. However, the operational issues

of backup and recovery for several physical databases must be taken into consideration.

5. Alternate paths to the data besides through the root segment can be provided. For example, we must know that with secondary indexing, IMS database records can be accessed on data elements other than the primary key.

6.5 SELECTION OF ACCESS METHODS

We often refer to the way that we store the data for subsequent retrieval as the file organization. The way that we retrieve the data is called the access method.

The types of access methods vary from manufacturer to manufacturer. The names also vary from DBMS to DBMS. The physical database designer must be familiar with several access methods. However, because of my background with IMS, I will discuss only those that are pertinent to IMS.

IMS allows us to define nine different types of databases. These are as follows:

DATABASE TYPE	GROUP	ACCESS METHOD
HSAM	Sequential	Hierarchical Sequential
SHSAM	Sequential	Simple Hierarchical Sequential
HISAM	Sequential	Hierarchical Indexed Sequential
SHISAM	Sequential	Simple Hierarchical Indexed Sequential
HDAM	Direct	Hierarchical Direct
HIDAM	Direct	Hierarchical Indexed Direct
MSDB	Direct	Main Storage
DEDB	Direct	Data Entry

6.5.1 Hierarchical Sequential Databases

HSAM databases use the sequential method of storing data. All database records and all segments within each database record are physically adjacent in storage.

HSAM data sets are loaded with root segments in ascending key sequence and dependent segments in hierarchic sequence. You don't have to define a key field in root segments. You must, however, present segments to the load program in the order in which you want them loaded. HSAM data sets use a fixed-length, unblocked record format (RECFM=F), which means that the logical record length is the same as the physical block size.

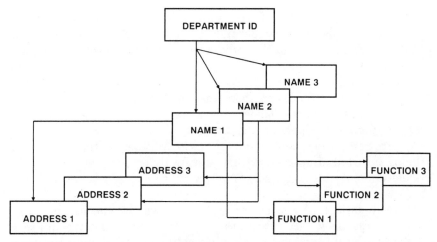

Figure 6.5 Representation of HSAM database in hierarchic sequence.

HSAM databases can only be updated by rewriting them. They are used primarily for low-use files. For example, audit trails or statistical reports or files containing historical or archive data.

Segments in an HSAM database are loaded in the order in which you present them to the load program. You should present all segments within a database record in hierarchic sequence. In the data set, a database record is stored in one or more consecutive blocks. If there is not enough space left in the block to store the next segment, the remaining space is filled with zeros and the next segment is stored in the next consecutive block.

Figure 6.5 illustrates the HSAM database records sequence. Figure 6.6 illustrates how HSAM database records are stored.

6.5.2 HISAM Databases

In a HISAM database, as with HSAM databases, segments in each database record are related through physical adjacency in storage. Unlike HSAM, however, for each HISAM database, you must define a unique sequence field in each root segment. These sequence fields are then used to construct an index to root segments in the database.

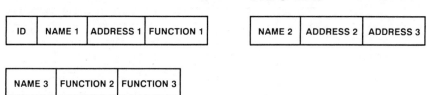

Figure 6.6 Storage of HSAM records.

HISAM is typically used for databases that require direct access to database records and sequential processing of segments in a database record. It's a good candidate for databases with the following characteristics:

* Most database records are about the same size.
* The database does not consist of relatively few root segments and a large number of dependent segments.
* Applications don't depend on a heavy volume of root segments being inserted after the database is initially loaded.
* Deletion of database records is minimal.

HISAM database records are stored in two data sets. The first, called the primary data set, contains an index and all segments in a database record that can fit in one logical record. The index provides direct access to the root segment. The second data set, called the overflow data set, contains all segments in the database record that cannot fit in the primary data set.

Figure 6.7 illustrates the HISAM database records sequence. Figure 6.8 illustrates how HISAM database records are stored.

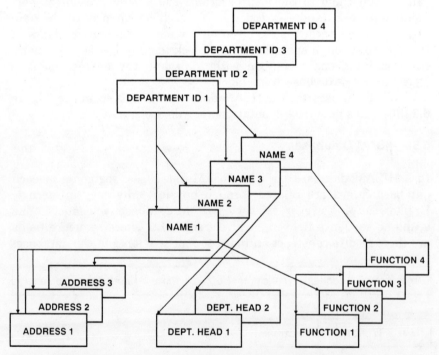

Figure 6.7 Representation of HSAM database in hierarchic sequence.

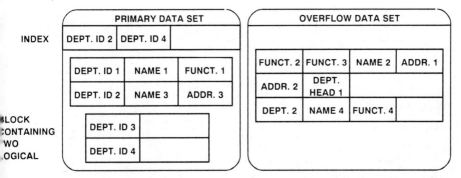

Figure 6.8 Storage of HISAM records.

There are several things you need to know about storage of HISAM database records:

- You define the logical record length of both the primary and overflow data set.
- You define the size of the control interval or block.
- Each database record starts at the beginning of a logical record in the primary data set.
- Segments in a database record cannot be split and stored across two logical records.

6.5.3 Hierarchical Direct Databases

Hierarchical Direct databases differ from sequentially organized databases in two important ways. First, they use the direct method of storing data; that is, the hierarchic sequence of segments in the database is maintained by having segments point to one another. Except for a few special cases, each segment has one or more direct-address pointers in its prefix. When direct-address pointers are used, database records and segments can be stored anywhere in the database. Their position, once stored, is fixed. Instead, pointers are updated to reflect processing changes.

Hierarchical Direct (HD) databases also differ from sequentially organized ones in that space in HD databases can be reused; that is, if part or all of a database record is deleted, the deleted space can be reused when new database records or segments are inserted.

HDAM databases are typically used when you need primarily direct access to database records. The randomizing module provides fast access to the root segment.

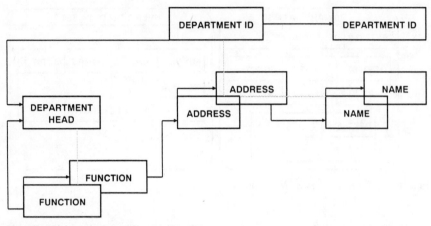

Figure 6.9 Hierarchic forward pointers.

HIDAM databases are typically used when you need both random and sequential access to database records and random access to paths of segments in a database record. Access to root segments is not as fast as with HDAM, because the HIDAM index database has to be searched for a root segment's address. However, because the index keeps the address of root segments stored in key sequence, database records can be processed sequentially.

The next few diagrams (Figures 6.9, 6.10, and 6.11) illustrate how hierarchical direct databases are stored and processed.

In hierarchic pointers, each pointer points from one segment to the next in either forward or forward-and-backward hierarchic sequence.

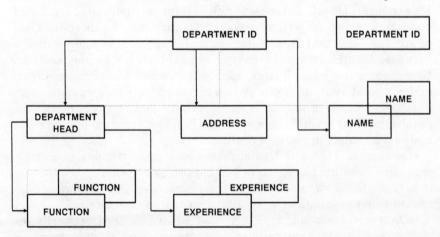

Figure 6.10 Physical child first pointers.

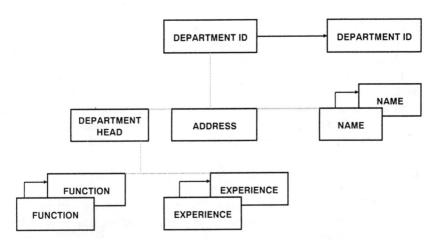

Figure 6.11 Physical twin forward pointers.

In physical child first pointers, each pointer points from a parent to the first child or dependent segment. You should notice that no pointers exist to connect occurrences of the same segment type under a parent.

In physical twin forward pointers, each segment occurrence of a given segment type under the same parent points forward to the next segment occurrence.

HDAM databases consist of two parts: a root addressable area and an overflow area. The root addressable area contains root segments and is the primary storage area for dependent segments in a database record. The overflow area is for storage of dependent segments that don't fit in the root addressable area.

Root segments in HDAM databases must have a key field, although the key field doesn't have to be unique.

A HIDAM database is actually composed of two databases. One is for storage of the database records; the other is for the HIDAM index.

Root segments in HIDAM databases must have a unique key field. This is because an index entry exists for each root segment based on the root's key.

6.6 SUMMARY

The chapter dealt with the logical and physical design aspects of database development. In the logical design phase, we discovered that the primary deliverable was a data model with the constructs of the relevant DBMS superimposed. In the physical design phase, we indicated that the important steps were calculating space and time estimates, selecting access methods, and learning the database.

The chapter discussed in some detail the access methods of IMS, an IBM-developed, hierarchical DBMS.

Finally, the chapter served as a forerunner of Chapter 7, where we will discuss specific designs of currently available DBMSs.

QUESTIONS

1. Define systems development life cycle. Discuss its phases.
2. What is the difference between process-driven and data-driven life cycles?
3. Discuss logical and physical database design in terms of their activities.
4. Discuss the deliverables of each phase of a data-driven system development life cycle.
5. What are constraints of database management systems? Discuss how they are used in mapping the logical data model to the particular DBMS.
6. What are access methods? Discuss those pertinent to Information Management System (IMS).

7

Design of Specific Systems and Databases

7.1 INTRODUCTORY REMARKS

In this chapter, we will apply the concepts of logical and physical database design which we discussed in earlier chapters to specific database management systems.

In addition to applying the concepts, we also want to introduce some tools and utilities into the design process. Some of these tools and utilities are:

• Prototyping Tools
• CASE Tools
• Data Dictionaries
• Performance Tuning Utilities
• Backup and Recovery Utilities

The specific databases that we will discuss include:

• IMS
• DB2
• IDMS
• SQL/DS

7.2 PROTOTYPING TOOLS

A valuable tool in the design of any database system is the screen and report prototype. This facility allows the systems designer to simulate for the user what the final product will look like and, at some level, how it will function. Prototyping tools have been available for most mainframe application development packages for many years.

Tools, like Excelerator from Index Technology, provide several useful features that together allow the designer not only to create sample screens and reports, but also to have the user enter data into specified files and run actual reports against that data without having to write code. Screen and report prototypes use the elements in the data dictionary and can reference tables of acceptable values set up by the designer.

The developer, when creating a screen, specifies a unique name for the screen and describes its function, then indicates the next screen. A screen painting facility allows the developer to add screen headings, field labels, and locations on the screen where specific elements will be entered. Elements can be set up with attributes such as blinking or skip, and these elements can use edit tables stored in the data dictionary. The screen painting facility also has options: cutting, pasting, deleting, blocking, and repeating screen elements.

Once the screen is completed, the designer can generate a data map for COBOL, C, BASIC, or PL/1. These tools generate files or print out the structure for the elements defined on the screen in the format for the language specified. Screens are associated with files; the designer can designate record and key lengths for screen data entry. The system presents a menu allowing the user to add, modify, and delete records in the file. Once these records are added to the file, they can be reported on to allow users to use screens prior to approving final design.

Creating report prototypes is similar to creating screens. The report can contain labels and elements that exist in the dictionary, has options for repeating elements, and can be printed as output to a file or the screen.

The tools give the designer total control over format, selection criteria, and sort order for reports generated. The report selection criteria allow selection of a single element or group of elements. Common selection conditions such as >, < and = are supported by most tools. The output sequence for the report can be on a single sort element or on a combination of elements with a primary sequence, a secondary sequence, and so on.

There are options in some of these tools that allow the designer to use a predefined output format, which simply prints the contents of the record, or a user-defined format, with which the designer can select the elements to be printed and the order of printing.

7.3 CASE TOOLS

Nearly every systems development organization has experienced problems with meeting development schedules, coordinating design efforts, and maintaining its systems. And they have also heard that Computer-Aided Software Engineering (CASE) can be a big help with such problems. This section introduces CASE tools and their functions. Chapter 9 will be devoted in its entirety to the rapid emergence and use of CASE tools.

7.3.1 Some Definitions of CASE

CASE, although now widely accepted as an acronym, does not yet have a single, widely accepted definition.

Because CASE can encompass so many aspects of systems development, the question of CASE must be addressed separately for each of the three types of CASE tools:

- Programmer/Project Productivity Tools — these provide support for designers and programmers of software, but only at the back end of the systems development life cycle. These may include tools for natural language programming, rapid prototyping, project management, and documentation.
- Systems Development Support Tools — these provide support for techniques and tasks of systems development at any or all stages of the life cycle, but do not necessarily enforce a systems development methodology. These may include diagramming tools, data dictionaries, and analysis tools, or any of the productivity tools.
- Systems Development Methodology Tools — most systems development methodologies are collections of techniques combined in structures made to minimize redundant effort and maximize coordination between tasks. These methodology tools provide support for and enforce a systems development methodology at any or all stages of the lifecycle. They may include any of the systems development support tools as appropriate for the methodology. In addition, they enforce methodology rules and thus provide systems development expertise to users.

The reader should turn to Chapter 9 for a more detailed discussion of CASE tools.

7.4 DATABASE SPECIFIC UTILITIES

The physical designer of database systems can't escape the use of utilities in his work. He has to use them to load the database, reorganize the database, and tune the database.

This section discusses some of the utilities that are available to service the more established DBMSs.

7.4.1 IMS Space Management Utilities

This set of utilities, in general, can help with the following tasks:

* Detecting DB pointer discrepancies
* Gathering statistics for DB tuning
* Restructuring and reloading segments during database reorganization

You can use four of the utilities to help monitor your database.

The Pointer Checker Utility In addition to validating pointers, the pointer checker programs produce detailed statistics about the segments and pointers in the database. This utility analyzes disk space used and gives you reports showing free space and pointer statistics. Also, output from this utility is used to determine the effects of changing parameters and/or randomizing routines.

The DB Tuning Aid This utility produces a map of how the DB data is actually stored throughout the database. You can use this information and the segment and pointer statistics from the pointer checker to optimize distribution of the data.

The Data Space Monitory Utility You can use this utility to monitor data space growth rate. You can select some or all data sets, on a volume or catalog, to be monitored.

The HDAM Physical Block Reload Utility You can analyze output from this utility to determine the effect of changing database parameters and/or randomizing routines.

7.4.2 IMS Database Tuning Utilities

You will want to tune your database either to improve performance or to better utilize database space. This section introduces the reorganization utilities, which can be used to make many types of changes to tune your database.

HISAM Reorganization Unload Utility   You use the HISAM unload utility to unload HISAM database or HIDAM index database.

HISAM Reorganization Reload Utility   You use the HISAM reload utility to reload a HISAM database. You also use the HISAM reload utility to reload the primary index of a HIDAM database.

Database Scan Utility   You use the database scan utility to scan databases that are not being initially loaded or reorganized, but contain segments involved in logical relationships with databases that are being initially loaded or reorganized.

Database Prefix Update Utility   You use the prefix update utility to update the prefix of each segment whose prefix was affected by the initial loading or reorganization of the database.

7.4.3 DB2 Database Utilities

DB2 utilities perform many of the same functions described earlier. Some of them are:

- LOAD — The LOAD utility is used to load rows into a table without using SQL.
- REORG — The REORG utility creates JCL for a reorganization.
- COPY — The COPY utility will copy the contents of a tablespace to a sequential dataset.
- MERGECOPY — The MERGECOPY utility can combine several incremental image copies into one or combine incremental image copies with a full image copy to produce a new full image copy.
- RECOVER — The RECOVER utility is used to restore tablespace from its backup dataset generated by the COPY utility.
- STOSPACE — The STOSPACE utility collects information and records it in the catalog.

7.5 THE DATA DICTIONARY

The logical and physical designer of database systems will find the data dictionary a very important tool.

The data dictionary acts as a central repository for holding the definitions and descriptions of the major entities and processes that comprise the original system.

The dictionary is used at each phase of the system development life cycle to document the deliverables from the phase. In the user requirement phase, the data dictionary will contain metadata about the entities, attributes, and relationships that satisfy the user requirement. In a process-driven environment, the data dictionary will contain metadata about the data flows, the systems, and the processes that satisfy the user requirement.

In the logical design phase, the designer will enter metadata about the data model into the data dictionary. The data model may be a single-user view of the business requirement or a composite and integrated view of all user requirements.

In the physical design phase, the designer may enter metadata about the storage requirements, the access methods, the key selection, the security requirements, and programming requirements into the data dictionary.

The data dictionary can be used as a re-engineering tool to assist the designer in developing new data models from existing programs and "copy" libraries. It can also be used to obtain usage statistics on entities, attributes, and relationships.

Finally, a detailed discussion of the use of the data dictionary in systems design will be given in the next chapter.

7.6 SPACE CALCULATIONS

Physical database design consists of choices among such things as access methods, indexing, block sizes, data set groups, root anchor points, root addressable area size, randomizing algorithms, and pointer options. This section discusses some choices which can aid in the task of finding the right combination of values for these parameters to produce efficient performance and economic space utilization.

7.6.1 Input to the Space Calculations

The required input for space calculations is obtained from information normally contained in the database definition statements. From the database definition statements, we use the names and lengths of the segments, their relationships to each other, and their average frequencies of occurrence.

7.6.2 Use of Subtrees in Space Calculations

The notion of subtrees is very useful when calculating database size estimates. A subtree of segment type X is defined to be one occurrence of segment type X plus the collection of all segments that are hierarchically subservient to that occurrence of segment X. Each segment occurrence that has children defines a proper subtree. Each segment occurrence without children defines a primitive subtree consisting of only that occurrence.

In Figure 7.1, occurrences of segment types C, D, and F are primitive subtrees because they are the low-level segments on their respective parts. The subtree of B1 is composed of segments B1, C1, C2, and D1. The subtree of B2 comprises segments B2, C3, D2, and D3. E1 and E3 are also primitive subtrees. E2's subtree contains E2 and F1. A1's subtree is A1 plus the collection of all the B, C, D, E, and F type segments subservient to A1. For purposes of calculation, it is convenient to think of a subtree as containing a defining segment occurrence plus the subtrees of all immediate dependents of that segment.

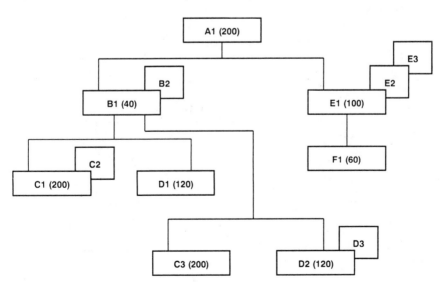

Figure 7.1 Example of a specific database record.

7.6.3 Calculating Subtree Length

The length of the subtree of a segment is merely the length of the segment itself plus the lengths of all its dependent subtrees. But it is impractical, and usually impossible, to determine the exact number of occurrences of the dependent types because the number of occurrences varies from record to record; it also varies dynamically within a record as inserts and deletions are made during processing. Hence, we calculate a segment's subtree size on the basis of an "average" record by estimating the expected number of occurrences of each subservient segment type.

7.6.4 Subtree Sizes Without Data Set Groups

For the initial example, assume the data set is not divided into groups. Assume 10,000 occurrences of the root segment A, and assume an "average" database record, as depicted in Figure 7.2, with segment frequencies (F) and lengths (L) as indicated.

The length calculations proceed in the following manner where $L(X)$, $S(X)$, and $F(X)$ represent the length of segment type X, the length of the subtree of segment type X, and the frequency of occurrence of segment type X, respectively:

$$
\begin{aligned}
S(F) &= L(F) = 60 \text{ bytes} \\
S(E) &= L(E) + S(F) \times F(F) \\
     &= 100 + 60 \times 0.8 = 148 \text{ bytes} \\
S(D) &= L(D) = 120 \text{ bytes}
\end{aligned}
$$

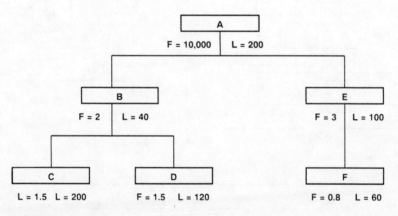

Figure 7.2 Example of an average database record.

S(C)   = L(C) = 200 bytes
S(B)   = L(B) + S(C) x F(C) + S(D) x F(D)
        = 40 + 200 x 1.5 + 120 x 1.5 = 520 bytes
S(A)   = L(A) + S(B) x F(B) + S(E) x F(E)
        = 200 + 520 x 2 + 148 x 3 = 1,684 bytes

Thus, the expected length of a record (each occurrence of the root, A, and all its dependents) is 1,684 bytes. The total number of bytes (TB) for the database is

TB   = S(A) x F(A)
        = 1,684 x 10,000
        = 16,840K bytes

7.6.5 Subtree Sizes With Data Set Groups

If the database is divided into groups, the space calculations must be performed on a "per group" basis, as each group will be defined to the system as a separate data set having its own storage characteristics. We can use Figure 7.3 with its indicated data set groups to determine the subtree size.

The space calculations for each group are performed as follows:

Group 1
S(C1)   = L(C1) = 200 bytes
S(B1)   = L(B1) + S(C1) x F(C1)
        = 40 + 200 x 1.5 = 340 bytes
S(A1)   = L(A1) + S(B1) x F(B1)
        = 200 + 340 x 2 = 880 bytes
TB(1)   = S(A1) x F(A1)
        = 880 x 10,000 = 8,800,000 bytes

Group 2
S(E2)   = L(E2) = 100 bytes
S(D2)   = L(D2) = 120 bytes
S(B2)   = S(D2) x F(D2)
        = 120 x 1.5 = 180 bytes
S(A2)   = S(B2) x E(B2) + S(E2) x F(E2)
        =180 x 2 + 100 x 3 = 660 bytes
TB(2)   = S(A2) x F(A2)
        = 660 x 10,000 = 6,600,000 bytes

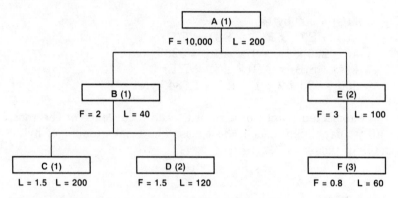

Figure 7.3 Example of a specific database record.

Group 3

$S(F3)$ = $L(F3)$ = 60 bytes
$S(E3)$ = $L(F3)$ x $F(F3)$
= 60 x 0.8 = 48 bytes
$S(A3)$ = $S(E3)$ x $F(E3)$
= 48 x 3 = 144 bytes
$TB(3)$ = $S(A3)$ x $F(A3)$
= 144 x 10,000 = 1,440,000 bytes

The total number of bytes for the database is the sum of the sizes of the data set groups.

TB = $TB(1) + TB(2) + TB(3)$
= 8,800,000 + 6,600,000 + 1,400,000
= 16,840,000 bytes

7.6.6 Basic Space Calculations Formulas

The total number of storage bytes required for the database is given by

TSS = NB x $BLKS2$

where

TSS = total storage space in bytes
NB = number of required blocks
$BLKS2$ = block size in bytes

The number of required blocks (NB) is given by

$$NB = \frac{TB}{EFFBLK \times (1 - FSB)}$$

where

TB	= Total Number of Segment Bytes
EFFBLK	= Effective Block Size in Bytes
FSB	= Percentage of Blocks to Remain Empty

The EFFBLK is the number of segment bytes to be stored in a block. This is given by

EFFBLK = (FLKS2) x (2-FSW) - OVHD - EOBW

where

FSW	= percentage of free space within the blocks
OVHD	= block overhead in bytes
EOBW	= end of block waste in bytes

7.7 TIME ESTIMATES

In estimating the I/O timings for a database design, a number of assumptions and probabilities must be stated. If, for example, we considered the IMS environment, we will have to consider

• The probability of a physical I/O operation in going from a parent segment to the first occurrence of one of its child segment types.
• The probability of a physical I/O operation in going from a segment to its next twin.
• The probability of a physical I/O operation in going from a segment to its physical parent.

We will not discuss, in any detail, how to derive these probabilities. We will rather refer the reader to other texts on this subject. Hence, for our purposes, we will just state two relations for determining CPU and physical I/O timings. There are:

1. CPU Time = E x PL x MIPS
   where

E = expected number of database calls
PL = average number of instructions for the call
MIPS = CPU speed in instructions per microsecond

2. I/O Time = E(I/O) x (ST + LT + XT)
    where
    E = expected physical I/O's
    ST = seek time
    LT = latency time
    XT = transfer time

7.8 PERFORMANCE TUNING OF IMS DATABASES

In an IMS environment, you may want to tune your database either
to improve performance or to better utilize database space. This section describes the various types of tuning changes you might want to
make and when and how the changes can be made using the reorganization utilities.

The types of changes you may want to make are as follows:

• Reorganizing the database
• Changing access methods
• Changing hierarchic structures
• Changing direct-access storage devices
• Adjusting HDAM options
• Adjusting buffers
• Adjusting VSAM options
• Changing amount of space allocated
• Changing the number of data set groups

Reorganization can be done using various vendor-supplied utilities.
In the case of IMS, we use a single program called Utility Control
Facility (UCF). In some cases, you may use the appropriate unload
and reload utilities.

7.9 USE OF SECONDARY INDEXES

Secondary indexes are indexes that allow you to process a segment
type in a sequence other than the one defined by the segment's key.
A secondary index can also be used to process a segment type based
on a qualification in a dependent segment.

COURSE SEGMENT

CLASS DATE	COURSE NUMBER	COURSE NAME	CLASS ROOM NUMBER	ROOM SIZE

Figure 7.4 Layout of course segment.

Let us demonstrate the need for a secondary index by the following (Figure 7.4):

Suppose the root segment, COURSE, has the fields shown in Figure 7.4 and the course number is a unique key field. This selection may not be appropriate for an application that would like to access the database by student name and then get a list of courses a student is taking. Given the order in which the database record is now organized, access to the courses a student is taking requires a sequential scan of the entire database. Each database record has to be checked for an occurrence of the STUDENT segment. When a database record for the specific student is found, then the course segment has to be referenced to get the name of the course the student is taking. This type of access is relatively slow. In this situation, you can use a secondary index that has a set of pointer segments for each student to all COURSE segments for that student.

7.9.1 Characteristics of Secondary Indexes

Secondary indexes can be used with HISAM, HDAM, and HIDAM databases. A secondary index is in its own database and must use VSAM as its access method.

Secondary indexes use three types of segments:

• Pointer Segment — is contained in the secondary index database and is the only type of segment in the secondary index database.
• Target Segment — is in the regular database and is the segment the application program wants to retrieve.
• Source Segment — is also in the regular database. The source segment contains the field that the pointer segment has as its key field. In other words, data is copied from the source segment and put in the pointer segment's key field.

Figure 7.5 illustrates the layout of a pointer segment.

In Figure 7.5 the RBA field is the address of the segment the application program wants to retrieve from the regular database.

DELETE BYTE	RBA OF THE SEGMENT TO BE RETRIEVED	KEY FIELD	OPTIONAL FIELDS	SYMBOLIC POINTER TO SEGMENT TO BE ACCESSED

Figure 7.5 Layout of course segment.

7.10 DESIGN CONSIDERATIONS OF IMS

In addition to deciding on the basic characteristics of the data structure, the designer must filter in certain relevant design characteristics. In the IMS specific database environment, some of these considerations are as follows:

- Specifying free space
- Estimating the size of the root addressable area
- Choosing a logical record length for the database
- Determining the size of the control intervals and blocks
- Determining which VSAM options
- Determining which ISAM/OSAM options
- Fast path design considerations

I will leave the reader to research some of these considerations. However, I will list some rules for choosing a logical record length for the database (HISAM):

- Logical record size in the primary data set must be at least equal to the size of the root segment, plus its prefix, plus overhead. If variable length segments are used, logical record size must be at least equal to the size of the longest root segment, plus its prefix, plus overhead.
- Logical record size in the overflow data set must be at least equal to the size of the longest segment in the overflow data set, plus its prefix, plus overhead.
- For ISAM/OSAM, the logical record length must be evenly divisible into physical block size. In other words, if physical block size is 2,048 bytes, four logical records per physical block can be used.
- For VSAM, the logical record lengths must be an even number.
- If you are using multiple data set groups, the rules for logical record size for the primary data set group are the same as the rules used when multiple data set groups are not used.

7.10.1 Determining the Size of Control Intervals

You can specify the VSAM control interval size for your database. To determine how many physical blocks ISAM or OSAM will use per track and then what percentage of track space will be utilized, use the following formulas:

- Blocks per tract = $\dfrac{Size\ of\ Track}{C + KL + LR}$

  where
  Size of tract = 19,254 bytes
  C = 185 if KL = 0
  C = 267 if KL $\neq$ 0
  KL = length of key field in the root segment
  LR = length of the logical record

- Percentage of space = $\dfrac{Blocks\ per\ track\ x\ block\ size}{Size\ of\ Track}$

7.11 PERFORMANCE TUNING OF DB2 DATABASES

Performance of DB2 databases is affected in both the design and processing phases. Poorly designed tables can make designing of good performing queries very difficult.

Items affecting DB2 performance that are part of the design phase are:

- Number of tables being joined
- Row size
- Primary key uniqueness
- Normalization of tables

7.11.1 Performance Tuning Hints

Database   Applications using DDL for tablespace, tables, and indexes should have their own database. Some types of processing within a database are restricted until DDL query execution is completed. Dynamic SQL cannot be performed with DDL execution. Likewise, binds cannot be performed or utilities executed during DDL execution. Since personal data is more susceptible to changes requiring DDL executions than shared data, it is a good idea to separate shared data from personal data at least by database.

Tablespace   Unless very small tables are being developed, use the guideline of only one table per tablespace. Many utilities operate at the tablespace level; thus, when one table is being processed, all tables in the tablespace are unavailable. Also, locking of a table actually locks at the tablespace level, and once again all of the tables in the tablespace are impacted.

Another reason to avoid placing more than one table in a tablespace is possible tablespace scan. If indexes are not used for a query, the entire table is scanned. This implies that every row of every table is processed regardless of the table referenced in the query.

Also of concern is the space occupied by deleted tables in the tablespace. The space is not reclaimed until reorganization. If only one table resides in the tablespace, the tablespace can be deleted and redefined to reclaim unusable space.

You can achieve performance tuning by the judicious use of utilities. For example, the load utility can be used to load data into DB2 tables in a more efficient manner than the corresponding SQL insert statements. If you have a unique index defined on a table being loaded, make sure you remove all duplicate rows. DB2 does not prevent duplicates from being loaded because the rows are inserted before the indexes are updated.

Finally, if you are planning mass deletes, consider unloading the rows to be kept and reloading with the replace option. Since the delete query is one of the more expensive queries, this could save considerable amounts of resources.

7.12 SOME CONCLUDING REMARKS

If the topics discussed in previous chapters can be labeled "the mechanics of database design," those discussed here can be termed the "fine tuning of the mechanics."

Chapter 7 sought to apply the specifics of database design to topics covered earlier. We took considerations for IMS, the representative database from the hierarchical group, and DB2, the representative database from the relational group and introduced them in such a way that the designer can easily apply them to his own database environment. This can truly be called the synopsis for the entire discourse on database design.

QUESTIONS

1. What are prototyping tools? Discuss their role in systems design and development.
2. Give a definition of a CASE tool. Discuss each of the three types of tools.
3. Discuss database utilities in terms of their involvement in tuning, reorganizing, loading, and monitoring the database.
4. Discuss the use of subtrees in space calculations.
5. Set up a database record for an IMS environment and calculate the space requirement for that record.
6. List the various changes required in tuning a database. Give reasons for those changes.
7. What is a control interval? How is its size determined?

8

The Data Dictionary in Systems Design

8.1 INTRODUCTION

The role of the data dictionary in the design, implementation, and maintenance of database systems has been well documented in the current literature.

The growing awareness of data as a corporate resource, resulting in data-driven, rather than process-driven, systems, has led to recognition of the impact of data on departments outside data processing. In this way, the system development life cycle has developed from a point where the focus of concern was on highly localized data processing problems. It is now recognized that the efficiency of a given system usually depends upon its end-user orientation and how well it represents and serves the organization as a whole. Current methodologies are becoming less process-oriented and more data-oriented.

It is because of this new awareness that the data dictionary can play a significant part in supporting the SDLC. It provides a wealth of detail on which early research work can be based and is, then, an invaluable communications tool between the different departments that are involved in the SDLC. It is for these reasons that the succeeding sections discuss the role of the data dictionary in the SDLC.

8.2 WHAT IS A DATA DICTIONARY?

The data dictionary can be defined as an organized reference to the data content of an organization's programs, systems, databases, collections of all files, or manual records.

The data dictionary may be maintained manually or by computer. Sometimes, the term data dictionary refers to a software product that is utilized to maintain a dictionary database. The data dictionary will contain names, descriptions, and definitions of the organization's data resource.

8.3 THE CONCEPT OF METADATA

In the broadest sense, a data dictionary is any organized collection of information about data.

In the real world, any information system, whether or not it is computerized, exists to store and process data about objects (entities). We then create data records to represent occurrences of these entities. We define specific record types to represent specific entity types. Frequently we also assign keys or identifiers, such as customer names and invoice numbers, to differentiate one record occurrence from another. A data dictionary can then be designed to contain data about those customer and invoice record types.

The customer and invoice records in the database contain ordinary data. The record in the data dictionary contains metadata, or data about the data. For example, the record in the data dictionary may contain the name, the record length, the data characteristics, and the recording mode of the record in the database.

8.4 ACTIVE VERSUS PASSIVE DATA DICTIONARIES

Data dictionaries are often categorized as active or passive. This refers to the extent of their integration with the database management system. If the data dictionary and the DBMS are integrated to the extent that the DBMS uses the definitions in the dictionary at run time, the dictionary is active. If the dictionary is freestanding or independent of the DBMS, it is passive.

An active dictionary must contain an accurate, up-to-date description of the physical database in order for the database management system to access the data.

In a passive dictionary environment, more effort is required to keep two copies of the same data, and great care must be taken to ensure that the two copies are actually identical.

8.5 THE ROLE OF THE DATA DICTIONARY IN THE SDLC

The role of the data dictionary in the system development life cycle is best exemplified in Figure 8.1.

Any analysis of Figure 8.1 will show that the data dictionary is at the core of systems design and development. The metadata collected in the dictionary about the different phases of the SDLC are demonstrated in the second layer of the diagram. The third layer depicts the various interfaces to the different phases of the SDLC. The directions of the arrows indicate that the interfaces act as input to the phases and also extract design information from the phases.

As we move in a clockwise direction around the second layer we notice, starting with the input from the end users, that the following types of metadata are collected:

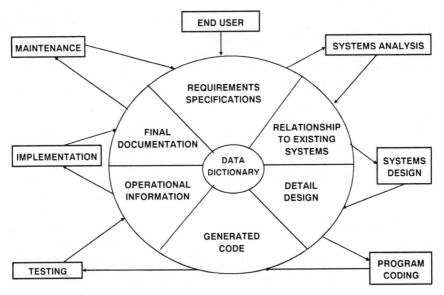

Figure 8.1 The SDLC showing the data dictionary as a communication and documentation tool.

- Requirements specifications
- Relationships to existing systems
- Detail design
- Generated code
- Operational information
- Final documentation

8.5.1 Requirements Specifications

As indicated in Chapter 2, the systems analyst or the data analyst collects data from the end user as to the entities in which he or she has a particular interest. The data collected may be definitions and descriptions about the entities, data characteristics, security requirements, attribute content, and the processes involved in moving the data across interfaces and manipulating that data.

The analyst synthesizes this data and then enters as much of it into the data dictionary as the constructs of the dictionary allow. For example, in the DATAMANAGER data dictionary marketed by Manager Software Products (MSP) the analyst can enter data about the system, file, groups of data, and data items that will constitute a solution to the user's requirements.

8.5.2 Relationship to Existing Systems

In arriving at what may be the optimum solution to the user's requirement, the analyst must seek to determine from the dictionary if:

- A system already exists that can solve the problem.
- No system exists, what portions of the existing systems can be used in his solution.
- Alternate solutions can be obtained.

8.5.3 Detail Design

During detail system design, the analyst will enter data about the data models, the process flows, the programming specifications, the file layouts, and report formats. If the current design has any relationship to existing designs already existing in the data dictionary, the analyst can extract that portion and implement it with the new metadata.

8.5.4 Generated Code

The data dictionary contains copy books (source statements) and source statements or pointers to source statement libraries that may be extracted to use for program testing.

It is now possible to generate code from process definitions and programming specifications stored in the data dictionary. Current CASE tools can generate this code for several languages and several different platforms, e.g., PC or mainframe.

8.5.5 Operational Information

The data dictionary may contain information which will enable the data processing staff to execute the programs. This information may include run instructions, job control language (JCL) setup, distribution information, test plans and requirements, and processing exceptions.

8.5.6 Final Documentation

The final documentation information stored in the data dictionary may include user-manual instructions, impact analysis information, acceptance testing and sign-off information, change control information, and job control language information.

8.6 INTERFACES TO THE DATA DICTIONARY

The interfaces to the data dictionary are many and varied. The interfaces act in two directions; the deliverables to the dictionary and the information extracted from the dictionary. These interfaces include:

• End user
• Systems analysis
• Systems design
• Program coding
• Testing
• Implementation
• Maintenance

8.6.1 The End User

The end user is the primary source of input to the requirements specifications phase of systems development. It is during this phase that data is collected on the objectives and scope of the project, the data and processing requirements, the operating environment, alternative processing, data security, and the input and output formats.

The advent of database management systems, structured design methodologies, and new development tools has signalled a larger role for the end user in a systems development. The end user is now as much a part of the systems development team as the data analyst or systems analyst. The success or failure of the system now depends in a large degree to the quality of the data collected on user requirements.

8.6.2 The Systems Analysis Phase

During the systems analysis phase, data is obtained from the end user and the user requirement specifications and fed into the systems design phase; the relationship to existing systems data is stored in the data dictionary.

During this phase, the data and systems analyst will iteratively extract data from the requirements specifications already stored in the data dictionary, augment it with that from the end user and any obtained from existing systems, to come up with data and process models which form the primary deliverables of the systems design phase.

If during the systems analysis phase no data is found in the data dictionary that connects the current system with other systems, the analyst enters any existing relationships into the data dictionary.

8.6.3 The Systems Design Phase

During the systems design phase, the data analyst extracts information from the analysis phase and relationship to existing systems stored in the data dictionary and develops a data model. This model is in turn stored in the data dictionary as detail design metadata. Meanwhile, the systems (process) analyst develops a process model with information from the data dictionary and the systems analysis phase. This data collected during the phase is stored in the detail design section of the data dictionary and used as input through programming specifications to the program coding phase.

8.6.4 The Program Coding Phase

During the program coding phase, the programmer analyst takes specifications from the systems design phase and couples it with metadata from the detail design information stored in the data dictionary to produce program codes for the testing phase and to be stored as metadata, and sometimes source data, in the data dictionary.

8.6.5 The Testing Phase

During this phase, the analysts take program codes from the program coding phase and generated code stored in the data dictionary and test it to obtain operational metadata to be stored in the data dictionary and program code for the implementation phase.

8.6.6 The Implementation Phase

During this phase, operational information metadata stored in the data dictionary is coupled with the tested program code to produce implementable systems. The results from the phase are stored in the data dictionary as a final document and are used as input to the maintenance phase.

8.6.7 The Maintenance Phase

During this phase, metadata from the final document stored in the data dictionary and input from the implementation phase are used to maintain the production systems.

This phase also sees the updating to requirements specifications stored in the data dictionary and the constant reporting to the user of the results of these changes.

8.7 THE DATA DICTIONARY AS A DOCUMENTATION TOOL

As was mentioned earlier, the data dictionary plays a significant role in the systems development life cycle. One major role is documenting the results of each phase of the SDLC. This section describes some of the entries that are documented in the data dictionary for the major phases of the SDLC.

8.7.1 Documenting the System Design Phase

The data dictionary can offer substantial assistance to the designer during the system design phase by providing the source and storage for the inputs and outputs of the design step.

The inputs to data design are full descriptions of the business processes and the data required by these processes. The outputs are the logical views and the logical database (also known as logical schemas). A logical database refers to a structuring of entities and relations between entities supporting the business processes of the application.

There are many different methods of transforming the business processes and their required data into a logical database. One is a top-down data design method identifying entities and the relationship between the entities before defining the attributes of each entity.

This is opposed to bottom-up data design techniques, which encourage the description of entities, and the attributes identifying the entities, before identifying relationships between entities.

There are five basic steps in top-down data design:

- Identify the business functions of the application.
- Identify the data required by each function and the procedure by which data is collected.
- Identify the entities of the application.
- Define the relationships between the entities.
- Ascribe attributes to their entities.

Nowhere is the importance of the data dictionary more obvious than it is in the building of the function's logical model. As the keeper of the "who," "what," and "how" of the organizational information system, the data dictionary provides full descriptions of:

- The business functions
- The data generated by and used by the business functions
- The application entities
- The relationships of the application's entities to one another
- The attributes of the entities

Frequently, data itself goes through an evolutionary process, its definition becoming more and more refined until it can finally be set. Data also can be perceived simultaneously from several user points of view. A data dictionary that has facilities for multiple logical dictionaries can document the history of a data item or process as well as hold these varied points of view. This can be a most valuable aid during the design stage.

8.7.2 Documenting the Detailed Design Phase

In a Business System Plan (BSP) the design phase is composed of two levels, the General Design and the Detailed Design, in which business activities, data, entities, relationships and attributes are described, not just on the application level, but from a higher level providing a corporate, transfunctional perspective. In BSP, the methodology is the same as with SDLC; it is simply engineered on a higher plane. Once these elements are plugged in, they remain in documented form on the data dictionary and can be accessed for future systems development as well. Another feature of the data dictionary which can prove to be most useful at this point in the SDLC is its facility for providing implicit, as well as explicit, relationships, and the systems designer, who might otherwise overlook these implicit relationships, is spared one more trap to fall into.

8.7.3 Documenting the Physical Design Phase

The details of physical design depend very much on the characteristics of the DBMS chosen for the database design.

In an IMS environment, the physical design included the following selections:

- Physical databases and types of logical relationships, whether unidirectionally or bidirectionally physically paired
- Access methods, whether HISAM, HIDAM or HDAM
- Segments and hierarchical structures and data representation, including type and size
- Secondary indexes
- Types of pointers in relationships

The data dictionary is a very useful tool to document these mentioned selections. In addition, volume and usage statistics necessary for the ordering of database segments and for determination of storage estimates can be documented in the data dictionary.

8.7.4 Documenting the Implementation Phase

The implementation phase is very often not considered a part of the SDLC because by that point, the system has been installed and consequently has entered a separate, operational period.

It is a stage which has enormous impact on, not just the system, but the entire organization as well. Maintenance is also a task which is especially well served by the data dictionary, which provides:

• Complete up-to-date documentation of the system
• A historical and multi-user perspective view of the development of the definitions of the systems entities, process entities, and the relationships among them
• Enforcement of the use of definitions in a logical manner
• Security of the integrity of these definitions
• The means of assessing the impact of system changes

Consequently, the maintenance staff is provided with a comprehensive and logically consistent picture of the system, its functions, processes, and data components. The staff is thus properly prepared to respond to the needs of change in ways which will minimize error, save time, money, and frustration.

The maintenance stage is also the point at which the use of the data dictionary as a systems development tool is most easily validated. Systems founded upon data dictionary resources are the most likely to be spared the unnecessary and yet most typical function of maintenance, namely rectification of bad systems planning and specifications. Consequently, they are the ones most likely to free the maintenance stage for its proper function of adapting the system to the organization's changing environment. Obviously, this frees up the staff for the development of new systems and reduces many of the external pressures otherwise imposed on all systems.

8.7.5 Documenting the Structured Maintenance Phase

Structured maintenance deals with the procedures and guidelines to achieve system change or evolution through the definition of data structure change to accommodate the requirements of system change. The inputs to structured maintenance are user change requests to the current system, including database design and systems design. These are held on the data dictionary. The output from structured maintenance is, ideally, a system reflecting the user change request.

There are five steps in structured maintenance:

* Identify the changes to the data structures required to accommodate the user request.
* Identify the program functions which currently process the data structures. These program functions are reviewed and systems changes are identified.
* Determine the cost of the change. One of the benefits of this method is that it quickly indicates significant costly changes, seen when the data structures required to accommodate the change are very different from the current data structures.
* Do the implementation — if the cost is acceptable
* Test the results.

Structured maintenance thus goes through all the steps of the structured system development methodology as defined here. This is an effective way to minimize the need to recover from past mistakes of the system, be they the result of unstructured or structured methodologies.

A system development life cycle is used to produce the means by which the organizational data is to be manipulated. Before it may be manipulated, however, it must be managed, and that is the function of the data dictionary.

8.8 THE DATA DICTIONARY AND DATA SECURITY

The data dictionary can be used in the database environment to protect the organization's data. Entries in the data dictionary can be used to indicate who has access rights to what data and who can update or alter that data. It can also be used to indicate who has responsibility for creating and changing definitions.

Current data dictionaries utilize several different protection mechanisms to effect data security in an environment. Also, data dictionaries can have pointers in an "AUTHORIZATION" section to various data security software packages. Some of these are:

* Access management
* Privacy transformations

- Cryptographic controls
- Security kernels
- Access matrix

Due to the constraint on space, I will not discuss all of these mechanisms at length. I will refer you to some of the current literature on data security. However, here is a brief discussion on some of them.

8.8.1 Access Management

These techniques are aimed at preventing unauthorized users from obtaining services from the system or gaining access to its files. The procedures involved are authorization, identification, and authentication. Authorization is given for certain users to enter the database and request certain types of information. Users attempting to enter the system must first identify themselves and their locations, and then authenticate the identification.

8.8.2 Privacy Transformations

Privacy transformations are techniques for concealing information by coding the data in user-processor communications or in files. Privacy transformations consist of sets of logical operations on the individual characters of the data. Privacy transformations break down into two general types — irreversible and reversible. Irreversible privacy transformations include aggregation and random modification. In this case, valid statistics can be obtained from such data, but individual values cannot be obtained.

Reversible privacy transformations are as follows:

- Coding — Replacement of a group of words in one language by a word in another language.
- Compression — Removal of redundancies and blanks from transmitted data.
- Substitution — Replacement of letters in one or more items.
- Transposition — Distortion of the sequence of letters in the ciphered text; all letters in the original text are retained in this technique.
- Composite Transformation — Combinations of the above methods.

8.8.3 Cryptographic Controls

Cryptographic transformations were recognized long ago as an effective protection mechanism in communication systems. In the past, they were used mainly to protect information transferred through communication lines.

There is still much debate about the cost/benefit ratio of encrypting large databases. My experience with encryption indicates that the cost of producing clear text from large encrypted databases is prohibitive.

8.8.4 Security Kernels

Security kernels, as the name suggests, are extra layers of protection surrounding operating systems. The kernels are usually software programs which are used to test for authenticity and to either authorize or deny all user requests to the operating system.

A request to the operating system to execute a task or retrieve data from the database is routed to the security kernel, where the request is examined to determine if the user is authorized to access the requested data. If all checks are passed, the request is transmitted to the operating system, which then executes the request.

8.9 DATA DICTIONARY STANDARDS

There are two types of data-related standards for data dictionaries: data definition standards and data format conformance.

"Data Definition" refers to a standard way of describing data. One example is the naming of data. The naming standard may be in the form of rigid rules or established conventions for assigning names to data entities. All user areas within the enterprise will know that, for instance, the data element "customer name" — used in files, programs and reports — means the same throughout the enterprise.

"Data Format Conformance" is content-related. It means that a data element, in addition to having the same name throughout the enterprise, also must conform to a common set of format rules for the data element to retain the same meaning. For example, all data elements involving "date" should have the same format throughout the enterprise — and only that format should be assigned. Similarly, if codes are to be used throughout the enterprise, these must be uniform. If an acceptable code for state is a two-letter code, that must be the universally accepted code in the enterprise, and no other code, whether one-, three-, or four-letter, should be used.

8.9.1 Standard Formats for Data Dictionary Entries

Standards are required for the format and content used in defining and describing meta-entities of the data dictionary. This means setting standards for the type of information that must be collected for each entry type and, most important, for the conventions that must be observed in defining these attributes. In effect, this amounts to defining a set of standards for methods of preparing attribute, entity, and relationship descriptions.

There are a number of general guidelines for establishing a standard. Several standard entries are available in commercially produced dictionaries. However, a typical standard entry for a data element may be, as illustrated in Table 8.1. A data element may be described in terms of the attributes in this table.

8.9.2 Standards for Programs Interfacing with a Data Dictionary

Data dictionary standards for programming interfaces basically fall into the area of the structure of the "call" statement from the programming language to the dictionary package.

Other standards in this area will indicate how high-level languages will use the data dictionary to build file structures and record layouts from "COPY" books. They will also indicate how these languages will access the dictionary itself.

8.9.3 Security Standards

Standards for access rules and controls will indicate who can access the dictionary, how the dictionary will be accessed, and whether the contents will be accessed in their original form or as copies.

Standards in the area of security will cover the use of the data dictionary as a protection mechanism and the entries that must be made in the data dictionary to achieve those standards.

Table 8.1 Sample Standard for Data Element Description

DATA ELEMENT	DEFINITION
Identification number	A 7-character unique identifier beginning with ELXXXXX.
Designator	A short name composed of the key words of the DE-SCRIPTION.
Programming name	An abbreviated form of the DESIGNATOR using only approved abbreviations. Example: LEGL-CUST-NAME.
Description	A narrative explanation of the data element; the first sentence must identify the real-world entity being described. The second sentence may expand on usage characteristics. Example: The name of a customer, which is the legal name. It may not be the commonly used name. It is usually derived from legal papers.

8.10 EXAMPLES OF DATA DICTIONARY ENTRIES

There are several commercially available data dictionaries, each with its own metadata entries and standards. This section illustrates entries for three available dictionaries:

- XEROX DATA DICTIONARY (XDD)
- MSP DATAMANAGER
- IBM DB/DC

8.10.1 The Xerox Data Dictionary

Functional Requirements — The dictionary software must process certain essential features to properly support the Xerox administrative and data processing environment, including:

- Local users and data administrators in controlling their data processing environment
- Multinational systems designers and users
- Technical designers and programmers in implementing and maintaining systems on a local and multinational level
- Audit, security, and systems control needs of Xerox management

These functions can be divided into ten categories:

Data Definitions

1. Describe data elements.
2. Describe physical and logical records.
3. Allow for mechanical generation of entity code or name.
4. Relate elements and records to program and modules.

Data Administration

1. Support data element definition.
2. Describe usage of standards and procedures in programs, systems, and data entries.
3. Relate entity definitions to authorized owners.
4. Rename dictionary entities.

System and Program Definition and Support

1. Describe programs.
2. Provide for description of functional interfaces.
3. Relate a program (module) to other programs (modules) that call and are called by the program (module).
4. Describe and generate on-line screen formatting characteristics.

User Access

1. Cross-referencing of all dictionary-defined entities.
2. Access to any dictionary-defined entity by its generic name, entity code, or ALIAS.
3. "Where used" reporting for all entities, single and full level.
4. COPY and MACRO library member generation
5. On-line access for inquiry and update

Database Definition Administration

1. Describe databases (one definition per database).
2. Relate databases to their components and to program.
3. Relate databases to elements.
4. Generate mechanically all data definitions and relationships for database development (e.g., DBDs, PSBs, etc.).
5. Provide interface for external entity editing and control for dictionary transactions.

Data Dictionary

1. All organizations involved in data definitions and usage will maintain records describing the data entities, usage, and relationship.
2. Corporate data naming standards and attribute definitions will be followed for all mechanized data dictionaries.
3. All information systems organizations should establish migration strategies to Xerox Data Dictionary for all operations systems.

Data Element Attributes

1. Element name — specifies the descriptive name of the data element.
2. Element description — provides narrative text/description of the data element.
3. Element length — specifies the number of positions required for one occurrence of the data element as entered.
4. Element format — specifies the character category of the element, such as numeric, alphabetic.
5. Responsibility — specifies the organization or function responsible for the data element definition.

Security

1. Registered
2. Private
3. Unclassified
4. Personal

Status

1. Draft — applies to data entered into the dictionary for the purpose of facilitating the early system design process.
2. Proposed — a user using the dictionary proposes an addition, deletion, or change to meet a system's requirement.
3. Approved — when testing is completed to the satisfaction of the Administrator, the specification's status is changed to "approved."
4. Active — indicates the entity is being used in a production system.

- Synonym — specifies a data element as having nearly the same name and/or meaning as another element.
- Coding/Edit Rules — indicates coding structures, conventions, composition, and any special edit rules.

Data Dictionary Naming Standard

1. Primary Name — primary names for elements and groups will be descriptive English, not exceeding 32 characters.
2. Higher-Level Entities — no password is required on items or groups, but for higher-level entities a leading password is to be used, such as SYS-XXXX.

8.10.2 MSP Datamanager

The MSP Datamanager is a data dictionary marketed by Manager Software Products (MSP). It has the following basic structure:

- System
- Program
- Module
- File
- Group
- Data item

The data structure is useful to both user and data dictionary in terms of establishing data relationships and the levels of importance of each of the listed member types.

Discussion of Member Types

- System — the highest level of the member type hierarchy. They can be subsystems to other systems; they can be declaration of the program, modules, files, groups, and data items processed in the system.
- Program — contains or calls other programs and/or modules, inputs, outputs or updates files, groups and/or data items.
- Module — an independent set of instructions. May be used by other programs.
- File — may be manual or automated. Contains records. Its records contain groups and/or data items. May also contain other files.

• Group — a combination of data items and/or other groups. May be an entire record or a subset of data items found on a record. May be used to describe information on a preprinted form.
• Data Item — the fundamental element of data. Smallest named unit into which data is divided in the user organization.

Entries in Datamanager

System
Effective Date	'10-9-85'
Obsolete Date	'12-31-99'
Alias	'MGA'
Contains	
	'MGA03001-XTRACT-IPMF'
	'MGA03002-CREATE-IPMF'
	'MGA03003-SELECT-IPMF'
	'MGA03003-CREATE-UPD'
	'MGA03004-TAG-PURGED'
Frequency Run	'Weekly'
Catalog	'System'
	'batch'
Catalog Owner	'Annette Green'
Note	'Year in Production-1988'
Administrative-Data	'Application Narrative'
Project ID:	'Project ID. MGAP'

Prepared By: Freida Roxax   Date: 10/19/88

A. System Objective
    To function as an interface between Cycare-based Medical Group systems and the new IPMF update processing.
B. System Functions
    1. Reformat IPMF and transmittal tapes for subsequent processing.
    2. Generate a summary of all changes done on a particular policy.
    3. Provide a copy of all updating trans. to all Cycare-based Medical Center, properly flagged according to changes undergone by each policy.
C. System Features
    MGA uses input from the registration and capitation systems.

8.10.3 The IBM DB/DC Data Dictionary

The DB/DC data dictionary is composed of a set of databases that are used to store and access information about an installation's data processing resources. (See Figure 8.2.)

The dictionary contains data about data.

Subject Categories
- IBM defined
  - Systems/subsystems
  - Jobs
  - Programs/modules
  - Databases
  - PSBs/PCBs
  - Segments/records
  - Data elements
- Installation defined
  - Business function
  - Logical transactions
  - Data classes
  - Physical transactions
  - Reports
  - OS files
  - Reusable packets

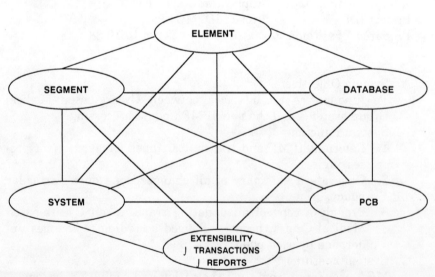

Figure 8.2 Dictionary databases.

Information on Subjects

* Name
  — Unique/meaningful
  — Primary/alias
  — 1 to 31 positions/language (BAL/CobolPL/I)
* Attributes
  Depends on category
  Language of program
  Length of a data element
* Description
  — Descriptive name (user name) on line one
  — Any descriptive matter starting on line three
  — 999 lines of 72 positions each
* User data
  — Provision for five separate types
  — Audit trail
  — Edit criteria
  — System identification
  — Reusable packet information
  — Application-related information
* Relationships (See Figure 8.3.)
  — To other entities
  — System to job
  — Job to program
* Relationship data
  — Information about the relationship between two entities
  — Indicative key (data element within segment)

Identification of Subjects (Dictionary Name)

* Components of name
  — Status code — Identifies status of entity
  — Subject category (code) — Identifies category
  — Name — Primary name on the dictionary
  — Occurrences — Distinguishes different physical attributes
* All the identifiers are required while working with a subject (Subject name).

Accessing the Dictionary

* Interactive on-line facility
  — Screens for each subject

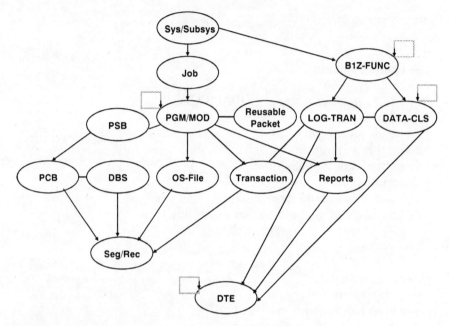

Figure 8.3 Data dictionary relationship diagram.

- —Prompting for action
- —Screen-to-screen access
- —Available through TSO terminals
- —Used for entry/update/retrieval
- • Batch forms
  - —Card image
  - —Identifying control info on each record
  - —Bulk data processing
  - —For entering only
  - —Available through TSO
- • Commands
  - —Interactive on-line
  - —Within batch processing
  - —Example: scan, change name, report

Procedure for Documentation

- • Application group fills out data dictionary input forms.
- • Data dictionary group reviews and enters data.
- • Data dictionary group runs reports and delivers to application group.

- Input forms may also be used for corrections.
- Order of entities follow order of the PLC.

Data Element Entry Procedure

- Application project team
  — Identifies and describes data elements by user name.
- Supplies data element I/P forms to data dictionary administration.
- Data dictionary administration
  — Assigns descriptors.
  — Performs redundancy analysis.
  — Develops Cobol names.
  — Assigns BAL name.
  — Enters data elements in dictionary.
  — Sends data elements and cross reference report to application project team

Table 8.2 Entry of Information into Data Dictionary

PROJECT LIFE CYCLE	DATABASE DESIGN	DATA DICTIONARY DOCUMENTATION
Feasibility	Conceptual design	System/subsystems business functions data classes
Functional analysis	Detailed conceptual design	Logical transactions data elements reports
System design	Logical DB design	Segments Jobs Program/modules Reusable packets OS files Physical transactions
Implementation	Physical DB design	Databases PSBs/PCBs

8.11 SUMMARY

This chapter discussed the role of the data dictionary in the development of systems in a database environment. It indicated what inputs and outputs the dictionary generated for each phase and the interface with the relevant phase personnel.

The chapter closed with a summary of the structure of three data dictionaries — the last two, very successful and widely used.

The author would like to refer his readers to a detailed coverage of data dictionaries discussed in his book Analysis, Design, and Implementation of Data Dictionaries.

QUESTIONS

1. What is a data dictionary? Discuss in terms of active and passive dictionaries.
2. Discuss the concept of metadata.
3. Discuss the interface between the data dictionary and the following:
   (a) End user
   (b) Systems analysis
   (c) Programmer
   (d) Data administrator
4. Discuss the role of the data dictionary in the following:
   (a) User requirements specifications
   (b) Detail systems design
   (c) Documentation
   (d) Program code generation
5. Discuss the data dictionary as
   (a) Protection mechanism
   (b) An item at risk
6. Discuss the role of the data dictionary in the implementation of standards.

9

Systems Design Using Case Tools

SOME INTRODUCTORY REMARKS

Computer-aided software engineering (CASE) has been promoted as the panacea for curing an organization's backlog problems in meeting development schedules, coordinating design efforts, and maintaining its systems. It has also been touted as the tool to increase programmer and systems designer productivity as much as two to ten times.

This chapter will introduce CASE tools as a design and development aid. It will discuss some selection criteria for deciding on the tool that will best suit a particular environment. Finally, it will list some vendors of CASE tools and the contacts within each vendor.

9.1 SEVERAL DEFINITIONS OF CASE

CASE, although now widely accepted as an acronym, does not yet have a single, widely accepted definition. Perhaps a more appropriate acronym would be CASD (Computer-aided systems development), which could be defined as "computers applied to aid in any aspect of systems development."

Because CASE can encompass so many aspects of systems development, the question "When is CASE the right choice?" must be addressed separately for each of three types of CASE tools:

1. Programmer/Project Productivity Tools — provide support for designers and programmers of software, but only at the back

end of the systems development life cycle. These may include tools for natural language programming, project management, and documentation.

2. Systems Development Methodology Tools — most systems development methodologies are collections of techniques, combined in structures made to minimize redundant effort and maximize coordination between tasks. These methodology tools provide support for and enforce a systems development methodology at any or all stages of the life cycle. They may include any of the systems development support tools as appropriate for the methodology. In addition, they enforce methodology rules and thus provide systems development expertise to the users.

3. Systems Development Support Tools — provide support for techniques and tasks of systems development at any or all stages of the life cycle, but do not necessarily enforce a systems development methodology. These may include diagramming tools, data dictionaries and analysis tools, or any of the productivity tools.

9.2 CATEGORIES OF CASE TOOLS

An individual CASE tool automates one small, focused step in the life-cycle process. Individual tools fall into these general categories:

- Diagramming tools for pictorially representing system specifications
- Screen and report painters for creating system specifications and for simple prototyping
- Dictionaries, information management systems, and facilities to store, report, and query technical and project-management system information
- Specification-checking tools to detect incomplete, syntactically incorrect, and inconsistent system specifications
- Code generators to be able to generate executable code from pictorial system specifications
- Documentation generators to produce technical and user documentation required by structured methodologies

CASE "toolkits" provide integrated tools for developers seeking to automate only one phase of the life cycle process, while "workbenches" provide integrated tools for automating the entire development process. "Frameworks" integrate CASE tools and/or link them with non-CASE software development tools, and "methodology companions" support a particular structured methodology and automatically guide developers through the development steps.

9.2.1 Well-Equipped Toolkits

Toolkits can focus on the design of real-time, information, or project management systems. They also can be classified by the hardware and operating system on which they run; by the ease with which they can be integrated into a family of compatible CASE tools; by their architecture — open, so that it can be used with products from other vendors, or closed; by the structured methodology or methodologies they support; and by development languages such as, ADA, COBOL, FORTRAN, C, and PL/1.

Many CASE toolkits run on an IBM PC or compatible under DOS. Some run on the Apple Macintosh, Wang PC, or Texas Instruments Professional PC. Others run only on 32-bit workstations, such as Sun, Apollo, or Digital Equipment Corporation (DEC) Vax Station II; on an IBM or Data General mainframe; or across the DEC Vax family. Many open-architecture products are not limited to one specific hardware, operating system, target programming language, or structured methodology.

The analysis toolkit has four basic components: structured diagramming tools, prototyping tools, a repository, and a specification checker.

9.2.2 Structured Diagramming Tools

Structured diagramming tools are computerized tools for drawing, manipulating, and storing structured diagrams such as data-flow and entity-relationship diagrams, which are required documentation for various structured methodologies.

Diagramming tools often reside on PCs or workstations that support graphics manipulation; at the minimum, they draw, update, and store data-flow and entity-relationship diagrams.

9.2.3 Prototyping Tools

Prototyping tools help determine system requirements and predict performance beforehand. Essential to prototyping are user-interface painters — screen painters, report painters, and menu builders —

that prototype the user interface to give users an advance view of how the system will look and to identify and correct problem areas. Screen dialog and navigation with data entry and edits can be simulated with or without compiles; source code for record, file, screen, and report description can be generated automatically.

Also essential are executable specification languages. These are the most sophisticated prototyping tools, which involve specifying system requirements and executing specifications iteratively to refine, correct, and ensure completeness of the system to meet user requirements.

9.2.4 The CASE Repository

The CASE repository is a design dictionary for storing and organizing all software system data, diagrams, and documentation related to planning, analysis, design, implementation, and project management. Information entered once can be maintained and made available to whomever needs it.

The repository stored more types of systems information, relationships among various information components, and rules for using or processing components than a standard data dictionary used in data management systems. The repository usually has many reporting capabilities that gauge the impact of proposed changes on the system, identify redundant or unneeded data elements, and resolve discrepancies. System diagrams and dictionary entities are linked within the dictionary, and some CASE tools provide automated means of verifying entities for completeness and correctness.

9.2.5 Data Design Toolkits

These support the logical and physical design of databases and files: logical data modeling, automatic conversion of data models to third-normal form, automatic generation of database schemes for particular database management systems, and automatic generation of program-code level file descriptions.

9.2.6 Programming Toolkits

Supported tools include hierarchical tree-structured diagramming tools with a syntax and consistency checker, procedural logic diagrammer and on-line editor, CASE repository with information manager, code generation, test data generator, file comparer, and performance monitor.

A code-generating tool is especially useful because it automatically produces codes from a program design. CASE code generators can generate compiled, structured codes in languages such as COBOL, PL/1, FORTRAN, C, or ADA, manage program specification and design information, generate documentation, and support prototyping.

9.2.7 Maintenance Toolkits

The most useful maintenance tools include documentation analyzers — to read source code from existing systems and produce documentation; program analyzers — to evaluate execution paths and performance; reverse engineering — to identify the model upon which a system is based; and restructures — to enforce structured programming and documentation standards.

9.2.8 Project Management Toolkits

Automated project management tools can help project managers better track, control, and report on software projects, thus improving software development and maintenance. To be most effective, these tools should be able to access the CASE repository in the toolkit or workbench. Besides storing technical system information, the repository should be the central location for current status, estimation, budget, and quality-assurance information.

Some of these tool kits include tools for word processing; interfacing to electronic mail; spreadsheets; project-management forms; configuration management for change, version, and access control; project plans; a calendar and task assignment system; and estimation of time tables and scheduling.

9.3 DEMONSTRATED USE OF CASE TOOLS IN THE SDLC

CASE tools have demonstrated their usefulness in all three components of the CASE environment: planning, systems design, and systems development.

9.3.1 CASE in the Planning Environment

CASE tools gather information about user problems and requirements, setting goals and criteria, generating alternative solutions.

They assist in the budget determinations, project duration and scheduling, manpower planning and scheduling, cost and time estimates, and project control.

9.3.2 CASE in the Systems Design Environment

CASE tools detail the design for a selected solution, including diagrams relating all programs, subroutines, and data flow. (See Figures 9.1 through 9.5.)

They can generate data modeling and relationship diagrams and functional models.

The functional modeling and data modeling processes have tools to construct the appropriate types of design diagrams. Data-flow diagrams, program structure charts, and entity-relationship diagrams are examples of diagrams.

More detailed tables and text contain the necessary concept descriptions, testable requirements, and data element definitions.

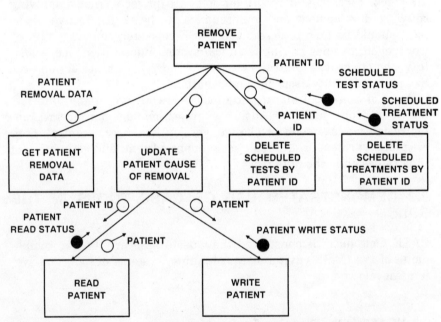

Figure 9.1 Yourdon structure chart. A structure chart is a tree or hierarchical diagram that shows the overall design of the program, including program modules and their relationships. This particular structure chart was produced by the Analyst/Designer Toolkit from Yourdon Inc.

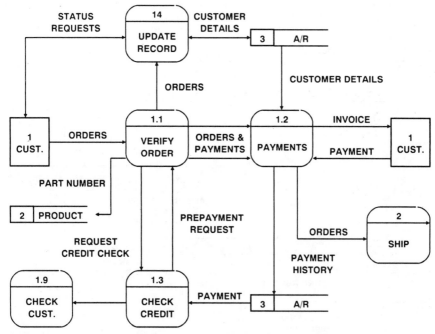

Figure 9.2 Excelerator produced data-flow diagram. A data-flow diagram traces the flow of data through a system. Data stores are indicated by open-end rectangles, processes by boxes with rounded corners, data flow by arrows, and external entities by squares. This diagram was produced by Excelerator from Index Technology Corp., using the Gane and Sarson technique.

9.3.3 CASE in the Systems Development Environment

CASE tools develop a construct of database information about the physical database scheme and the requirements for building, testing, and checking databases.

They produce language codes from definitions of data and processes stored in the data dictionary.

9.3.4 Samples of Deliverables from CASE Tools

The next several pages illustrate the deliverables from the three components of the CASE environment.

The deliverables illustrated below were produced from the following sample problem:

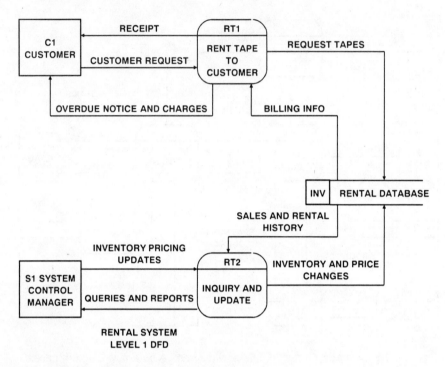

Figure 9.3 Excelerator produced data-flow diagram.

SAMPLE PROBLEM   Our sample problem concerns a video rental store with the following:

- Customer rents tapes and makes rental payments.
- Customer returns tapes and may pay late charge of $1 per day.
- Time to notify overdue borrowers.
- Time to report rentals.
- Store submits new tape.
- Store submits rate changes in some movie titles.
- Customer changes address.
- Customer requests particular movie title.

OTHER DETAILS   The standard time period for a rental is two days after the borrowed tape is rented. If the customer fails to return the tape on time, then it is time to send a tape overdue notice to the customer address with the title and copy number and past due return date.

A tape is a cassette of video tapes with a prerecorded movie that can be rented. Each tape has a movie title and copy number. All

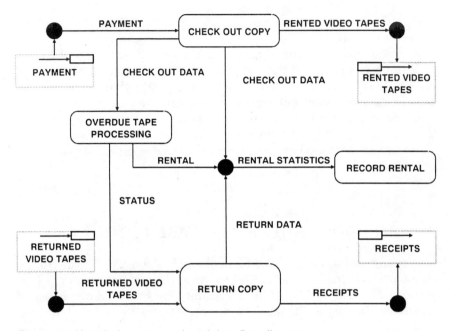

Figure 9.4 Knowledgeware produced data-flow diagram.

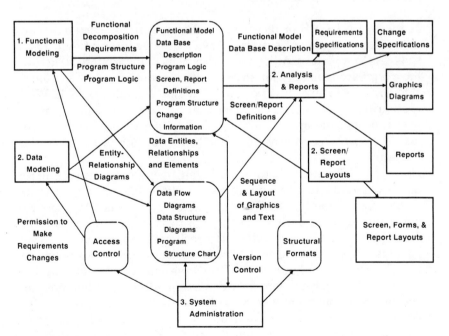

Figure 9.5 Components of a typical case tool.

copies of a movie have the same rental rate. Not all movies have the same rental rate.

A rental is the lending of a tape to a person in exchange for cash. A rental has a checkout date, a return date, and a rental charge. If a tape is late, there is a standard $1 per day late charge paid on return. A customer can rent more than one tape at a time.

A tape can be rented, on the shelf waiting to be rented, or overdue. This video store has no membership plan and doesn't take American Express. All transactions are in cash on the spot; no deposits are accepted.

9.4 SELECTION CRITERIA FOR CASE TOOLS

The ever-growing array of CASE tools makes it very difficult to decide on which tool is best suited for a particular environment. This section attempts to ease that uncertainty by setting down a list of questions the buyer should seek to get answers for before buying a tool.

The questions are as follows:

- Is the tool a DBMS or dictionary software system? Dictionary and database management systems provide greater integration capabilities. As a result, CASE tools with these underlying structures have a greater capacity for sharing specifications across functions.
- What is the future direction and functionality of the tool? When evaluating CASE tools, remember that CASE systems development is still in its infancy, so don't reject a tool with valuable attributes just because it currently does not have the full capabilities that you want.
- Does the tool's manufacturer have an open-architecture philosophy? A manufacturer's willingness to share file formats with all viable, noncompeting CASE manufacturers means that you can move smoothly from planning through to systems development because you will be able to integrate specifications across CASE components. Moreover, you will have a healthy variety of options for CASE software configurations. CASE manufacturers entering into exclusive hierarchical integration agreements with other noncompeting CASE tool manufacturers ultimately limits choice.
- Does the CASE tool produce utility software that will read procedure and source libraries and create CASE component specifications for existing systems? The acquisition of CASE tools in a non-

CASE environment creates a potential for inconsistencies in maintenance activities. Design and development specifications for systems designed and implemented before the installation of CASE components will not be consistent with those created after installation of CASE tools. Thus, a multiplicity of maintenance activities will be necessary. Certain CASE tools offer utility software that will make ready procedure and source libraries and create development specifications for existing systems, thereby mitigating the difference between pre-CASE and post-CASE systems documentation.

- Does the tool have an effective interface to other CASE design tools already purchased or under evaluation? Often, several methodologies are used to design a system, so it is important that a CASE tool provide a healthy array of methodological techniques to use in the process. The dictionary entries must be capable of being shared across these methodologies, so the dictionary should be strong and versatile.

- Does the tool have graphical methodologies capable of "exploding" design diagrams and dictionary specifications to a reasonable depth? Most of the CASE design tools provide graphical methodologies for representing proposed systems design. The graphical diagrams and the dictionary entries behind the components of the graphical diagrams must be capable of exploding to a reasonable number of lower, more specific levels.

- Will the tool be capable of executing with windowing capabilities? An advantage of the windowing capability is that multiple portions of the design can be displayed simultaneously and can therefore compensate for weaknesses in embedded explosion capabilities. As a result, the levels of explosion will not be restrictive and the comprehensiveness and integration of CASE design and development specifications should improve.

- Does the planning model in the CASE planning component provide comprehensive coverage of corporate and functional unit strategic planning and systems planning? The planning component contains a model for representing the corporation and for use in determining the direction of the corporation and systems development. The strength of the CASE top-level components lies in the comprehensiveness of this planning model.

- Does the tool provide a thorough means of prototyping? CASE development tools, rather than CASE design tools, provide the strongest prototyping methods. While it is not necessary that both types provide strong prototyping capabilities, at least one must provide this capability.

- Will the tool soon be able to generate automatically first-cut physical design specifications from logical design specifications? The conversion of logical design diagrams into initial physical design diagrams should be automatic because it involves simply the exchange and addition of graphical display table entries. Although most CASE design tools currently do not offer this feature, ask your CASE vendor if the tool will offer it in the future.
- Does the CASE design tool provide analysis support for design documentation? This concerns the capacity of the CASE tool to analyze design documentation and determine if the specifications entered by the analyst conform to prescribed methodological rules. The analysis should also indicate where design dictionary entries are incomplete. For example, a DFD diagram with a freestanding block should be highlighted as violating one of the rules of structured methodology. In addition, blocks on a DFD not having corresponding dictionary entry should be highlighted.
- Does the tool have the capacity to generate design specification reports automatically? The specifications created during logical and physical design activities serve as a source of documentation for the system. While they are permanently stored on disk devices, it is often advisable to get hardcopy printouts of the design specifications for reference. Many CASE tools provide various report formats for this purpose, including the capability of indicating design flaws.
- Does the lower-level CASE development component provide methods for convenient and comprehensive customization of the generated system? The CASE development component can already generate the major portions of the code's systems. Systems development activity using CASE involves providing the customization of the generic code to fit the system. The custom specifications must provide comprehensive coverage of the system requirements. The generated programs must also be able to call on existing routines to prevent the system from "reinventing the wheel."
- Do the tool permit distribution of design/development responsibilities? CASE design and development tools must provide a serviceable means of segregating job responsibilities and interfacing the individual efforts into a single system project.
- Does the CASE design and development tools have the capacity to export portions of the design and development dictionary specifications? This is important, as design and development specifications for one system may be reusable in the design and development of

other systems. "Reusable design" will join "reusable code" as a result of this capability.

• Can the tool interface design and development specifications to the functional DBMS be used to maintain the company's data? It is rare to develop systems that are not affected by the database environment, and the development of systems using CASE tools is no exception. Therefore, it is important that the CASE tools can interface design and development specifications of application systems to mainframe DBMSs and database creation or modification.

• Does the tool have word-processing capabilities? In addition to built-in word-processing capabilities, the tool should have an effective interface with standard word-processing systems. An added feature of some tools is the ability to pass documentation to a desktop publishing software system for more professional representation.

• Does the tool enhance project management? The use of CASE tools does not preclude the need for effective project management. In fact, their use can enhance such management. Specifications that are entered using a planning component provide a boundary for design and development activities. This boundary provides a built-in means of determining when design and development activities diverge from originally planned specifications. Some CASE design and development tools can generate reports on the progress of individual project assignments and some can interface to existing project management software systems. Currently, this interface is a temporary exit from the CASE tool into the project management system, but the interface will become much stronger in the future and provide more automatic updating of the project schedule.

• Is it possible to modify the CASE design and development tools relative to your firm's internal or existing methodology? CASE tools are prepackaged systems and may need modifications to make them more suitable for individual installations. Thus, it is important that the system has the ability to add or delete menu options or to modify the style of graphical or dictionary entry screens.

• Can the tool automatically generate design, operations, and end-user documentation? As systems are designed and developed with CASE tools, documentation concerning components and users of the system are entered into the dictionary. Thus the majority of design, operations, and user documentation required for documentation manuals is available from these dictionary entries. CASE systems should provide this documentation in either on-line or hardcopy form, with little additional work required from the project development team.

- Does the tool have facilities for maintaining design as well as systems? When conditions in business warrant changes in the information systems function, the people responsible for maintenance should be able to effect the required system changes in the system's design specifications automatically. Or, once those changes are made, the development tool should be able to designate where the current systems need changing, as well as indicate which users need to be notified of the changes and what they need to be told. Some development systems already provide some of these capabilities. As the interface between CASE design and development software systems becomes stronger, modifications to design specifications entered into the design software will be able to modify development specifications, and, ultimately, the entire system. Since the planning component was the last to emerge, the interface between it and the design component is weak. Subsequently, as the interface between it and the design strengthens, it should have the same effect on those activities as the strengthening of the interface between design and development did.

- Can the tool generate programs that span a range of systems? The hardware and software to create a transparent micro, mini, and mainframe environment are not far off. Consequently, the programs that the CASE tool generates must be able to provide the same execution services on a desktop micro as on a mighty mainframe. Some of today's CASE development systems already offer this.

It goes without saying that the CASE tool manufacturer should be willing to provide a list of installations using its software and grant permission to contact them. This major criterion should govern the purchase of any software system. Should a software vendor refuse to supply this information, you have reason to doubt the validity and comprehensiveness of its product.

9.4.1 Analysis of Selection Criteria

A subset of the above questions were sent to about a dozen vendors of CASE tools. Their responses are recorded in APPENDIX B.

9.5 VENDORS OF CASE TOOLS

This section lists some of the major vendors of CASE tools and gives a brief summary of their products.

9.5.1 Vendor List

ADPAC COMPUTING LANGUAGES CORP. Adpac Computing Languages Corporation develops, markets, and services technology support tools for the IBM mainframe operating under MVS. Adpac's CASE tools (DPDP and DESIGN) provide a front-end CAD/CAM diagramming technique that assists analysts in drawing any type of diagram and design analysis with the capability to verify the contents of diagrams.

AGS MANAGEMENT SYSTEMS INC. AGS/MS is recognized as the world's leader in systems development methodologies and project management systems. MULTI/CAM, the micro-mainframe CASE system created by AGS/MS, integrates software development tools, software design and production models, project management, and any other user-selected CASE tools into a unified, automated work environment.

AMERICAN MANAGEMENT SYSTEMS AMS is a major computer services firm specializing in applications development. AMS's Life-cycle Productivity System (LPS) integrates productivity tools from AMS and other vendors for strategic system planning, design, development, maintenance, and project management. LPS produces all deliverable work products required by most methodologies. Major portions of LPS operate on PCs. Implementation, configuration control, and foundations software modules operate on IBM mainframes.

ANALYSTS INTERNATIONAL CORP. Analysts International Corporation, a professional data processing software and services company, and a leader in the computer industry for over 22 years, introduces CORVET. CORVET is a graphics-oriented, PC-based, interactive CASE design and development product that generates stand-alone COBOL programs and comprehensive documentation for IBM mainframe environments.

ARTHUR ANDERSON & CO. FOUNDATION is a computer-integrated environment for software engineering developed by Arthur Anderson & Co. Consulting practice. Covering the entire systems development life cycle, FOUNDATION consists of METHOD/1, a PC LAN-based tool for planning and design, and INSTALL/1, an IBM mainframe-based environment for implementation and support of DB2 applications.

ARTHUR YOUNG & CO. Arthur Young is an international accounting, tax and management consulting firm that is working with KnowledgeWare to develop the Information Engineering Workbench (AY/IEW); it markets KnowledgeWare products internationally and uses the AY/IEW for systems building. Arthur Young will present its experience building systems using the AY/IEW and Information Engineering techniques.

ASYST TECHNOLOGIES, INC. The DEVELOPER provides multi-user, automated support for the systems development process, through its repository located either at the PC, at the mainframe (using DB2), or at both sites. The DEVELOPER and its CUSTOMIZER module allow the use of any methodology at all levels of compliance and rigor. Repository integrity is maintained through a menu-driven SQL query language and built-in ASYSTants capabilities.

BACHMAN INFORMATION SYSTEMS, INC. Bachman Information Systems, Inc. is exhibiting The Bachman Product Set, which supports the development of new applications while supporting existing applications. It provides the powerful maintenance, enhancement, and migration capabilities MIS departments need to control the largest component of their workload.

CATALYST CATALYST, an information technology firm of Peat Marwick, will present PATHVU, RETROFIT, ReACT, and DataTEC. PATHVU provides analysis and detailed reporting of program logic and structure. RETROFIT restructures COBOL code. ReACT translates Assembler programs to structured COBOL. DataTec provides data element analysis, standardization, and migration capabilities. These products make up the re-engineering baseline necessary to migrate existing systems to advanced technical environments.

CGI SYSTEMS, INC. PACBASE is a full-cycle CASE product. It integrates mainframe and PC-based analysis and design workstations for the development and maintenance of application specifications. This is done through active prototypes, a centralized enterprise-wide dictionary that controls and manages all business specifications directly into complete COBOL applications, including all code and documentation.

CHEN & ASSOCIATES, INC. Chen & Associates provides products, training, and consulting in data-oriented systems development. Products (PC-based) are ER-Designer, which defines information requirements in entity-relationship diagrams; SCHEMAGEN, which generates schemas for your database systems (from micro-based to mainframe-based); Normalizer, which normalizes data or words.

COMPUTER SCIENCES CORP. The Technology Activity's Design Generator is an object-oriented, expert system that automatically selects a central transform from a data-flow diagram and generates an initial design represented in structure chart notation. The graphic-intensive user interface features intelligent pop-up menus and multipane browsers.

CORTEX CORP. CorVision is an application development system that automates the entire software development cycle for the DEC VAX/VMS environment using a technique called Picture Programming. Picture Programming allows DP professionals to visualize an application by diagramming the design and then automatically generating a production-ready application directly from the pictures.

DIGITAL EQUIPMENT CORPORATION As a leading manufacturer, Digital provides a range of integrated Application Development tools for solutions to business and engineering problems. The offerings are workstation-based and address all aspects of the Applications Development Life Cycle. They are integrated into the VAX hardware, software, and network architecture to provide enterprise-wide solutions.

ETECH ALGORITHMS AND SYSTEMS, INC. ETECH SOFTROBOT is an intelligent workbench built on PSDDL (Problem Statement and Diagram Description Language). ETECH-D is a fully automatic diagramming toolkit without screen editing. ETECH-M intelligent project manager driven by Project-Makefile, ETECH-R reusing language and ETECH-G language independent code generator based on reusability. It reaches many professionals' goals.

HOLLAND SYSTEMS CORP./DELOITTE HASKINS AND SELLS Deloitte Haskins & Sells and Holland Systems Corp. have pooled their proven consulting and software product expertise in the IRM area. The result is a line of products that address the entire information resource management process...from business modeling...to database design and analysis...to application development and implementation. The companies will feature the 4Front Family of IRM products.

I-LOGIX, INC. I-Logix, Inc. pioneers system design automation with STATEMATE, the only available tool that models the dynamic behavior of real-time systems as well as system functions and architecture. With STATEMATE, users produce a specification that is compiled allowing its execution to be viewed on screen. STATEMATE includes three graphic languages for modeling, execution, and simulation capability; rapid prototyping in ADA; and 2167A documentation.

INDEX TECHNOLOGY Index Technology markets the Excelerator family of products that automate systems development. Products include PC PRism for systems planning, Excelerator and Excelerator/RTS for analysis and design, plus links to application generators and programming environments. Excelerator and Excelerator/RTS support a variety of techniques and methodologies and can be tailored for each organization's needs.

INFODYNE INTERNATIONAL, INC. InfoDyne, Inc. markets and distributes MASTER, a PC-based CASE tool and methodology, based on the E-R (Entity-Relationship) approach to systems planning and design. MASTER accommodates numerous approaches to the problem of analysis, design, and documentation of all design activities relating to the conceptual, logical, and physical model of data and international processes in an information system.

INFOREM PLC Inforem's Professional Application Generation Environment (PAGE) is a unique CASE offering. A multi-user product, it combines on-screen graphics with a systems encyclopedia and uses a relational database on networked PCs. PAGE is based on the Inforem Method, which provides a seamless transition right from analysis to program code for both PC and mainframe systems.

INTEGRATED SYSTEMS, INC. AutoCode focuses on the needs of Real-Time Software Engineers and addresses all steps from analysis to design, simulation, and code generation. The graphical specification environment features engineering block diagrams, data flow/control flow, state transition, and process descriptions. Ward-Mellor real-time software methodology with Boeing-Hatley extensions are included in an environment where simulation and analysis can be performed for design verification; and real-time code in C, Ada, or Fortran can be generated automatically.

INTERACTIVE DEVELOPMENT ENVIRONMENT (IDE) IDE's product, Software through Pictures, is a set of integrated graphical editors and error-checking tools supporting definition of names, types, constants, and associated text. Users can generate Ada declarations and define process and module templates to generate specifications.

JAMES MARTIN ASSOCIATES James Martin Associates, an international consulting firm established by James Martin, is considered the leader in creating systems development methods and CASE tools to support those methods. With more than 250 professionals throughout the world, JMA's teams provide commercial and government clients with technical and management services.

KNOWLEDGEWARE, INC. KnowledgeWare, Inc. provides complete Integrated Computer-Aided Software Engineering (I-CASE) environment for the planning, analysis, design, construction, and maintenance of computer-based information systems. The Information Engineering Workbench (IEW) provides enterprise modeling, data modeling, process modeling, systems design, and code generation experts. The "Knowledge-Coordinator/Encyclopedia" team uses state-of-the-art artificial intelligence technology.

LANGUAGE TECHNOLOGY Language Technology provides CASE products to the IBM mainframe market. The company's flagship product RECODER is the leading COBOL structuring tool. RECODER automatically transforms difficult-to-maintain, unstructured COBOL into structured COBOL. Language Technology's INSPECTOR is the only quality assurance tool based on scientific measurement of COBOL quality and maintainability.

MANAGEMENT SYSTEMS, INC. LBMS will present its PC-based tools, SUPER-MATE and AUTO-MATE PLUS. SUPER-MATE provides a powerful set of automated facilities for strategic planning, including business area/activity analysis, analysis of competitive strategies, the prioritization of applications, and the development of the strategic plan. Results of this plan may be passed to AUTO-MATE PLUS, which provides full support for systems analysis, logical design, automatic generation of physical designs, and data dictionary syntax for ADABAS, DB2, and other DBMS.

MANAGER SOFTWARE PRODUCTS (MSP)   The MANAGER Family of Products (PC and mainframe) is dedicated to automating all phases of the systems life cycle, from strategic information planning to the generation of enabled code. MSP will present managerVIEW, the intelligent workstation-based graphical information engineering tool driven by the central knowledge base resident on the corporate dictionary. ManagerVIEW is integrated with the mainframe corporate dictionary and also runs on the IBM PC family and PS/2.

MICHAEL JACKSON SYSTEMS, LTD.   Jackson CASE tools automate the widely acclaimed Michael Jackson methods of system development and program design. SPEED-BUILDER supports the analysis phases of development through powerful graphical and text facilities and automates documentation production. The cooperating Program DEVELOPMENT Facility (PDF) generates complete, well-structured program code from Jackson structure charts.

MICRO FOCUS   Micro Focus COBOL/2 Workbench puts a mainframe programming and testing environment on a PC platform under MS-DOS or OS/2. It is used by developers of COBOL, CICS PL/I, and IMS DB/DC applications to improve productivity and cut applications development backlogs. Micro Focus COBOL compilers and CASE tools are the choice of IBM, AT&T, Sun Microsystems, Microsoft, and others.

NASTEC CORP.   Nastec Corporation develops tools for commerical, government, and engineering software developers. CASE 2000 DesignAid is based on an interactive, multi-user database with features for process modeling, real-time system modeling and documentation. Operating in the IBM PC and Digital VAX environment, CASE 2000 also includes tools for requirements management, project management and control, and consulting and training in CASE technology.

NETRON INC.   The NETRON/CAP Development Center is a CASE system for building custom, portable COBOL software using a frame-based software engineering process called Bassett Frame Technology. NETRON/CAP unifies the prototyping/development/maintenance life cycle into an automated specification procedure. The open design architecture allows unlimited automation of additional application functionality for IBM mainframes and PCs, VAX systems and Wang VS minis.

OPTIMA, INC. (Formerly known as Ken Orr & Associates) Optima,   Inc. integrates the use of tools and technology with the experience of people. DSSD (Data Structured Systems Development), the flagship product, is a lifecycle methodology that serves as the base of the product offering. CASE tool products that automate the methodology are Brackets, for the diagramming process, and Design Machine, for requirements definition and logical database design.

ON-LINE SOFTWARE INTERNATIONAL On-Line Software International presents CasePac — Automated Software Development with a powerful DB2 data dictionary. As the foundation for On-Line Software's CASE platform, CasePac provides a complete, fully active central repository; software engineering facilities including a graphics front end; change management and maintenance facilities.

PANSOPHIC SYSTEMS, INC. Pansophic   Systems,   Inc.   presents TELON. The TELON application development system captures design specifications to generate COBOL or PL/I applications. TELON assists the transition from analysis to design by providing interfaces to leading front end analysis tools. TELON components include directory, data administration, screen/report painters, prototyping, specification facilities, automated documentation, generator, and test facility.

POLYTRON CORP. POLYTRON offers the leading configuration management system for MS/DOSPC and VAX/VMS software development. PVCS maintains versions and revisions of software systems. PolyMake automatically rebuilds any desired version of the system. PolyLibrarian maintains libraries of reusable object modules. The tools work together or independently with ANY language and your existing tools.

POPKIN SOFTWARE & SYSTEMS INC. Popkin Software & Systems offers SYSTEM ARCHITECT, a PC-based CASE tool running under Microsoft Windows. Its set of process- and data-driven methodologies for structured analysis and design include DeMarco/Yourdon, Gane and Sarson, Ward & Mellor (real-time), structure charts, and entity-relationship diagrams. SYSTEM ARCHITECT's Data Dictionary-Encyclopedia utilized dBase II file format.

READY SYSTEMS Ready Systems will present CARDTools, which supports automatic DoD 2167 documentation generation, specific Ada requirements, including object-oriented design, packages, information hiding and rendezvous. CARDTools offers real-time perfor-mance deadline analysis on multitasking architectures and hard-ware/software interface specification, including intertasking synchro-nization and communication designs, allowing for design analysis verification prior to actual implementation.

SAGE SOFTWARE, INC.   Sage Software, Inc. develops, markets, and supports a family of CASE tools for developers of IBM-based infor-mation systems. The company's product family (known as the APS Development Center) encompasses the software development cycle and supports the physical design, interactive prototyping, coding, testing, and maintenance of COBOL-based applications software.

SOFTLAB, INC.   Softlab, Inc., will present MAESTRO, the integrated Software Engineering Environment. MAESTRO organizes, manages the software cycle through real-time project management, time ac-counting, and your standards. MAESTRO integrates customizable tools for design; coding, testing, documentation, and maintenance; is language independent; and fits in numerous hardware and software environments.

TEKTRONIX   TekCASE is a family of automated software develop-ment tools that help software engineers and project managers ana-lyze, design, document, manage, and maintain complex real-time sys-tems. Because they support Digital's complete VAX line and inte-grate with VAXset software, TekCASE products are flexible, extensi-ble, and especially well-suited for large projects.

TEXAS INSTRUMENTS   Texas Instruments' integrated CASE product, The Information Engineering Facility, is designed to automate the complete systems development life cycle. It consists of a powerful mainframe encyclopedia and PC-based, graphical toolsets to support analysis and design. TI can demonstrate today the major components of this product, including strategic planning, analysis, design, COBOL code and database generation.

THE CADWARE GROUP, LTD.   The CADWARE Group, Ltd. designs, produces, and markets rule-based frameworks and modeling tools for development of complex systems. Managers, planners, systems ana-lysts, and designers use these tools to help manage the complexity of defining and evaluating mission-critical business, industrial, and technical systems.

TRANSFORM LOGIC CORP. Transform addresses the development and maintenance of the entire application life cycle. Using expert system technology, complete COBOL applications are produced for IBM mainframe DBMS's DL/I and DB2. The concepts behind automated development, data-driven design architecture, prototyping, and maintenance are reviewed with examples of user accomplishments.

VISUAL SOFTWARE, INC. Visual Software, Inc. markets personal CASE tools for workstations, LAN, and mainframe design environments. The base package, vsDesigner, is a methodology-independent workbench supporting shared access to LAN-based information repositories. Several default design syntaxes come with the product, including those for real-time design. Extensive analyses are supported and an optional SQL interface to the design data is available.

YOURDON INC. The YOURDON Analyst/Designer Toolkit supports both the traditional and real-time YOURDON Techniques and allows for the creation of all the diagrams associated with the techniques. The diagramming facilities of the Toolkit are integrated with a powerful project dictionary, which features dBase III compatibility. The Toolkit provides error checking to insure the accuracy of diagrams and dictionary entries.

9.6 GETTING CASE IN PLACE

There are three basic steps for implementing CASE technology in a software development organization:

- Determine methodology and automation support requirements.
- Select a CASE product.
- Implement the CASE product.

This is a lengthy process involving numerous people, so do not expect major results for a couple of years. Even then, the biggest and longest-term benefits may come in application maintenance. CASE tools make it much easier to maintain specifications.

9.6.1 Determine the Methodology

Following agreement on the organization methodology, whether data-flow or entity-relationship diagrams, your next step is what you need most in automation support. For a larger organization with complex applications, you may want some of the following capabilities:

• Interactive drawing of analysis diagrams
• Automatic data normalization
• Consistency checking
• Initialization of physical design from requirements
• Prototyping tools
• Directory of reusable code modules
• Analysis methodology enforcements
• Interface with application development environment

A second key decision is whether you want a single integrated environment or a CASE front end to a more classical development environment.

9.6.2 Select a CASE Product

Once you have determined your methodology and decided that CASE capabilities will be useful, you need to select a product. You may do this on the basis of:

• What environment — PC or mainframe?
• What application does the tool support? Some tools support a specific database (e.g., DB2), or language (e.g., ADA).
• Does the tool support your methodology?
• Is the vendor financially secure?
  — You may want to talk to people who have experience using the vendor's CASE tool.

9.6.3 Implement the CASE Product

An aggressive strategy for CASE implementation in smaller organization is to automate many software engineering techniques simultaneously on a small trial project. The basic steps are as follows:

• Select a new development project to be used for the CASE trial situation.
• Staff the trial project with your best requirements and design analysts.

• Assign a full-time CASE administrator to learn the tool, make detailed methodology decisions, enter information, run analysis reports, and generate specifications.

A large organization with thousands of users nationwide must take on a different approach. Most such organizations find it physically impossible to decide on a complete automated methodology and then get hundreds of people trained on it in a short time period.

In this circumstance, a method or support group acts as change agent, introducing a few techniques at a time and supporting them with automation.

9.7 REMARKS IN CONCLUSION

This chapter introduced a tool that has literally "taken the software development world by storm." CASE tools are making a big impact on software development and will continue to do so for years to come.

The chapter introduced the "what are CASE tools" topics and showed how they could be selected and used in small or large organizations.

Finally, I would like to point my readers to APPENDIX B, where a number of unedited responses from CASE tool vendors are displayed.

QUESTIONS

1. What is a CASE tool? Discuss its role in systems development in terms of your definition.
2. What is the difference between a CASE toolkit and a CASE workbench?
3. Discuss the role of a data dictionary or repository in the CASE tool environment.
4. Discuss the demonstrated uses of CASE tools in the systems development life cycle.
5. List some selection criteria for CASE tools.
6. What recommendation would you make to an enterprise that is considering the purchase of a CASE tool, but has no structured design methodology in place?

10

Data Security in a Database Environment

Data security is defined as the procedural and technical measures required to:

• Prevent any deliberate denial of service.
• Prevent unauthorized access, modification, use, and dissemination of data stored or processed in a computer system.
• Protect the system in its integrity from physical harm.

The access control requirements are particularly important in time-shared and multiprogrammed systems in which multiple users must be prevented from interfering with each other and users must be prevented from gaining unauthorized access to each other's data or programs.

Privacy is an issue that concerns the computer community with maintaining personal information on individual citizens in computerized record-keeping systems. It deals with the right of the individual regarding the collection of information in a record-keeping system about his person and activities and the processing, dissemination, storage, and use of this information in making a determination about him.

Integrity is a measure of the quality and reliability of the data on which computer-based information systems depend. Many computerized databases in use today suffer from high error rates in the data they receive and consequently are riddled with bad data. With incorrect data, even the most efficient and sophisticated system is well-nigh useless.

Computer privacy is concerned with the moral and legal requirements to protect data from unauthorized access and dissemination. The issues involved in computer privacy are, therefore, political decisions regarding who may have access to what and who may disseminate what, whereas the issues involved in computer security are procedures and safeguards for enforcing the privacy decisions.

Privacy issues affect all aspects of computer security because of legislative measures enacted. With due consideration of its social implications, legislation for computer privacy determines the type of information collected and by whom, the type of access and dissemination, the subject rights, the penalties, and the licensing matter.

In 1973 the Department of Health, Education, and Welfare proposed several actions that should be taken to help protect individual privacy. This report proposed the following fundamental principles of fair information practice to guide the development of regulations and laws concerning privacy.

- There must be no personal-data record-keeping systems whose very existence is secret.
- There must be a way for an individual to find out what information about him or her is in a record and how it is used.
- There must be a way for an individual to prevent information about her or him obtained for one purpose from being used or made available for other purposes without her or his consent.
- There must be a way for an individual to correct or amend a record of identifiable information about him or her.
- Any organization creating, maintaining, using, or disseminating records of identifiable personal data must assure the reliability of the data for their intended use and must take reasonable precautions to prevent misuse of the data.

Guidelines and procedures may be established for accountability, levels of control, type of control, rules, and checklists. Preventive measures and recovery due to internal threats and external intrusions are also a part of data security. For these threats and intrusions, the causes, effects, and means must be studied. More difficult aspects of data security research include risk analysis, threat analysis, assessment, and insurance. By knowing the risks involved, data security may be expressed in terms of quantitative indicators, cost factors, and options. These discussions are included in the remaining sections of this chapter.

10.1 CONDUCTING A THREAT ANALYSIS

A threat is defined as that which has the potential to menace, abuse, or harm. A threat can either modify or destroy the functional purpose of an object, and hence is a source of potential danger. In the context of our discussion of threat analysis and data security, we shall express a threat as the danger to which the data is exposed.

A threat analysis is defined as the methodology employed to assess the level of the system's security and the protection mechanisms in place to counter the threat. Threat analysis is also useful in designing cost-effective security systems.

A good threat analysis is an important element in the review of security needs. Together with an analysis of vulnerability, it provides the basic data needed to assess the risks. Even if threats are not expressed in probabilistic terms, their existence should be recognized and priority ratings should be assigned.

The threats considered in this chapter will be limited to those faced by the data. We will not consider those threats to physical security that are usually countered by the installation of some physical measures. In this category of threats are fire hazards, illegal entry into a specific computer installation, and hardware failure.

The methodology most frequently used and employed in studies that produced most of the data for this chapter is the checklist method. This approach consists essentially of a series of questions asked to determine what protection measures are in place to counter threats against specific objects.

Considerable attention should be devoted to planning the questionnaire and the follow-up interviews with respondents. The researcher should set specific objectives and have clearly measurable goals for each associated task. The scheduling and coordinating of interviews with the various respondents should also receive considerable attention.

10.1.1 Threat Analysis Case Study

The threat analysis detailed in this section was conducted in a database environment using IMS as the database management system (DBMS). The objects selected for the study included>
* Program specification blocks (PSB) library
* Database description (DBD) library.
* Application control block (ACB) library
* Data dictionary
* Source and object modules for COBOL, Mark IV, and Application Development facility (ADF)
* Cobol Message Processing Programs (MPP)
* Data files

The primary goal of the questionnaire was to determine what protection existed to counter the following categories of threats:

* Unauthorized access to the library
* Unauthorized manipulation of the members of the library
* Authorized users browsing the library
* Unauthorized use of utility routines
* Inadequate auditing and monitoring of threats
* Obtaining access to the database by bypassing the PSB library
* Illegal use of processing options
* Destruction of the storage medium
* Unauthorized distribution or exposure
* Unauthorized copying or altering of the libraries
* Illegal deletion of stored data
* Passing of sensitive data by authorized users to unauthorized users
* Access to residues of data
* Unauthorized use of terminals
* Collusion of employees
* Denial of access to system resources
* Inadequate documentation and historical change data to establish audit trails
* One programmer having sole knowledge or access to, and maintenance responsibility for, sensitive programs
* Inadequate training and attitude toward data security
* Exposure of sensitive data following abnormal ending of job.

An example of a typical question found on the questionnaire follows:

Does the computer give a dump of memory if an abnormal end of job occurs during the running of a sensitive program?

The response to the several questionnaires are then analyzed to determine the level of protection available to each specific object.

10.1.2 Analysis of Results

The results obtained from the responses to the questionnaire agreed favorably with results from similar surveys. They indicated that the following threats existed:

- Inadequate authentication of user identification
- Inadequate controls over the use of utilities and special purpose programs
- Inability to identify terminals and users in the event of a breach of security
- Need for risk assessment

Some of the major systems surveyed required identification for access to data that depended on personal knowledge of corporate structure, manager's position code, or manager's signing authority, and in general on information that can easily be obtained by corporate customers. The ease with which such information could be obtained presented considerable security problems.

In view of the ease of obtaining such information the authentication process should be stringent enough to provide some protection for the passwords, user identification, or sign-on identification. The authentication process should not be based on further personal knowledge of the authorized user. For example, requiring a user to give the birth date, name of first child, or high school attended as authentication for an already weakened identification scheme only serves to further weaken the system. The unauthorized user armed with such easily obtainable knowledge of the authorized user will be in a position to pass the authentication requirements with little difficulty.

It was demonstrated that it was possible for an authorized user to retrieve a user's source program and alter the code without detection. The unauthorized user could illegally embed statements in the user's code, recompile the code, and return the object code to the load library.

Existing controls did not restrict by, for example, a user profile the access to user's source libraries by other users. A user profile would restrict that user to certain libraries, programs, or portions of stored data.

In a similar manner control should exist over certain specialized routines, utility programs, and programs that allow specially trained programmers to bypass standard procedures to gain access to stored data. Administrative controls should be in place that outline what procedures one should follow to gain access to routines and utilities. These controls should include who can authorize use of such programs, signatures required, logs to be completed, and any follow-up reporting that should be done.

The responses to the survey showed that there was almost no ability to make a positive identification of a terminal or its user in the event of a security breach. The failure was due to the following:

- Inadequate authentication
- Use of logical terminal identifications
- Inadequate audit trails

The protection mechanism to counter this threat should include restricting the use of certain terminals to certain types of transactions, certain terminals to processing during certain periods, and include in the authentication process certain transformations that require keys that would link the terminal to the corresponding identity.

Finally, the analysis of the responses reveals that consideration should be given to some or all of the following protection mechanisms:

- Frequent changing of password
- Levels of authority and processing functions
- Terminals' sign-off automatically after a period of inactivity
- Fixed time to bring up terminals and period processing
- On-line auditing — one terminal used to maintain monitoring and surveillance
- Dedicated telephone lines
- Encryption of files
- Administrative control of utilities

- Erasure of residues on tapes/disks
- Log of all terminal users
- Hardwired terminals for entering specific transactions
- Individual libraries — users restricted by either password or user identification to libraries for which they have authorization

10.1.3 Conducting a Risk Assessment

Another useful exercise, in addition to conducting a threat analysis in implementing security safeguards in an organization, is conducting a risk assessment.

A risk assessment is an analytical process designed to quantify the data security required by an organization. It considers the threats to data and the loss that would occur if a threat were to materialize. The purpose of a risk assessment is to help an organization establish priorities for cost-effective safeguards to reduce the probability of given threats or aid in recovery from a loss.

For some potential threats, a risk assessment may show the potential loss to be catastrophic to the organization. In some cases, when a security breach can be evaluated in terms of cost, delay, disclosure, or other measure, establishing a base level of security may be a desirable first step.

The risk analysis provides a rational approach toward choosing security safeguards. A security program should logically provide protection in the most economical manner. The following questions, therefore, should be answered in the course of a risk assessment:

- What are the specific results desired; that is, exactly how much security is required?
- What is the proper balance between security program cost and potential benefits?
- When trade-offs can be made between protection and recovery, how much effort should be expended on each?

Several full-length checklists and questionnaires for conducting risk assessment are available in current literature on the subject. The author developed a questionnaire as part of the database security research conducted during the past five years. This questionnaire is illustrated as EXHIBIT 10.1, following.

Exhibit 10.1   User Risk Analysis for ___System

PREPARED BY _____
ORIGIN DATE   _____

Uses of the Application Output (LIST)

A. _____
B. _____
C. _____
D. _____

DEPENDENCIES
Are there other uses of the Application Output outside of your specific area? Please list.

USE   USER

_____   _____

_____   _____

_____   _____

3. Critical Dates or Time Periods
Please list any critical dates or time periods (e.g., fiscal year end, Christmas checks)

Date   Reason   Brief Description
OF: _____   Criticality

4. Dollar Risk vs EDP Application Outage Duration
Please complete Table 1 (attached)

5. Critical Files
    A. Please List Critical Files

_____

_____

_____

_____

    B. File Backup requirements
        Are the files backed up by EDP resource?   _____
        If so, how often?   _____
        How are the files backed up?   _____
        a) Magnetic tape in vault   _____
        b) Microfilm   _____
        c) If Microfilm, where stored?   _____

d) Estimate time to recover if Microfilm
> or

listing is only backed up partially?   _____

e) If backup is by Microfilm, how often is
  it updated?   _____

6. Revenue Estimate

Revenue earned is _____ per _____

7. Fall-Back Model

A. Is a manual fall-back system feasible?
   a) If so, how long to put it in place?   _____
   b) Cost to put it in place?   _____
   c) Estimated running of manual system is
      _____ per _____

B. Time frame when manual fall-back system ceases to be feasible?   _____

C. Estimated loss as a result of interruption.
   Please complete Table 2.

8. Remote Access System Data

Is the application run remotely from the
computer centre?   _____
If yes,

A. What type of terminal is used _____

B. Is your terminal connected to the computer via:
   a) leased lines
   b) Dial up plus acoustic coupler
   c) Other (State)

_____

_____

C. Is your terminal in the same building
   as the computer?   _____

D. Do you use a password to sign in
   on the system?   _____
   If so,
   a) who determines the password
      (User/Technical Branch)?   _____
   b) How?   _____
   c) How often will passwords be changed
      and by whom?   _____
   d) Would you change the password when an
      employee who knows the password ter-

minates his/her employment?   _____
  e) How many people know the password?   _____
E. Would you consider the information
    transmitted/received over the terminal   _____
    a) Business Confidential?   _____
    b) Personally Private?   _____
    c) Information whose dissemination should
       be controlled?   _____
    d) Used in making management decisions?   _____
    e) Information that may be disseminated to
       anyone within a department without control?   _____
F. Do you employ any cryptographic methods to protect vital
    data? If so   _____
    a) Are software or programmatic techniques
       used?_____
    b) Are hardware devices used?   _____
       If so, name the manufacturer and model number
    _____
    c) The cryptographic methods are used because of
       i) Pertinent legislation ii) User priorities
       iii) Other
G. What programming language can you utilize from
    your terminal? Please list and encircle those
    not required _____
H. Which of the following security measures pertaining
    to terminals have you considered adequate for your needs?
    a) Non-display screen mode for entering the sign-on
       parameters and update passwords?
    b) The defined terminal access be restricted to time of day?
    c) The defined terminal to be automatically signed off after
       extended periods of inactivity?
    d) In the case of attempted violations, the system
       identifies the responsible terminal/user?
    e) The transaction can only be entered from the terminals so
       authorized?
I. Security Audit Report(s)
    Please indicate reports applicable to this application:
    a) RACF
    b) Access Matrix Model
    c) Generated from DBMS Log Tapes
    d) Security Audit Trail
J. Other Potential Problem Areas Not Covered Above

Table 1   Risk (In Dollars vs EDP Application Outage Duration

OUTAGE DURATION	DOLLAR RISK	REASON FOR RISK	TIME*	COST*	REMARKS
1 Day					
2 Days					
3 Days					
4 Days					
5 Days					
6 Days					
7 Days					
2 Weeks					
3 Weeks					
4 Weeks					
2 Months					
3 Months					

Note
*Time — Time when you would start Manual

Table 2   Est. Business Lost (Rev) as a Result of Interrupted or Degraded Service

DURATION	REVENUE LOST (%)	REVENUE LOST ($)	CRITICAL TIME*	REMARKS
1 Day				
2 Days				
3 Days				
4 Days				
5 Days				
6 Days				
7 Days				
2 Weeks				
3 Weeks				
4 Weeks				
2 Months				
3 Months				

Note
*Time — Time when you would start Manual

10.1.4 Achieving Database Privacy

Privacy of information in a database is lost either by accident or deliberately induced disclosure. The most common causes of accidental disclosures are failures of hardware and use of partially debugged programs. Improvements in hardware reliability and various memory protection schemes have been suggested as countermeasures. Deliberate efforts to infiltrate an on-line database can be classified as either passive or active.

Passive infiltration may be accomplished by electromagnetic pickup of the traffic at any point on the system.

Active infiltration — an attempt to enter the database to directly obtain or alter information — can be overtly accomplished through normal access procedures by:

* Using legitimate access to the database to ask unauthorized questions, or to browse in unauthorized date.
* Masquerading as a legitimate user after having obtained proper identification by other means
* Having access to the database by virtue of your position

The above spectrum of threats can be countered by a number of techniques and procedures. Some of these were originally introduced into time-shared, multi-user systems to prevent users from inadvertently disturbing each other's programs and then expanded to protect against accidental or deliberately induced disclosures of data. In the following discussion, we cite some of these countermeasures.

10.1.5 Access Management

These techniques are aimed at preventing unauthorized users from obtaining services from the system or gaining access to its files. The procedures involved are authorization, identification, and authentication. Authorization is given for certain users to enter the database and request certain types of information. Any user attempting to enter the system must first identify himself/herself and his/her location, and then authenticate that identification.

10.1.6 Privacy Transformations

Privacy transformations are techniques for coding the data in user-processor communications or in files to conceal information. Privacy transformations consist of sets of logical operations on the individual characters of the data.

Privacy transformations break down into two general types — irreversible and reversible. Irreversible includes aggregation and random modification. In this case valid statistics can be obtained from such data, but individual values cannot be obtained.

Reversible privacy transformations are as follows:

- Coding — a word in one language replaces a group of words in another.
- Compression — removes redundancies and blanks from transmitted data.
- Substitution — letters from one or more items are replaced.
- Transposition — all the letters in the clear text appear in the ciphered text, but in a distorted sequence.
- Composite transformation — combinations of the above methods.

10.1.7 Cryptographic Controls and Data Transformation

Cryptographic transformations were recognized long ago to be an effective protection mechanism in communication systems. In the past they have been used mainly to protect information that is transferred through communication lines.

There is still much debate as to the cost/benefit of encrypting large production databases. The author's experience with encryption indicates that because of the need to produce clear text from large encrypted databases the cost of this type of control makes it prohibitive.

10.1.8 Database Integrity

A database integrity system is used to prevent certain types of inconsistencies introduced by errors of the users of the application programs from affecting the contents of the database. By enforcing semantic restrictions on the information, it is possible to insure that the contents of the database is correct and that no inconsistencies exist between related information. The increased use of data dictionaries has gone a long way in ensuring integrity of databases.

The data dictionary documents what validity and edit rules are to be applied to the data. These rules can be classified into a few basic categories that correspond to specifications of range, sets of values permitted, format, uniqueness of some values, non-missing values for a field, and interfield assertions.

Systems surveillance, measurement, and auditing are critical elements in providing the technical base for adequate integrity. The effectiveness and operability of the entire system, especially the protection mechanisms, must be continually scrutinized and measured. Management must also be able to detect and to respond to events that constitute system security threats.

Finally, the introduction of a properly functioning audit system should allow the Internal Auditors to indicate that the occurrence of certain events should trigger audit trails that cannot be destroyed deliberately.

QUESTIONS

1. Give definitions for data security, integrity, and privacy.
2. What is a threat? Discuss the steps involved in conducting a threat analysis.
3. What is a risk? Discuss the steps involved in conducting a risk assessment.
4. How would you achieve database privacy in a database environment?
5. Discuss privacy transformations in terms of irreversibility and reversibility.

Chapter

11

Development of Security Controls

This chapter discusses some features of database security, privacy, and integrity beyond a level that the author may consider introductory. The features are termed advanced because they are features that a worker, wishing to install security mechanisms in an organization, may select for direct implementation. The chapter does not give a step-by-step approach to the implementation of these features, but discusses the issues a security analyst must consider when deciding to implement security measures.

The chapter starts off by discussing top-level management involvement in database security, privacy, and integrity. The author has discovered that one of the main causes of inadequate database protection, or no protection, in several organizations is because top-level management does not see the need to incur the cost of protecting database contents. The analyst who wants to pursue the installation of security measures at the organization must first convince management of the need for security and get their support not only during the implementation of the measures but for the constant monitoring of the performance and adequacy of the measures and the upgrading of those measures as warranted.

To determine the adequacy of existing security measures, the level of protection required for the database content, and the cost to install these measures, the analyst must conduct a risk analysis. The risk analysis and the need for a risk analysis are discussed in later sections of this chapter.

The chapter concludes by discussing some protection mechanisms that may be implemented by organizations to achieve data security.

Protection mechanisms may be defined as the controls implemented by the organization to achieve data security and protection. The mechanisms discussed in this chapter can be divided into two categories. There are those mechanisms or controls implemented external to the computer system and operating software, and those implemented as part of the operating or management systems software. Administrative controls would fall into the category of external protection mechanisms, whereas the following controls could be considered as internal protection mechanisms:

• Auditing and monitoring the database
• Authorization schemas such as an access control matrix
• Resource access control facility (RACF)

11.1 TOP-LEVEL MANAGEMENT INVOLVEMENT IN DATABASE SECURITY, PRIVACY, AND INTEGRITY

My four years of research in database security, privacy, and integrity revealed that one of the major reasons for the non-effort or failure of database security efforts in most corporations is the lack of involvement and support by the top-level management.

We would have assumed that with the overwhelming statistics relative to the ease with which computer systems are penetrated, and the resulting loss, that management will support a program to provide adequate security. But this assumption is not necessarily valid.

For one thing, most managers are inundated with immediate problems. The one thing they feel they do not need is to be further burdened with hypothetical problems. But security deals with hypothetical problems, i.e., things that might happen.

Further, these are things that management hopes will not happen. And they involve "bad" human behavior, in most cases, whereas managers prefer to deal with "good" behavior such as how employees can get their work done more efficiently, get company problems solved, and increase company profits.

The net result, as one might expect, is that security considerations tend to be postponed. They are postponed, that is, until some serious consequence occurs from a breach of security. Then there may be a flurry of excitement, as an attempt is made to bolster security measures.

Management's willingness to consider the security problem is the most important single factor in the whole security program. For one thing, management makes the critical decision at the outset as to whether the security problem will be approached. They must set the policies, ground rules, and scope of the security project. They create the reviews to determine whether things have changed to the point where major new protective measures must be considered.

Management sets the guidelines and procedures for an effective system of internal controls. These controls deal with handling the assets and liabilities of the organization. They identify the sensitive data and programs that need to be protected. They classify and itemize their existence, importance, or need for protection.

Further, these assets and liabilities can be protected, in part, by protecting information about them. For example, if a fictitious payment transaction is entered into the accounts receivable database, an asset is lost. Also if a fictitious invoice is entered into the accounts payable database and is paid, an asset is lost. If a manipulated transaction causes a valuable piece of property, a vehicle, or a piece of equipment to be written off as salvage and is taken by some unauthorized personnel, an asset is lost. Protection against these threats is accomplished by controls set up by management that make it difficult to enter such fictitious transactions into the system. Management support for a security program may be in any of the following forms:

- Assignment of major responsibilities for the program
- Organization and assignment of the team for the security program
- Setting policies and general control objectives
- Undertaking a cost/benefit study to determine what protection features to implement

Management can set the desired tone for the whole security program by identifying those general control standards that it wishes to emphasize by the following means:

- Study existing protection to point out where additional or improved protection is needed.
- Design and install the needed protection, under the responsibility of operating management.
- Check the effectiveness of the whole internal protection system by means of periodic audits.

11.2 ADMINISTRATIVE CONTROLS

Administrative controls may be defined as management policies formulated to ensure adequate maintenance of a selective access program, whether it be selective authorization to data files or physical areas. They may include the development and implementation of security policies, guidelines, standards, and procedures.

Effective administrative controls can go a long way in helping to ensure that an organization has a secure operating database environment. These controls will certainly assist in reducing or eliminating both deliberate and accidental threats. Once an intruder realizes that his/her chances of being detected are good, that intruder may be deterred from attempting to breach the security. This determination of probability of being detected can be made from the intruder's knowledge of the existing administrative controls. For example, if the intruder knows that there is a requirement for the user's name and terminal log-on times to be recorded, then he/she will very likely not use the terminal.

The probability of accidental threats succeeding decreases with an increase in the user's knowledge of the operating environment and requirements. Clear and precise administrative procedures and assertions help to increase that knowledge and in turn decrease the probability of successful accidental threats.

Administrative controls, and security features in particular, should be developed in parallel with the actual systems and programs development. A group consisting of internal auditors, development team, and users should be assigned to develop these controls and standards.

Administrative controls can be defined in the following areas:

• Top-level management decisions — decisions pertaining to the selection and evaluation of safeguards
• Security risk assessment studies to identify and rank the events that would compromise the security of the database and the information stored in it
• Personnel management — pertains to employee hiring and firing procedures, employee rules of conduct and enforcement
• Data handling techniques — a well-defined set of rules describing the precautions to be used and the obligations of personnel during the handling of all data
• Data processing practices — include the methods to control accountability for data, verification of the accuracy of data, inventories of storage media

- Programming practices — pertain to the discipline employed in the specification, design, implementation, program coding, and debugging of the system
- Assignment of responsibilities — assign each individual a specific set of responsibilities toward carrying out certain security functions for which that individual is held responsible
- Procedures auditing — an independent examination of established security procedures to determine their ongoing effectiveness

11.3 AUDITING AND MONITORING THE DATABASE

Auditing and monitoring are integral features of database security. Should a violation be attempted, the system must be able to detect it and react effectively to it. Detection then implies that the system has a threat-monitoring capability. Threat monitoring requires the following actions:

- Monitoring the events of the system as related to security
- Recognizing a potential compromise to the security system
- Diagnosing the nature of the threat
- Performing compensatory actions
- Reporting the event
- Recording the event

While threat monitoring is an active form of surveillance, an equally important, but more passive, form is auditability of the database. A security audit should be able to cover the past events of the system and, in particular, cover all security-related transactions.

Audit trails that can lead to the identity of users, terminals, and authorizing bodies should be a feature of all applications.

The monitoring process within an organization should include the ability to determine whether

- The controls over the database administration function are effective.
- The process by which sensitive data is determined is adequate.
- The procedures by which security violations are detected are in place and effective.
- The extent to which data access is restricted to only authorized individuals is workable.
- The ability to restrict access by a program to data, other programs, and libraries exists.

- Terminal security features such as log on, log off, and restart are adequate and effective.
- The procedures to follow during processing interruptions are effective.

The importance of keeping records and logs of events affecting the database and its environment cannot be overemphasized. The events recorded should include performance data, all error or abnormal events, all transactions related to sensitive information, and all overrides of established systems controls.

Several database management systems provide logging capabilities as part of their package. These logs should be investigated for their adequacy and ability to meet the auditing requirements of the environment. Organizations should not be hesitant to design and implement their own in-house logging facilities if the manufacturer's prove inadequate.

Any security effort in an organization should eventually involve internal auditors. This involvement becomes mandatory because of the changing requirements for evaluating and verifying controls in a secure database environment.

Personnel responsible for security can offer considerable assistance to the auditors in determining the accuracy, integrity, and completeness of systems.

Researchers are now suggesting that the internal auditors become involved in the development stages of a system and not only in the post-installation evaluation. The auditors' experience should provide the development teams with an insight into the various methods they can use to approach their responsibilities in controlling and auditing the total information processing system.

Because of the rapidly changing database technology, internal auditors need to constantly upgrade their skills. System development teams with current knowledge should assist the auditors in filling the gaps in their knowledge of techniques and concepts of integrated database system design.

The development teams should strive to increase management's awareness of changes in the data processing environment as they affect internal audit and the controls governing data processing.

Finally, the following list of management activities should enhance the internal auditing capabilities within a corporation and especially as they affect the database environment:

- Ensure that all staff realize the importance of internal auditing in the security effort.

- Issue a clearly defined internal audit mandate that specifies the responsibility of the internal audit as it relates to all phases of the security effort.
- Clearly define the working relationship among users, internal auditors, and development teams responsible for database security, privacy, and integrity.
- Encourage the development of new techniques and internal audit approaches to ensure the security, privacy, and integrity of the database.
- Require the development of security control guidelines.
- Ensure that internal auditors participate in the security effort.

11.4 TYPES OF PROTECTION MECHANISM

In an earlier section, I introduced two classes of protection mechanisms. There are those built into the computer operating system (internal mechanisms) and those not linked to the operating system (external mechanisms). The next few sections of this chapter discuss some of those protection mechanisms in more detail.

11.4.1 The Access Matrix as a Protection Mechanism

The access matrix is an internal protection mechanism built into the operating system. It is essentially a set of tables that indicate who has access to what data. The access matrix consists of the following components:

- Objects that are to be protected
- Subjects seeking access to these objects
- Different protection levels for each object
- Rules that determine how the subjects access each object
- A monitor that mediates all access of a subject to an object
- Directories containing information about the objects and subjects. The information on the object consists of such things as the unique identifier, protection level, types of access permitted, and data types. The information on the subject consists of the unique identifier and class of subjects.

The interaction between the subjects and objects can be represented by an access control matrix (see Figure 11.1). The protectable objects are the row-components of the matrix. The subjects seeking access to the objects are the column-components of the matrix. Each entry in the access matrix determines the access rights of the subject to the object and is defined as the access attribute in the model.

The access matrix model is dynamic enough to include any class of objects or subjects within the data processing environment. It can provide a high level of protection for any object, irrespective of whatever application the organization's personnel develops and runs against the integrated database.

Each object will be placed in a class determined by the level of protection required for that object. Each subject will be a member of a hierarchy. The hierarchical classifying of the subjects will allow subjects to create other subjects while ensuring that the created subject will not have more privileges than its creator. Some of the subjects that will be considered in the model are as follows:

• Database Administrator
• Development Teams
• System and Application Programmers
• Maintenance
• Operations
• Terminals
• Programs and Utilities

Some of the objects that will be considered in the model are the following:

• Programs and Utilities
• Terminals
• Database Files
• OS Files
• Database Segments
• Database Fields
• Data Dictionary Entries

The Access Matrix — Case Study   A typical case of an application of the access matrix is in Figure 11.1. Each entry in the access matrix determines the access rights of the subjects to the objects. For example, the "01" in the first column and second row indicated that the ACCOUNTING department can READ the EMPLOYEE NAME; the "11" in the first column and row indicates that the PERSONNEL department can both READ and WRITE the EMPLOYEE NAME on the EMPLOYEE database; the "00" in the fifth column and second row indicates that the ACCOUNTING department can neither READ

EMP. NAME	EMP. ADDRESS	EMP. PHONE #	EMP. S.I.N.	EMP. EDUCA.	EMP. SAL HIST.	EMP. MEDICAL	EMP. PENSION	
11	11	11	11	11	11	11	11	PERSONNEL
01	01	01	01	00	01	01	01	ACCOUNTING
00	00	00	00	00	00	00	00	MARKETING
00	00	00	00	00	00	00	00	PURCHASING
11	11	11	11	11	11	11	11	D.B.A.
10	10	10	10	10	10	10	10	MAINTENANCE
10	10	10	10	10	10	10	10	PROGRAMMERS
10	10	10	10	10	10	10	10	OPERATIONS
01	01	01	00	00	00	00	00	CLERICAL

LEGEND:
01 — READ
11 — READ AND WRITE
00— NO ACCESS
10 — WRITE ONLY

Figure 11.1 Typical access matrix.

nor WRITE the EMPLOYEE EDUCATION information; and the "10" in the first column and sixth row indicates that the MAINTENANCE department can only WRITE the EMPLOYEE NAME on the EMPLOYEE database.

The matrix can accommodate several other access attributes such as EXECUTE, DELETE, UPDATE, APPEND (add something to the end of a data item without altering its original contents), SORT, CREATE, and OWN. This can be accomplished by adding appropriate codes.

The elements of the access matrix usually contain bits that represent accesses that can be performed by the subject on the object. However, if desired, the elements may contain pointers to PROCEDURES, DIRECTORIES, or PROGRAMS. This feature is useful since programs or procedures contain greater processing capabilities than a simple WRITE command, for example.

The additional processing information from the procedures, directories, or programs will be made available at each attempted access by a given subject to a given object. The information will allow those access decisions that depend on information not easily represented in the access matrix to be made.

11.4.2 Rules Governing Accessing Decisions

The accessing decisions are governed by a set of rules, listed below:

- Permits a subject to transfer any access attribute it holds for an object to any other subject.
- Permits a subject to grant to any subject access attributes for an object it owns.
- Permits a subject to delete any access attribute from the column of an objects it owns or the row of a subject it created.
- Permits a subject to read the portion of the access matrix it owns or controls.
- Permits a subject to create a non-subject object. The creation of an object consists of adding a new column to the access matrix. The creator of the object is given "owner" access to the newly created object and may then grant access attributes to other subjects for their object.
- Permits the owner of an object to destroy that object. This corresponds to deleting the column from the access matrix.
- Permits a subject to create another subject. This consists of creating a row and column for the new subject in the access matrix, giving the creator "owner" access to the new subject, and giving the new subject "control" access to itself.
- Permits only the "owner" to destroy a subject. This corresponds to deleting both the row and the column from the access matrix.
- Permits access based on the access history of other objects: subject A may write in object F only if he or she has not read from object G.
- Permits access based on the dynamic state of the system: subject B may read object H only at a time when the database in which the object resides is in a predetermined state.
- Permits access based on the prescribed usage of the object: A subject may sort an object in a protection level higher than that of the subject provided no data is returned to the subject.
- Permits access based on the current value of the object: a given subject may not read the salary field of any personnel record for which the salary value is greater than $20,000.

- Permits access based on the class of certain subjects: no access to certain objects can be made by a class of subjects between certain time periods, e.g., between 12 a.m. and 8 a.m.
- Permits access based on the class of certain objects: certain terminals or portions of the database can't be accessed between 12 a.m. and 8 a.m.

The access matrix is really the heart of the security system. By including more information on it, the complex aspects of data security such as data-dependent checks can also be achieved.

11.4.3 Protection Levels of Access Matrix

In the access matrix described above, authorization to access object is based on the protection levels of the objects and the classification of the subjects. Access requests are denied unless the classification of the subject requesting access equals or exceeds the protection level of the object requested.

Access can be controlled beyond the file level of the database if desired. By using directories that allow access to other directories and eventually to actual files, hierarchies of successively more restrictive access can be set up. This approach will provide adequate protection at the field level of the database.

The protection level of each object will be determined by the team that does the risk analysis. Each protection level will then be assigned to a directory. The movement of an object from one directory to another will indicate that the protection level of that object has been either increased or decreased.

The protection levels of the model will be increased as the need for more security is uncovered. Some levels that may be considered are as follows:

- No sharing at all (complete isolation)
- Sharing copies of programs, files, or the database
- Sharing originals of programs, files, or the database
- Sharing entire programming systems
- Permitting the cooperation of mutually suspicious systems
- Providing subsystems with the ability to perform a task but guaranteeing that no secret records of or from that task are kept by subsystems

11.4.4 The Access Matrix Monitor

The monitor of the access matrix is that part of the software that ensures that there is no violation of the protection levels of the objects. It should be designed in such a way that any attempted violation of the protection levels or the database will trigger an audit or logging capability. To accomplish this one must ensure that there can be no unauthorized alteration of the monitor.

The monitor can be either some software mechanism or administrative control that validates and then permits or denies each and every request for access to protectable objects.

A security program is effective to the extent it reaches and affects all elements of the organization. One of the most effective mechanisms for assuring widespread distribution and uniform enforcement of security policy is through an existing or newly created standards program. A good standard can be defined as a precept that is enforced because the benefits outweigh the costs.

When initially developing a computer security program, it is essential that meaningful policy and standards be set forth and disseminated to all personnel, so that each individual is fully aware of mandatory security requirements.

As a minimum, these standards should address the following areas:

• Background of security policy
• Purpose
• Responsibilities for security
• Personnel security
• Physical access controls
• Media and facility protection
• Communication and network security
• Hardware and software
• Password control
• Controlling release of sensitive data
• Integrity controls and error detection
• Security violation

Before dissemination to the organization as a working document, standards must be fully coordinated among the various organization departments.

Procedures must be fully coordinated among the various organization departments.

Procedures are more definitive: They provide step-by-step direction in performing a course of action. They should be specific and oriented to a given task in a given department. Security procedures should be detailed enough to be usable as a working document. For example, procedures regarding password changes should read, "Passwords will be changed by system administrator at least once per month," and not "Passwords will be changed regularly."

In any organization, probably the most difficult aspect of security procedure is enforcement. It is one thing to declare the programmers will not leave on-line terminal unattended, but quite another problem to enforce the rule. In this regard, security procedures should be subjected to the three rules of effectiveness:

- economic feasibility — are the procedures too costly?
- operational feasibility — a 10-digit password might be secure, but is it a reasonable solution?
- technical feasibility — can the procedure be implemented with the existing technical knowledge and equipment?

11.4.5 Administrative Controls in Access Matrix Environment

The organization about to use the access matrix should develop policies and standards that will form the basis of the administrative controls that can assist the access matrix in its efforts to deny or grant access to protectable objects. If adequate controls exist, attempts at unauthorized access may be thwarted before they enter the computer system.

Interviews should be conducted with data security personnel to determine what procedures are already in place to control subject's requests to resources.

All aspects of the requesting process should be examined and the adequacy of the existing controls evaluated. It is hoped that the study will lead to new controls that will reflect the current environment and need for adequate data security.

11.4.6 The Software Version of the Access Matrix Monitor

The monitor, the part of the access matrix model that enforces the security policy, should be designed according to the following three principles:

- Complete mediation — the monitor must mediate every access of a subject to an object.
- Isolation — the monitor and its database must be protected from unauthorized alteration.
- Verifiability — the monitor must be small, simple, and understandable so that it can be completely tested and verified to perform its functions correctly.

11.4.7 Design of the Monitor

Some considerations in the design of the monitor are as follows:

- An interface between the monitor and other parts of the system such as user programs
- How control is to be passed across the interface — in terms of invoking or calling the monitor
- Means of identifying processes that interact with the monitor
- Means of queuing and assigning priorities to request for services of the monitor
- Interfacing of the monitor with other auditing programs
- Protection of monitor against modification
- Interfacing of the monitor with subject and object directories

11.4.8 Functions of Monitor

The main functions of the monitor can be listed as follows:

- Responsible for creating and deleting subjects and objects
- Creates a process containing the subject ID, the object's protection level, and associated access attributes
- Terminates the subject's process and cleans up on his behalf
- Releases all reserved objects, closes any objects that are opened, removes the subject from the request queue, and purges the portion of memory that acted as the work area
- Maintains data consistency and seeks to avoid or resolve data interference
- Reserves and holds objects

11.4.9 Design of Subject and Object Directories

The directories to be established for the access matrix model will include the following:

- Information on subjects
- Information on objects
- Protection levels
- Pointers to other directories

11.5. SUBJECTS AND OBJECTS OF THE ACCESS MA-TRIX

The subjects of the matrix should be members of a hierarchy and have functions in relation to that hierarchy. For example, the DBA could be in the universal subject and have the following functions:

- Establish new subjects
- Impose logical limits on the resources
- Remove subject's ability to access the database
- Determine maximum protection level of each subject
- Define resource limitation of each subject
- Monitor and display all subjects and protection levels of objects
- Reclassify a subject
- Reclassify an object

The objects of the matrix must have a unique identifier, access attributes, description, and value set. The access attributes can be any of the following: READ, WRITE, UPDATE, etc. The description must indicate the format, and size.

11.5.1 Processing Details of Access Matrix Model

Figure 11.2 outlines the processing components of the access matrix system. A request to access an object will undergo the following steps:

- User program or transaction makes a request to access a protect-able object to the monitor.
- Monitor checks user program (subject) identifier, retrieves access matrix row containing the object to which access is requested. Access matrix points to a relevant directory.
- Monitor gets relevant information about subject and object from directory.
- Monitor verifies that the subject is authorized to access the requested object.

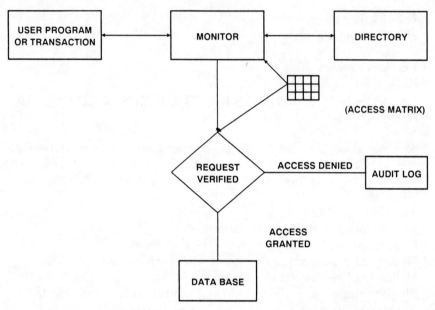

Figure 11.2 Schematic of components of the access matrix control system.

• Decision about request is made by the monitor. If request is denied, the monitor triggers an on-line terminal that creates an audit trail or log. If request is granted, the monitor accesses the database and returns the requested data item to the user program.

11.5.2 Processing Alternatives of Access Matrix Model

The design of the monitor is very critical in cutting down on overhead during processing. The monitor should be flexible enough to incorporate some of the following processing alternatives.

• Monitor should be able to determine whether the class of subjects making a request is authorized to access the requested object. This would prevent having to get the information from the access matrix or the directory.
• Monitor should be able to make determinations from either the access matrix or the directory and not necessarily have to access both.
• Monitor should be able to go directly to the database, bypassing access matrix and directories, after request is verified.

• Monitor should be able to update directories and put special emphasis on history- (time-) sensitive information.

11.6 THE RISK ASSESSMENT AS AN AID TO SELECTING A PROTECTION MECHANISM

Many organizations hesitate to initiate a security program because of their ignorance of the sensitivity of the data in their environment and the cost/benefit in instituting security features. This ignorance exists mainly due to reluctance of the organization to conduct risk analysis. Many of them prefer to institute security features only after a break in security occurs.

The purpose of performing a risk assessment is to obtain a quantitative statement of the potential problems to which the data processing facility is exposed, so the appropriate cost-effective security safeguards can be selected. It is assumed that, once armed with such information, no security measure will be selected that costs more than tolerating the problem. The risk assessment should establish that threshold.

The risk analysis provides a rational approach toward choosing security safeguards. A security program should logically provide protection in the most economical manner. The following questions, therefore, should be answered in the course of a risk assessment:

• What are the specific results desired, that is, exactly how much security is required?
• What is the proper balance between security program cost and potential benefits?
• When trade-offs can be made between protection and recovery, how much effort should be expended on each?

An important part of the security program involves determining what functions are performed or supported by the database environment that is vital to the organization's survival. The advisability of providing security beyond this minimum can be determined largely through the cost/benefit analysis.

Freedom of information legislation may require organizations to allow their customers access to their records. How such requests would affect the current structure of the organization's database can only be determined by a risk assessment.

Any risk assessment conducted at an early developmental stage of database design will be less costly and will allow more adequate security features to be built into developing systems at a lower cost than at a later stage, when systems are completed and may have to go through tremendous redesign phases and cost to implement similar and necessary security features.

The risk assessment conducted by corporations at an early stage of development need not be expensive. A useful set of baseline data can be obtained by conducting simple interviews and surveys in all departments and data processing groups.

11.7 RESOURCE ACCESS CONTROL FACILITY (RACF) AS A PROTECTION MECHANISM

RACF is a program product from IBM that is designed to identify system users and control their access to protected resources.

RACF's authorization structure can be contrasted with a data set password mechanism. With typical password protection a password is assigned to a specific data set. The system insures that the data set can be accessed only when that password is supplied.

Protected data sets can be accessed by anyone who knows the password. Obviously, there are control problems associated with restricting knowledge of the passwords.

There are also problems in withdrawing access to data sets. If three people know the password for a particular data set and an administrator wants to take away one person's access rights, the password must be changed and the new password communicated to the users.

11.7.1 RACF Concepts

The RACF authorization structure is based on principles different from password protection. RACF eliminates the need for data set passwords.

With RACF, an administrator or auditor can tell which users are authorized to access which data sets. A user's right to access a data set can be withdrawn simply by changing the structure.

The RACF authorization structure contains three kinds of elements: users, groups of users, and protected resources. It stores descriptions of users, group, and resources in profiles contained in a special data set called the RACF data set. The types of resources RACF protects are Direct Access Storage Device (DASD) data sets, tape volumes, DASD volumes, terminals, and applications.

Users, groups, and resources can be interrelated. A user can be a member of one or more groups. This membership allows the user to administer the group or simply to function within the group when accessing data. Both users and groups can be authorized to access protected resources. The type of access allowed corresponds to the different types of operations that can be performed in data handling.

RACF interfaces with the operating system in three main areas:

- Identification and verification of users
- Authorization checking for access to protected resources
- Monitoring to provide both immediate notification of security problems and a log for post de facto analysis

Once RACF has verified the user's identity, it builds a description of the user. This description is kept in memory for the duration of the job or on-line session. Comparing this description with what the user can do is the basis for authority checking.

Authority checking is the basis for deciding whether a processing function or an access to RACF performs authority checking without any user or operator intervention. If the access is authorized, it is allowed; if unauthorized, it is denied.

RACF follows very specific rules for authority verification. First, it checks to see if the user is authorized to the resource by inspecting the resource profile in the RACF data set. If this is not the case, then RACF uses its description of the protected resource. RACF determines if the user is on the access list. If so, then RACF can decide whether the user should be authorized to perform the requested function. If the user is not on the access list, RACF then checks to see if the user's group is on the access list.

Monitoring or logging is used to record and subsequently report the occurrence of unauthorized access attempts. It also serves to provide evidence that the general security guidelines that have been implemented are being enforced. RACF uses two general types of monitoring:

- Logging if access to data or to the system
- Logging if changes to the RACF profiles that define the authorization structures

If an access attempt is unauthorized, it will not be permitted or the profile change will not take place. Depending on options set by administrators or by the resource owner, a log record will be written, and a message will be sent to a designated security console.

The log record will contain the following:

• Normal time stamp
• Identification of the user and group causing the action being logged
• Reasons for logging
• Levels of authority required and granted
• Identification of the resource in question
• Operands specified and the values specified for these operands when the RACF profiles are changed

11.8 SUMMARY

This chapter has discussed some of the advanced features of database security, privacy, and integrity. It discussed the need for management's involvement and support of any effort in data security, a risk assessment to determine the sensitivity of the organization's data, and audit trails to determine who did what and when in terms of breaching the security.

In terms of protection mechanisms we discussed two. The access matrix developed by the author and Resource Access Control Facility (RACF) developed by IBM. The chapter concluded by giving a detailed account of these protection mechanisms for the benefit of researchers interested in installing any of them in their organization.

QUESTIONS

1. What are security controls? Discuss them in terms of external and internal controls.
2. Discuss the need for top-level management involvement in data security.
3. What are administrative controls? List areas in which they can be defined.
4. What are the two types of protection mechanisms? Give examples of each type.
5. Discuss the access matrix as a protection mechanism.

B

Case Histories and CASE Tools

Systems Development Case Study — Marketing

NOTE: The entire contents of this appendix were developed directly from the User Requirements discussed in Chapter 2.

1.0 INTRODUCTION

This appendix contains the specifications that are required to code programs to satisfy the data processing needs of the users as set out in the Business Requirements Document.

The document describes the flow of processing from the entering of data at the terminals, through updating the various master files, and to final storage in the IDMS database or other spool databases. It also gives descriptions of the various input and output data, the detail processing that must be done, the editing that must be carried out on the input data, and any subprograms that are used in the course of processing the data.

The document concludes with detailed representation of the various reports that are produced on a daily basis by the system and the spool database from which other reports can be produced on request.

SCOPE OF THIS DOCUMENT

The major processing objective of the project is to produce application programs that will allow the Sales and Marketing Department
to maintain their Master files on-line.

The application, through the use of Program Function (PF) keys,
will add, update, and delete data items from the Master files. Error
messages will be standardized and displayed at intervals to allow for
on-line correction of errors.

The programs will produce images of the input transactions in a
spool database environment. These images will be used to update the
Total database and produce Daily Update Reports.

All programs will run against the current IDMS database.

ENVIRONMENT

The following sections outline the hardware and software environment for which the programming specs were developed.

Hardware	Model Number
Computer	IBM 3081-3083
Terminal	IBM 3178/3179 3278/3279
Controller	IBM 3274-41C

Software	Release/Level
MVS JES-2	
IDMS-DC	10.0
CULPRIT	6.1
ADSO	1.1 - May, 1985
COBOL	IDMS Rev. 1.3 - Rel. 5.7 May, 1984
TOTAL	8.0

2.0 PROGRAM NARRATIVE

The set of programs described here processes the screen input; updates the Customer Master File, the Product Master File, the Zip
Code Master File, and the Buying Group Master File; and produces
batch reports of the transactions on a daily basis.

The system is designed to operate in two modes. The on-line mode
accepts the screen input, updates the Master Files, and produces the
spooled records that act as input to the batch portion of the system.

The programs that operate in batch mode take the spooled records and produce the various daily reports.

The programs access six major areas of the IDMS database. These areas are: (See Figure A.1.)

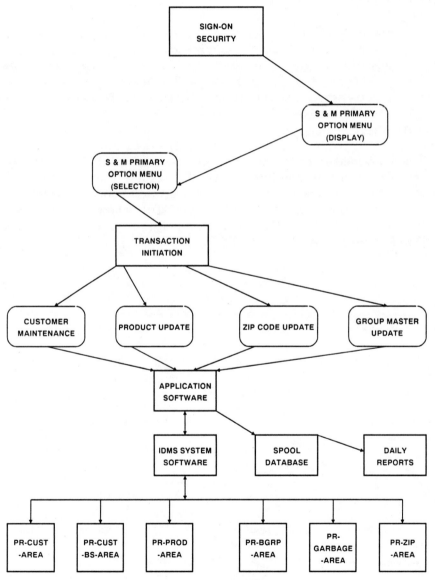

Figure A.1 Physical model for S & M on-line system.

- PR-CUST-AREA
- PR-CUST-BS-AREA
- PR-PROD-AREA
- PR-BGRP-AREA
- PR-GARBAGE-AREA (Table Data Base)
- PR-ZIP-AREA

The programs will do both field-by-field edits of the input and global edit/validation for data security and integrity.

Finally, the programs will create print lines to be spooled for future production of the daily reports. The details of producing the daily reports are discussed in other sections of this document.

3.0 SYSTEM FLOW CHART

The following two diagrams illustrate how data will be processed by the Marketing On-Line System. The first figure, the logical model, shows the data flow between the input operators and the machine. The second figure, the physical model, illustrates how the data flows from the terminal to IDMS databases and, finally, to daily reports. (See Figures A.1, A.2.)

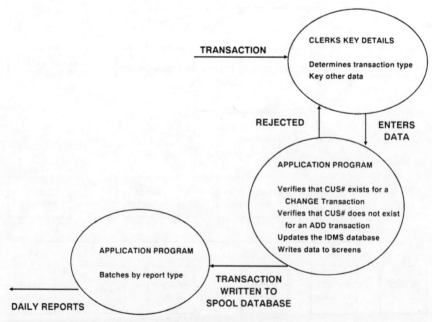

Figure A.2 Logical model for S & M on-line system.

4.0 DESCRIPTION OF INPUT

The input to the system consists of two parts:

• The input from terminal operators
• The spooled transactions that are processed to produce daily reports

The formats of the screen input, the data characteristics, and the field-by-field editing are discussed in more detail.

The spool database will consist of two tables set up in a CALC-VIA set.

The TABLE MASTER record will have a compound key containing:

• The ID of the program that will use it
• The current date.

The TABLE DETAIL record will contain the data stored in the format dictated by the currently used Input Transmittal Forms (see section A.1)

5.0 DESCRIPTION OF OUTPUT

The output from the system consists of two parts:

• The daily reports of changes to the Master Files and Tables
• Hard copy printouts of the Master File.

The record layouts for the daily reports and sample reports of the updates are given in section A.2.

6.0 DETAILED PROCESSING REQUIREMENTS

This section of the programming specs offers some suggestions to the programmers as to what approaches they should take when coding the programs. The section covers the following areas:

• Processing details
• Editing details
• Security controls

- Database retrieval
- Subprograms
- Spool database

PROCESSING DETAILS

The processing details cover processing requirements as expressed by the users and some suggestions as to screen processing and retrieval from the database. The details required by the users are as follows:

1. For an Add function, a blank screen with required data fields must be displayed.
2. A new product that is being entered into the system should allow for at least 10 report line codes to be assigned to that product.
3. Physical characteristics of the screen should be 80 characters per line and 20 lines per page.
4. Upper limit of customers assigned to a major code should be 10.
5. All fields in error to be highlighted. The cursor will be placed under the first field in error.
6. A message will be generated after all errors on the screen have been validated.
7. Scrolling of a screen will be limited to the second page of the transaction screens.
8. The use of colors are
   - Detail Headings - Turquoise
   - Updatable Fields - Amber
   - Other Areas - White
   - Validation Errors - Red
9. There must be some interactive feedback to indicate that a screen has been successfully updated.
10. Changes to the major code (llxxx series) that are now carried out by Transaction 44 can be achieved from the Customer Master screen.
11. The user requirements call for split screen processing for certain transaction types. These will be handled on a case-by-case basis when more detailed specs are written.
12. Required fields for transaction 37 and 43 are group code number, name and address, trade class, and region identification. For transaction 44 and 45, the required fields are group number, customer number, and start and end dates.

NOTE: The programmer is asked to see section A.3 for more detail on retrieval from the database.

EDITING DETAILS

The editing for the programs will be done in two passes: (a) field by field; (b) global.

The field-by-field editing will be outlined in a separate document. The global editing calls for validation of certain data field against tables.

SECURITY CONTROLS

The security controls requested by the users are to be put in place to control terminal operators' access to data and to ensure the integrity of the database. The following controls were requested by the users:

1. Checks for attempts to delete SIS numbers.
2. Checks for attempts to change TERRITORY numbers.
3. Checks for attempts to delete data fields from the PRODUCT INFORMATION FILE.
4. Allow for CUSTOMERS changing from one GROUP CODE to another.
5. Allow for CUSTOMERS to be added to multiple groups.
6. Allow for deletions of MAJOR CODE NAMES and MAJOR CODES.
7. INPUT OPERATORS cannot update MAJOR CODES less than llxxx series.
8. DEPARTMENTS other than MARKETING cannot update the on-line Master files.

SECURITY CHECKS

The programmer must check for the following:

1. For a Customer file, you must have a SIS Number before a CHANGE or an ADD can be implemented.
2. For an ADD, the Calls Address and Supplementary Information must be entered.

3. If the Customer is both OTC and ETHICAL, then the Calls Address, Supplementary Information, and OTC information must be entered.

4. If the Customer is both ONCOLOGY and ETHICAL, then the Calls Address, Supplementary Information, and Oncology Information are required.

5. For Product updating, the Product Code, Name, Department, Activity, Unit of Use, and Report Group Codes are required when ADDING a new product to the file.

6. For a CHANGE, only the Product Number and one other related field are required.

7. For an ADD to the Zip Master File, one requires the Zip Code and all three current input cards.

8. For a CHANGE, only the Zip Code is required.

9. For MAJOR CODE, a major code is required before ADDING customers associated with that code.

10. For MAJOR CODE, the name and address of the major code is required when ADDING customers.

DATABASE RETRIEVAL

See section A.4.

SUBPROGRAMS

The subprograms and utilities that are used to support these programs will be discussed in a separate document.

SPOOL DATABASE

See section A.2.

7.0 EDIT/VALUATION RULES

Some edit criteria were discussed in section 6 of this document. Detailed Edit/Validation rules will be discussed in a separate document.

8.0 DESCRIPTION OF SUBPROGRAMS AND UTILITIES

The discussion of subprograms and utilities used in these programs will be discussed in a separate document.

9.0 RECORD LAYOUTS

Samples of record layouts and daily reports that are produced by the batch portion of this system are shown in section A.3.

10.0 SPOOL DATABASE

A detailed discussion of the creation of the spool database and the format of the database records is given in section A.3.

A.1 Batch Input and Source Documents for Marketing System

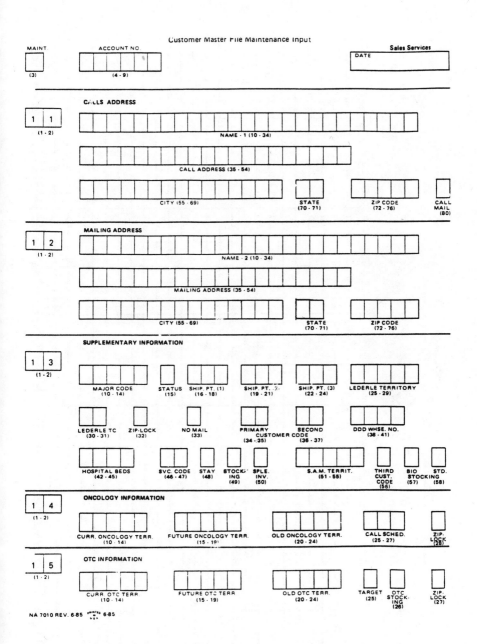

Customer Master File Maintenance Input

NA 7010 REV. 6-85   PRINTED 6-85

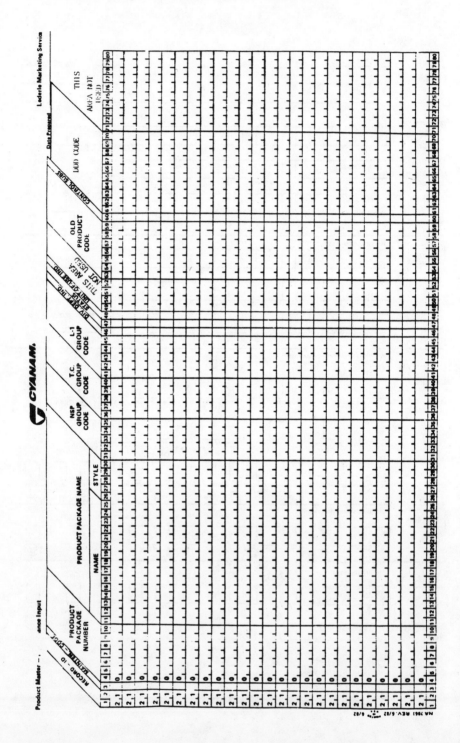

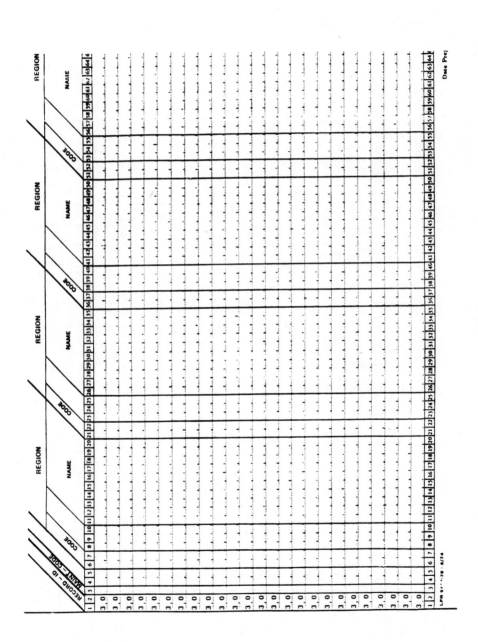

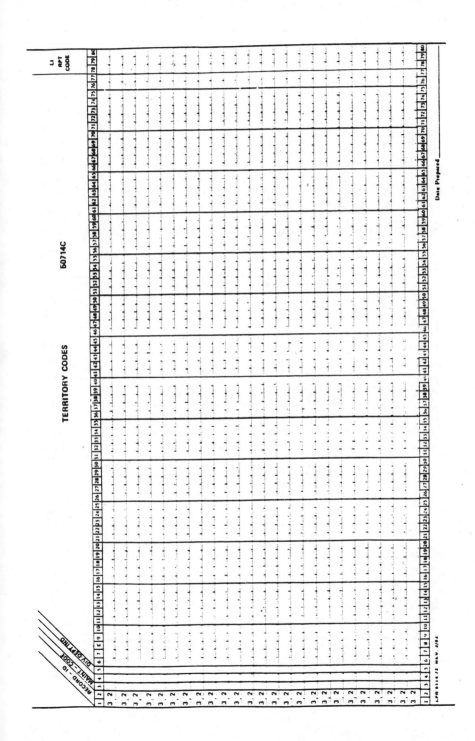

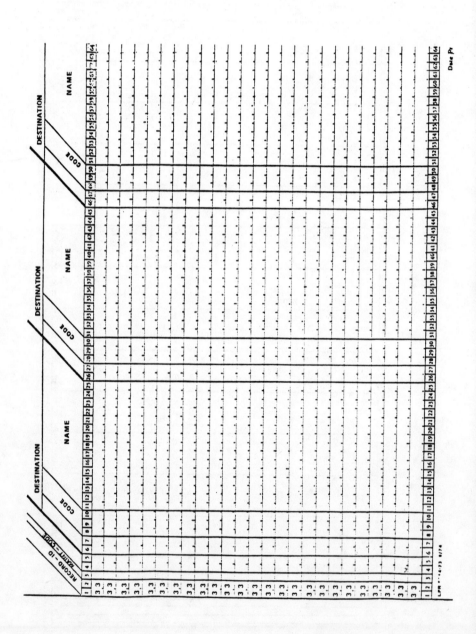

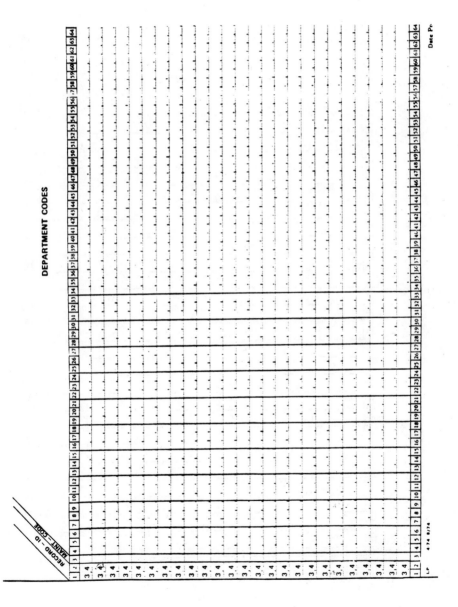

236   Systems Design in a Database Environment

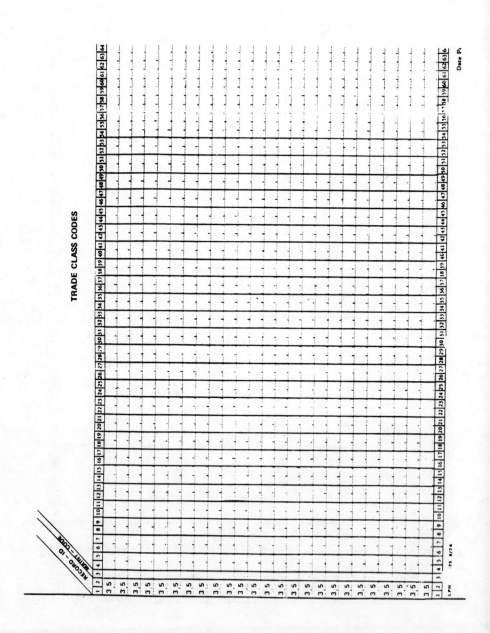

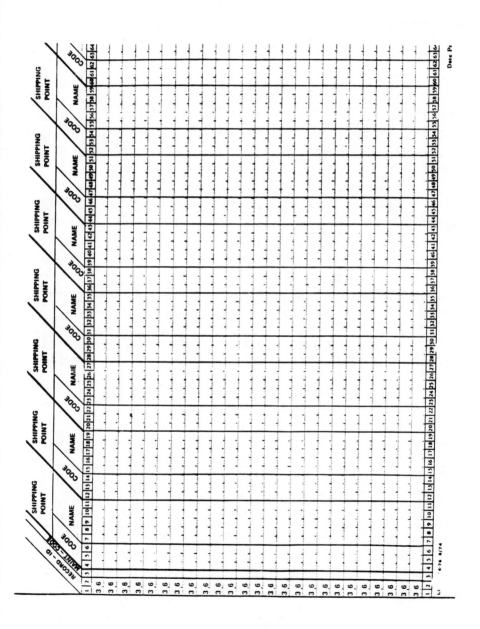

GROUP MEMBERS

JOB #PR50703G

ACTIONS

1 = ADD
2 = UPDATE
3 = DELETE

*DATES IN MMDDYY FORMAT

TRANS CODE	ACTION	GROUP NUMBER	CUSTOMER NUMBER	JOIN DATE*	EXIT DATE*		

Date Prepared _____

NA 7021-02 1 8U

A.2 On-Line Screens for Sales/Marketing System Developed from Batch Input Using ADS-Online with Dialogs)

```
C6404M                          IDMS-DC MAP UTILITY              DATE: 12/24/86  TIME: 104827 PAGE  3

REPORT FOR MAP  PPSM100M            VERSION   1      COMPILE DATE: 12/22/86     COMPILE TIME: 093944

DEVICES: 24X80, 32X80, 43X80, 27X132

    5   10   15   20   25   30   35   40   45   50   55   60   65   70   75   80   85   90   95  100  105  110  115  120  125  130
SSM1    $ CUSTOMER MASTER FILE          SDATE:$........SID:$=====
                                        (CURSOR) -
SCUSTOMER $:$======*          SSTATUS:$=
SNAME:$=                    ---------SSHIP POINT:$=== == ==
$---- CALLS  ADDRESS --------------SLEDERLE TERR:$====   SZIP-LOCK:$=
SSTREET:$============         SLEDERLE TC  :$==       SNO MAIL:$=
SCITY  :$=======            SSTATE:$==                 SSPLE INV:$=
SZIP   :$===== ===   SMAILLOCK:$=
S--------       SUPPLEMENTARY INFORMATION --------------------
SCUSTOMER CODE:$:== == =    SS.A.M. TERR:$====   SLENGTH OF STAY:$=
SMAJOR  CODE:$:====     SSVC.  CODE:$:==      SNO. OF BEDS  :$===
SWAREHOUSE # :$====      SSTOCKING  :$= SBIO STOCKING:$= SSTD STOCKING:$=
S--------       BUSINESS SEGMENT INFORMATION --------------------
SBUSINESS SEGMENT:$=== SSALES FORCE:$=== STRADE CLASS:$:== STARGET:$= SZLOCK:$=
STERRITORY:SCUR:$==== SFUT:$==== SOLD:$:S==== SCALL SCHED:$=== $STOCK:$=
S--------       KEY ASSIGNMENTS       PF24 - CUSTOMER MASTER FILE - 2
SPF5  - ADD   CUSTOMER
SPF6  - UPDATE CUSTOMER
SPF12 - DISPLAY CUSTOMER
```

```
C6404M                    IDMS-DC MAP UTILITY                      DATE: 12/24/86 TIME: 104827 PAGE  18

REPORT FOR MAP  PPSM101M            VERSION   1      COMPILE DATE: 12/22/86    COMPILE TIME: 093619

DEVICES: 24X80, 32X80, 43X80, 27X132

    5   10   15   20   25   30   35   40   45   50   55   60   65   70   75   80   85   90   95  100  105  110  115  120  125  130
***************************************************************************************************************************************
SSM       S     CUSTOMER MASTER FILE - 2 SDATE:S.......SID:S======
                            (CURSOR) -

SCUSTOMER #:S=======
SNAME:S==================
S---- MAILING ADDRESS -----          S-------- SALES INFORMATION --------
SNAME-2:S================            SCURRENT YEAR TO DATE TOTAL:S==========
SSTREET:S================            S LAST YEAR TO DATE TOTAL:S==========
SCITY  :S========SSTATE:S==          S PRIOR YEAR TO DATE TOTAL:S==========
SZIP   :S===== ===
                                     S---- SALES BY BUSINESS SEGMENT ------
S-------                             SBUSINESS SEGMENT:S=== SSALES FORCE:S====
SREPORTING AREA  :S======            SCURRENT YEAR TO DATE TOTAL:S==========
SREPORTING AREA  :S======            S LAST YEARS  TOTAL:S==========
SREPORTING AREA  :S======
SREPORTING AREA  :S======
SREPORTING AREA  :S======
S-------

SDATE OF LAST CHANGE:S== ==          SDATE ADDED TO FILE:S== == ==                                          P
S------------     KEY ASSIGNMENTS              PF24 - CUSTOMER MASTER FILE
SPF5  - ADD    CUSTOMER
SPF6  - UPDATE CUSTOMER
SPF12 - DISPLAY CUSTOMER
................................................................................................................................
***************************************************************************************************************************************
    5   10   15   20   25   30   35   40   45   50   55   60   65   70   75   80   85   90   95  100  105  110  115  120  125  130
```

```
C8604M                       IDMS-DC MAP UTILITY                    DATE: 12/24/86  TIME: 104827  PAGE   29

REPORT FOR MAP  PPSM200M              VERSION    1      COMPILE DATE: 12/08/86      COMPILE TIME: 101704

DEVICES: 24X80, 32X80, 43X80, 27X132

       5   10   15   20   25   30   35   40   45   50   55   60   65   70   75   80   85   90   95  100  105  110  115  120  125  130
     *******************************************************************************************************************************
SSBM            SPRODUCT INFORMATION UPDATE      SDATE:S........SID:S:====3
                                    (CURSOR) -

SPACKAGE NO:S======

SPACKAGE NAME:S========================  SPACKAGE STYLE:S====

SBUSINESS  SEGMENT:S===      SSALES FORCE:S===

SGROUP CODES:SN.S.P.:S===== ST.C.:S===== SL - 1:S=====

SDIVISION DEPARTMENT INDICATOR:S= SSTATUS:S=  SUNIT-OF-USE INDICATOR:S=

SOLD CODE:S======   SCONTROL SUBS:S=

S------------ KEY ASSIGNMENTS ------------
                    SPF12 - DISPLAY
SPF5  - ADD PRODUCT        S    PRODUCT          ===>S=======
SPF6  - UPDATE PRODUCT     S    BUSINESS SEGMENT ===>S===
                                SSALES   FORCE   ===>S===

                                                                          P
     .....................................................................................................................

       5   10   15   20   25   30   35   40   45   50   55   60   65   70   75   80   85   90   95  100  105  110  115  120  125  130
     *******************************************************************************************************************************
```

C860MH   IDMS-DC MAP UTILITY   DATE: 12/24/86 TIME: 104827 PAGE 39

REPORT FOR MAP PPSM300M   VERSION   1   COMPILE DATE: 12/08/86   COMPILE TIME: 140102

DEVICES: 24X80, 32X80, 43X80, 27X132

```
     5   10   15   20   25   30   35   40   45   50   55   60   65   70   75   80   85   90   95  100  105  110  115  120  125  130
*************************************************************************************************************************************
SSM              SZIP CODE UPDATE             SDATE:S.......SID:S======
                          (CURSOR) -

SZIP CODE:S===== ====             SCITY:S:============ SSTATE:S==
SCOUNTY:S===============   SSHIPPING POINT:S===   SGEO CODE:S=====
S-------- TERRITORIES ----------
SBUSINES SEGMENT:S===  SSALES FORCE:S===   SPRIME TERR:S=====   SLOCK INDICATOR:S=
S=====         ====         ====         ====         ====
S=====         ====         ====         ====         ====
S-------- BUSINESS SEGMENT TERRITORY DESIGNATIONS --------

SBUSINESS SEGMENT:S===    SSALES FORCE:S===

SCURRENT:S===== SFUTURE:S===== SOLD:S===== SOLD-OLD:S=====

SOLD PRIME:S===== SOLD-OLD PRIME:S=====

S-------- KEY ASSIGNMENTS --------
                           SPF12 - DISPLAY
SPF6  - UPDATE ZIP CODE       S  - ZIP CODE        ====>S=====
                              S  - BUSINESS SEGMENT ====>S===
SPF24 - ZIP CODE UPDATE - 2   $  - SALES FORCE      ====>S===
.................................................................................................................................
     5   10   15   20   25   30   35   40   45   50   55   60   65   70   75   80   85   90   95  100  105  110  115  120  125  130
```

244   Systems Design in a Database Environment

```
C8404M                          IDMS-DC  MAP UTILITY                        DATE: 12/24/86  TIME: 104827  PAGE  50

REPORT FOR MAP  PPSM400M                   VERSION    1      COMPILE DATE: 12/09/86      COMPILE TIME: 111021

DEVICES: 24X80, 32X80, 43X80, 27X132

     5   10   15   20   25   30   35   40   45   50   55   60   65   70   75   80   85   90   95  100  105  110  115  120  125  130
*********************************************************************************************************************************
SSM              STERRITORY UPDATE              SDATE:S.......SID:S======
                                                (CURSOR) -

SBUSINESS SEGMENT:S===                    SSALES FORCE:S==

SF NUMBER        S----- TERRITORIES -----
         DESCRIPTION          F NUMBER          DESCRIPTION
S= ====  ===========  ==============  : ====  =======================
S= ====  ===========  ==============  : ====  =======================
S-               REGION UPDATE --------------
SF CODE  NAME          F CODE   NAME          F  CODE   NAME
S= ==    ========      = ==     ========      =  ==     ========
S= ==    ========      = ==     ========      =  ==     ========
S-               DISTRICT UPDATE -------------
SF CODE  NAME          F CODE   NAME          F  CODE   NAME
S= ===   =========     = ===    =========     =  ===    =========
S= ===   =========     = ===    =========     =  ===    =========
S-               TRADE CLASS UPDATE ----------
SF CODE  F CODE  F CODE  F CODE  F CODE  F CODE  F CODE  F CODE
S= ==    = ==    = ==    = ==    = ==    = ==    = ==    = ==
S-               KEY ASSIGNMENT
SF COLUMN: A = ADD   C = CHANGE   D = DELETE

SPF6 -- UPDATE DATA
                                                                                  P
.................................................................................................................
*********************************************************************************************************************************
     5   10   15   20   25   30   35   40   45   50   55   60   65   70   75   80   85   90   95  100  105  110  115  120  125  130
```

```
C860MM                          IDMS-DC  MAP UTILITY                        DATE: 12/24/86  TIME: 104827 PAGE  58

REPORT FOR MAP   PPSM410M              VERSION    1        COMPILE DATE: 12/09/86      COMPILE TIME: 134902

DEVICES: 24X80, 32X80, 43X80, 27X132

     5   10   15   20   25   30   35   40   45   50   55   60   65   70   75   80   85   90   95  100  105  110  115  120  125  130
*****************************************************************************************************************************
SSMM          SSHIPPING INFORMATION UPDATE        SDATE:S........SID:S=====         (CURSOR) -

S---------------- SHIPPING POINT -------------
SF  CODE      NAME                   F  CODE      NAME
S=  ===   ====================   =   ===   ================
S=  ===   ====================   =   ===   ================
S=  ===   ====================   =   ===   ================

S------------- DESTINATION CODE ------------
SF  CODE      NAME                   F  CODE      NAME
S=  ===   ================   =   ===   ================
S=  ===   ================   =   ===   ================
S=  ===   ================   =   ===   ================

S--------- DEPARTMENT CODES ---------
SF  CODE   F  CODE   F  CODE   F  CODE
S=  ===    =  ===    =  ===    =  ===

S---------- KEY ASSIGNMENT ----------
SF COLUMN: A = ADD  C = CHANGE  D = DELETE
                                                                     P
SPF6 - UPDATE DATA
.......................................................................................................................
*****************************************************************************************************************************
     5   10   15   20   25   30   35   40   45   50   55   60   65   70   75   80   85   90   95  100  105  110  115  120  125  130
```

```
C8404M                        IDMS-DC  MAP UTILITY                    DATE: 12/24/86  TIME: 104027  PAGE  73

REPORT FOR MAP  PPSM500M            VERSION   1    COMPILE DATE: 12/11/86      COMPILE TIME: 133214

DEVICES: 24X80, 32X80, 43X80, 27X132

     5   10   15   20   25   30   35   40   45   50   55   60   65   70   75   80   85   90   95  100  105  110  115  120  125  130
SS#M             SMAJOR  CODE  UPDATE           SDATE:S........ SID:S======
                                       (CURSOR) -

SMAJOR  CODE:S====

SGROUP NAME:S===================================

S    STREET:S================
S    CITY:S=========== SSTATE:S==
SZIP  CODE:S===== ====

STRADE CLASS CODE:S==     STERRITORY NUMBER:S====


S--------------- KEY  ASSIGNMENT ----------------
                                                   PF 9 - DELETE MAJOR CODE
SPF6  - UPDATE MAJOR CODE

SPF12 - DISPLAY MAJOR CODE
        MAJOR  CODE  ====>S=====                              P
        SGROUP NAME  ====>S==================
....................................................................................................................
     5   10   15   20   25   30   35   40   45   50   55   60   65   70   75   80   85   90   95  100  105  110  115  120  125  130
```

S&M   SUPER CODE MEMBERS   DATE: 12/29/86 ID: =======

SUPER CODE: ===== *1*
SUPER CODE NAME: *2*
MAJOR CODES

CODE	CODE	CODE	CODE	CODE
3				

FF12 - DISPLAY SUPER CODE   KEY ASSIGNMENT *4*
       SUPER CODE <===> ==== *5*
       SUPER NAME ====>
PLEASE SELECT NEXT FUNCTION

```
C86404M                        IDMS-DC MAP UTILITY                    DATE: 12/24/86 TIME: 104827 PAGE  65

REPORT FOR MAP  PPSM420M            VERSION    1      COMPILE DATE: 12/11/86      COMPILE TIME: 105148

DEVICES: 24X80, 32X80, 43X80, 27X132

     5   10   15   20   25   30   35   40   45   50   55   60   65   70   75   80   85   90   95  100  105  110  115  120  125  130
===================================================================================================================================
SS4M            SMAJOR CODE REPORT LEVEL           SDATE:S........ SID:S=====
                                        (CURSOR) -

S     BATCH            BATCH IDENTIFICATION
S     TOTAL
S     ===

$ F--LEVEL0--------- REPORT LEVEL DESCRIPTION ------------------------------------

S = ===
S = ===
S = ===

SMAJOR CODE -------- SUPER STRUCTURES LEVEL NUMBERS ---------------
S F         $01   $02   $03   $04   $05   $06   $07
S = ====  ====  ====  ====  ====  ====  ====
S = ====  ====  ====  ====  ====  ====  ====
S = ====  ====  ====  ====  ====  ====  ====
S F COLUMN: A = ADD  C = CHANGE  D = DELETE
S         KEY ASSIGNMENTS

SPF20 - PROCESS REPORT
SPF24 - MAJOR CODE REPORT LEVEL - 2
...............................................................P...................................................................

     5   10   15   20   25   30   35   40   45   50   55   60   65   70   75   80   85   90   95  100  105  110  115  120  125  130
```

A.3 Report Format for Sales/Marketing System

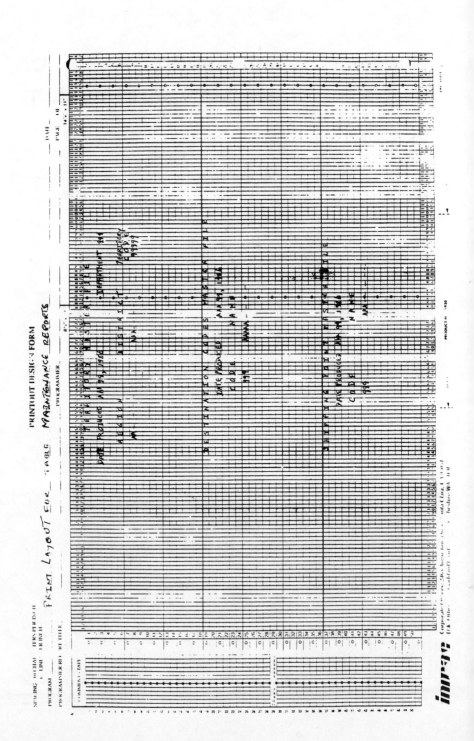

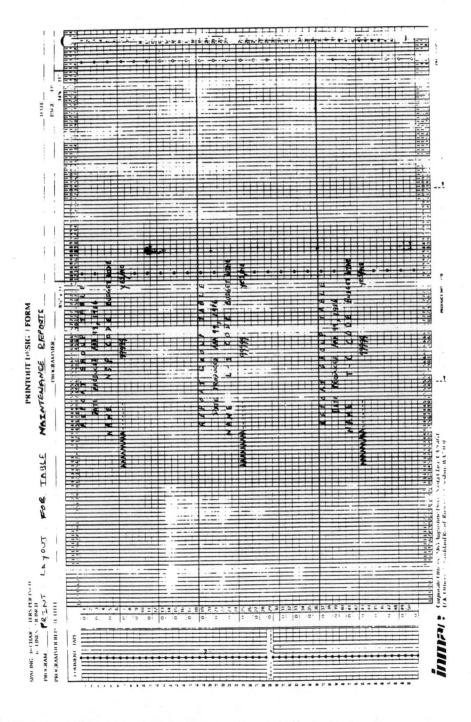

252   Systems Design in a Database Environment

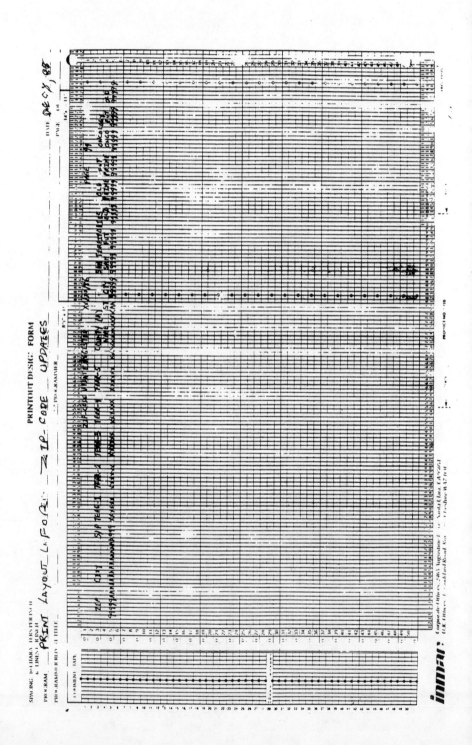

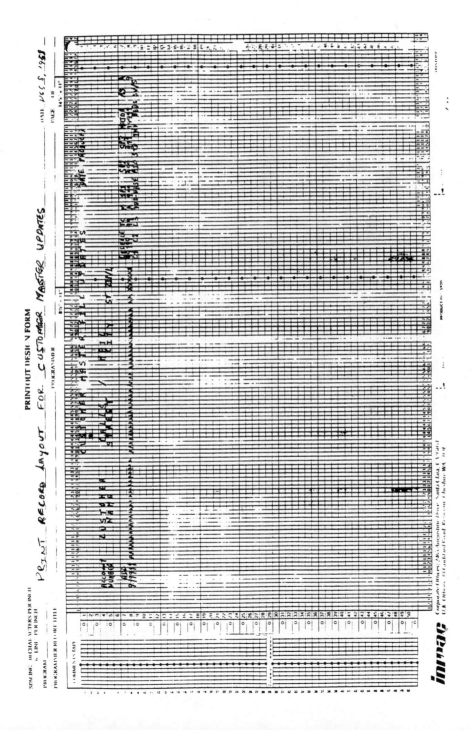

234 Systems Design in a Database Environment

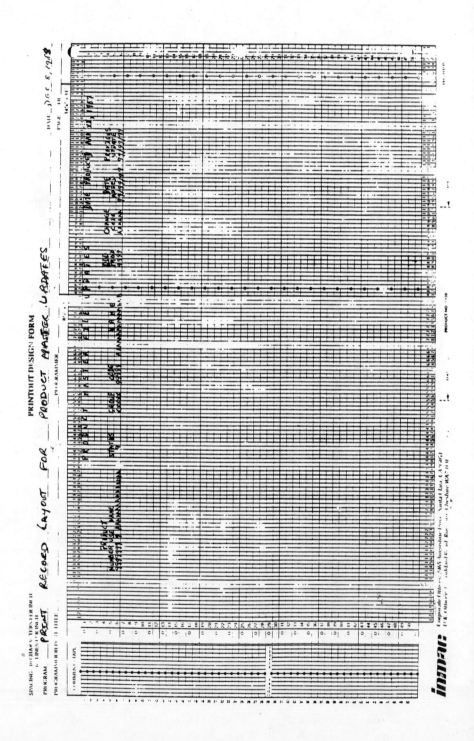

A.4 Processing Details for Sales/Marketing System

Retrieval from Database

Retrieving data for editing or display will depend on satisfying the many times compound-key requirements of the given record type.

CUSMST can, for example, be retrieved by CALC on customer number or by index using customer name.

CUSBS requires a key field (in this case, customer number), plus business segment and sales force values, as does TERMSC (territory, REGMSC, and DISMSC).

Screen 1.0 Record Types and Sets

```
PR-CUSTMST            CALC
PR-CUSMST--CUSCAD     via using:
                         P1003-BS-CODE
                         P1003-BS-SALES FORCE-TYPE-CODE
PR-CUSMST-CUSDC       via using:
                         P1003-SHIP POINT-CODE
PR-CUSBS              CALC
PR-CUSBS-CUSSTC       via using:
                         P1019-CUST-TO-SUBCLASS-CODE
PR-BGMST-BGCUS-       via using:
                         P1040-SIS NUMBER
```

Screen 1.1

PR-CUSMST   CALC: P1001-SIS NUMBER
PR-CUSMST-INAME   via using:
                            P1001-CUST-NAME
PR-CUSMST-CUSMAD   via using:
                            P1004-SF-KEY: P1004-BS-CODE
                            P1004-BS-SALES FORCE-TYPE-CODE
PR-CUSBS   CALC: P1018-SIS-NUMBER
                            P1018-B-SCOPE
                            P1018-BS-SALES-FORCE-TYPE-CODE

Screen 2.0

PR-PPMST   CALC: P1011-PROD-PKG-NUMBER
PR-BGMST   CALC: P1038-BUY GROUP NUMBER
PR-BGMST-INAME   Index using:
                            P1038-BUY GROUP-NAME
PR-SFORCE   CALC: using:
                            P1066-BL-CODE
                            P1066-BS-SALES-FORCE-TYPE-CODE

Screen 3.0

PR-ZIPMST   CALC   P1025 ZIP CODE
                       P1025 EXT-ZIP CODE
PR-TERMSC   CALC   P1026-TERR NUMBER
PR-DISMSC-TERMSC   P1026-BS-CODE
                       P1026-BS-SALES FORCE-TYPE CODE
PR-ZIPMST-ZIPGEO via
PR-STCNTY   CALC: P1037-ZIP-GEO-STATE-CODE
                       CALC: P1037-ZIP-GEO-CNTY-CODE

Screen 4.0

PR-TERMSC	CALC: P1026-TERR NUMBER
	P1026-BS-CODE
	P1026-BS-SALES
	FORCE-TYPE-CODE
PR-REGMSC	CALC: P1028BS-CODE
	P1028-BS-SALES
	FORCE-TYPE-CODE
	P1028-REG NUMBER
PR-DISMSC	CALC: P1030-BS-CODE
	P1030-BS-SALES
	FORCE-TYPE-CODE
	P1030-DIST NUMBER
PR-TCMST	CALC: P1063-CUST-TC-CODE

Screen 4.1

PR-DCMST	CALC: P1069-DC-CODE

Screen 4.2

PR-BGMST	CALC: P1038-BUY-GROUP NUMBER
PR-BGMST-INAME INDEX	P1038-BUY-GROUP-NAME
PRBGNEST	
PR-BGMST-EXPLODE via	
PR-BGMST-IMPLODE via	

Screen 5.0

PR-BGMST	CALC: P1038-BUY-GROUP-NUMBRR
PR-BGMST-INAME INDEX	P1038-BUY-GROUP-NAME

Screen 5.1

PR-BGMST CALC	P1038-BUY-GROUP-NUMBER
PR-BGMST-INAME INDEX	P1038-BUY-GROUP-NAME
PR-BGMST-EXPLODE via (PR-BGNEST)	
PR-BGMST-IMPLODE via (PR-BGNEST)	

Screen 5.3

```
PR-BGMST CALC            P1038-BUY-GROUP-NUMBER
PR-BGMST-INAME INDEX P1038-BUY-GROUP-NUMBER
PR-BGMST-BGCUS via
PR-CUSMST CALC           P1001-SIS-NUMBER
PR-CUSMST-CUSCAD via P1001-SIS-NUMBER
```

B

A Guide to Selecting Case Tools

(Sample responses to a questionnaire on selection criteria for CASE tools for a hospital insurance plan)

B.1 AMS' RESPONSE TO QUESTIONNAIRE: SELECTION CRITERIA FOR CASE TOOLS

American Management Systems, Inc. (AMS) offers a practical solution to Computer-Aided Software Engineering: the Life-cycle Productivity System (LPS). LPS treats the productivity problem the way it should be treated: as a total life-cycle concern, rather than as the need simply to produce lines of code faster.

LPS is not just another paper methodology. Rather, it is a comprehensive set of computer software, user guides, and training designed to help you accomplish all life-cycle activities faster and better. It is compatible with all popular system development methodologies and can also be used with most in-house development standards.

LPS consists of the following five major components:

- Strategic Systems Planner
- Systems Designer
- System Implementer
- CORE Foundation Software
- Life-cycle Project Manager

Each of these major components has several modules corresponding to key life-cycle activities.

Because LPS is more than just a design aid, it would be possible to write a book and still not explore thoroughly each of the enclosed questions. However, the following adequately addresses the questions, and coupled with our presentation should give you a more complete representation of LPS.

QUESTION 1: *Is the underlying structure of your CASE tool a DBMS or data dictionary?*

The Life-cycle Productivity system is composed of many modules encompassing the entire systems development and maintenance process. The Excelerator (by Index Technologies) portion of the LPS System Designer uses a data dictionary as the underlying structure, but also adds database capabilities for keeping track of other entities (like processes, data flows and graphs). Other modules in LPS (Incident Tracking, Test Logging, Deliverables Tracking, etc.) are implemented with dBASE III+, utilizing that inherent database framework.

Although the Life-cycle Productivity System is composed of many modules from disparate sources, most modules can share data. Excelerator can feed data-flow diagram information to the Matrix Organizer and Analyzer. Project Workbench data drives the Deliverables Tracking System. Screens and Reports designed in Excelerator are used to directly generate mainframe code. Record layouts and field lengths are converted to COBOL data divisions for use with the COBOL workbench.

By combining the best tools available for system design, planning, implementation, and management, LPS avoids being locked into one data structure or format. With bridges linking the parts together LPS becomes far greater than just the sum of its parts.

QUESTION 2: *Does your CASE tool share or will it share, in the near future, file formats and specifications with other noncompeting CASE manufacturers? If yes, please explain.*

The microcomputer portion of LPS is built around Excelerator, Project Workbench, dBASE III+, Lotus 1-2-3, and the Micro Focus COBOL compiler. All share data among themselves, and all can share data with other programs. The following is a program-specific file-sharing overview:

Excelerator: Excelerator data file formats are published, and many interfaces to popular programs have been developed.

Project Workbench: Project Workbench exports most of its data to ASCII files for import into most popular programs.

dBASE: dBASE III can read and write ASCII data and comma delimited data. Most programs can write ASCII files easily read by dBASE.

Lotus 1-2-3: 1-2-3 can read and write ASCII data and comma delimited data. Most programs can write ASCII files easily read by 1-2-3. AMS supplies a direct interface to Excelerator export files.

Micro focus COBOL compiler: Reads and writes ASCII text files.

QUESTION 3: *Describe your CASE tool's ability to read procedure and source libraries and create CASE components specifications for existing systems.*

We are currently developing reverse engineering programs for inclusion into LPS. These programs will evaluate current systems and place specifications into the Excelerator dictionary.

QUESTION 4: *Describe how your CASE tool interfaces with other CASE design tools.*

As described in question 2, LPS can communicate data to any program that reads ASCII data. In addition, Excelerator graphs data can be converted into almost any format with C language programs.

QUESTION 5: *Does the tool have graphical methodologies capable of exploding design diagrams and dictionary specifications to a reasonable depth?*

The Excelerator portion of Systems Designer allows for up to 9 levels of data-flow diagram explosion, as well as 9 levels of structure chart and 9 levels of data-modeling explosion.

QUESTION 6: *Is your tool capable of executing with window capabilities?*

Because LPS is composed of system components built by other companies we are dependent upon the windowing plans of other vendors. We intend to commit to a graphical interface, but must wait until implemented by our core products. Excelerator will offer windowing support in the future, as will 1-2-3 in version 3.0G. Ashton-Tate and Project Workbench's windowing plans are presently unclear, but both can run as dominant tasks under Microsoft Windows.

QUESTION 7: *Describe the tool's ability to do strategic planning on a corporate or functional unit basis.*

One portion of The Life-cycle Productivity System is the Strategic Systems Planner. In conjunction with the data modeling facility in Excelerator, and the LPS Matrix Organizer/Analyzer, our system offers a complete implementation of IBM's Business Systems Planning methodology (BSP), as well as supporting the TIP variation. This methodology makes extensive use of matrices to describe organizational characteristics. In addition to BSP strategic planning, Index Technology offers a program called PRISM, used primarily for strategic planning. PRISM works with Excelerator, and with all of the LPS modules.

QUESTION 8: *Does your tool provide a thorough means of prototyping?*

The System Designer allows for screen and report creation, using data structures defined in the data dictionary. These screens can be linked together, as well as transferred to the System Implementer for conversion into program code.

Prototypes can be created with the System Implementer using the on-line screen generation capabilities of LPS's CORE Foundation Software.

QUESTION 9: *Describe the tool's ability to provide physical design specifications from logical design specifications.*

System Implementer generates COBOL code for the data division of a program. A program is defined as a structure chart. In addition, the entire procedure division of COBOL programs can be generated, with each paragraph relating to function names on the lowest level structure chart, and the function description appearing as a comment below the procedure name. If the function description is entered as actual program code, then all the programmer needs to do is remove the comment character.

QUESTION 10: *What design specification reports does your tool provide?*

The Excelerator portion of System Designer produces many specification reports. These reports include:

• Record content analysis
• Key validation analysis
• Data model validation
• Data normalization analysis

- Screen report data usage
- Element access and derivation
- Graphical analysis

In addition to predefined reports, the System Designer contains a report writer that allows the analyst to create and save his own reports.

QUESTION 11: *Does your tool provide analytical support from design documentation? For example, does it indicate the completeness of relevant documentation?*
LPS provides several tools that generate portions of the design documents. A new mainframe-based capability of LPS will add "configuration management" of documentation in a future release.

QUESTION 12: *Can your tool's design and development specification interface with particular DBMs and data dictionaries? For example, DATA MANAGER.*
LPS has been interfaced to several DBMs and data dictionaries. We have built an interface from the System Designer to DATA MANAGER for one of our clients. Using the Excelerator Programmers Interface, it is possible to build data links with most DBMs and data dictionaries, several of which currently exist in the public domain.

QUESTION 13: *Can your tool be modified relative to an organization's existing design methodology? Please describe*
LPS supports most design methodologies. DFDs can be either Yourdon or Gane and Sarson. Data modeling can utilize Chen or Merise. Both structure charts and structure diagrams can be used to model program logic. Most of the other modules are supplied with the program code, allowing them to be modified in any way required. LPS is compatible with the most popular system development methodologies and can also be used with most in-house development standards.

QUESTION 14: *Describe your tool's ability to generate design, operations, and end-user documentation.*
The LPS System Documentation tools extract information from the Excelerator System Dictionary for combination with other graphical and word processing files. These can be manipulated with a desktop publishing system for direct production of user and operation documentation.

QUESTION 15: *Describe your tool's ability to maintain design and system changes.*

The new LPS mainframe-based repository will maintain all system documentation, from the planning and design to the implementation and testing. In addition, LPS allows system changes to be made at the PC level, tested, and then uploaded to the primary operating platform. Changes can also be made to the design documents by reverse engineering the changed program.

QUESTION 16: *Describe your tool's ability to generate programs for a range of platforms from design specifications. For example, COBOL programs for PC and mainframe.*

LPS utilizes the Micro Focus COBOL Compiler for PC development of programs. System Designer interfaces with this compiler, automatically generating data divisions and procedure divisions. In addition reports and screens created within System Designer are automatically generated to work with COBOL programs and our own CORE routines.

Our own CORE foundation software runs on the PC as well as on VAX machines and IBM mainframes. By allowing for COBOL compilation, IMS and CICS development, and CORE to run on a PC, a system can be developed up to unit testing on an IBM PC running OS/2. In fact, an entire mainframe system can be developed and then maintained on a PC for testing and implementing changes. In the vast majority of cases, programs developed on the PC need only be uploaded and recompiled to work on the mainframe.

B.2 INDEX TECHNOLOGY'S RESPONSE TO QUESTIONNAIRE: SELECTION CRITERIA FOR CASE TOOLS

QUESTION 1: *Is the underlying structure of your CASE tool a DBMS or data dictionary?*

Excelerator is built on an integrated and active dictionary: the XLDictionary. All of the facilities available in Excelerator are integrated with the XLDictionary. This integration provides the user with access to a comprehensive design database that collects information on over 50 unique entity types.

Unlike other CASE products, Excelerator's XLDictionary is both customizable and extensible. It is based on an open architecture that allows users to easily interface with other products. The XLD-ictionary is also highly differentiated. It is able to store, and report on, design information unique to each entity type defined to the system. In addition, it automatically collects detailed audit information for each entity, as well as information about the entity's relationship to other entities defined in the system. This information is extremely valuable in managing the overall design process.

QUESTION 2: *Does your CASE tool share or will it share, in the near future, file formats and specifications with other noncompeting CASE manufacturers. If yes, please explain.*

Index Technology's product line strategy emphasizes an open, customizable, and flexible approach to supporting the systems development life cycle (SDLC). Excelerator, the premier systems analysis and design product, functions as the core technology to which numerous other CASE tools are connected. Index Technology is committed to continuing to enhance Excelerator's base functionality in order to expand the depth of its support for systems analysis and design.

Future product and product line enhancements will include further integration with tools that support phases of the systems development life cycle not directly addressed by Index Technology's product line.

This integration includes additional connections to planning tools, code generators, databases and other systems development processes as well as specific project-related activities. Improved functionality in Excelerator and other Index Technology products will also include support for additional methodologies, operating systems, and software environments such as IBM's Systems Application Architecture (SAA).

QUESTION 3: *Describe your CASE tool's ability to read procedure and source libraries, and create CASE components specifications for existing systems.*

Excelerator currently addresses the maintenance phase of the systems development life cycle through interfaces to other tools that are designed to help the user work with existing system design components. These interfaces include programs available throughout XL/Group User Exchange Library as well as products available from other companies such as AMS' RECGEN and RECBUILD.

QUESTION 4: *Describe how your CASE tool interfaces with other CASE design tools.*

A commitment to open architecture is a key element of our product strategy. Excelerator is built on an extensible architecture that allows users to add/change/delete virtually any aspect of the product.

Using standard features, users are able to exchange information between our products, as well as between other software tools they might be using. The data file formats used by our products are published in our user manuals. These specifications provide the information necessary for most needs.

Our XL/Programmer Interface supports the integration of user processes and other software products. It gives a "C" programmer direct access into the Excelerator dictionary for building a seamless interface to other software.

Index Technology's open architecture approach to product development, and our Customizer and XL/Programmer Interface products, have resulted in a broad library of utilities that allow our users to successfully connect to a variety of software products. There are presently more than 20 interfaces to other CASE tools, 4GLs, database management systems, physical construction tools, and desktop publishing systems such as:

- COBOL/2 Workbench — Micro Focus
- APS — Sage
- TELON — Pansophic
- PowerHouse — Cognos
- Personal Leverage — D. Appleton
- Ventura Publisher — Xerox
- Project Workbench — ABT

QUESTION 5: *Does the tool have graphical methodologies capable of exploding design diagrams and dictionary specifications to a reasonable depth? Please describe.*

Yes. Objects in a diagram can be "exploded," or decomposed, to either additional levels of graphical detail or to an Entity Definition Screen in the XLDictionary. Decomposition from one level to another can involve multiple diagram types. These explosion, or XLDictionary navigation, paths are customizable for each entity and type of graph. There is no limit on the number of "exploded" levels a diagram can contain.

QUESTION 6: *Is your tool capable of executing with window capabilities?*

Index Technology is committed to using new and emerging technologies to continue to enhance Excelerator's functionality in response to our user's systems development needs. It is our intent to provide support for windowing environments such as the OS/2 Presentation Manager, XWindows, and its derivatives.

QUESTION 7: *Describe the tool's ability to do strategic planning on a corporate or functional unit basis.*

PC Prism, Index Technology's business and strategic planning product, is a flexible tool for modeling and evaluating an organization. PC Prism supports information systems planning, strategic business planning, enterprise modeling, data modeling, process modeling, to name a few. It translates business goals into systems requirements by furnishing an automated environment for strategic planning, enterprise modeling and priority setting. Information developed in PC Prism can be shared with Excelerator, or other tools being used to design and develop systems.

The connections between Excelerator and PC Prism links the information developed in the planning phases of systems development with the analysis, design and other phases of the life cycle.

QUESTION 8: *Does your tool provide a thorough means of prototyping? Please describe.*

Yes. Excelerator offers integrated screen and report design facilities. Each field in a screen and report mock-up can be tightly linked to elements and their associated attributes stored in the XLDictionary. Screen data entry facilities allow users to easily prototype their designs, including the testing of edit criteria. The screens can also be used to create an actual database for testing or on-line usage (Index Technology uses these related screen data files on its own internal specifications projects). In addition, the designs can be passed to many of the other tools that interface with Excelerator, eliminating the need to re-enter design information.

QUESTION 9: *Describe the tool's ability to provide physical design specifications from logical design specifications.*

Index Technology will continue to offer tight connections between Excelerator and tools that generate either application code or Data Definition Language (DDL). For example, we currently generate SQL/DDL for tables and views with our DB2 interface. The company is also committed to providing its own "design-to-code" solution.

QUESTION 10: *What design specification reports does your tool provide?*

Excelerator offers many different reporting options. These include standard XLDictionary reports that provide detailed information about an entity's dictionary definition, audit attributes, and relationships to other entities; graph analysis reports that provide verification as to a graph's contents and correctness; extended analysis reports (standard and matrixed) that provide structured and data analysis information including affinity analysis, process analysis, and data normalization up to third normal form; and an ad hoc dictionary Report Writer that allows the user to create reports about information currently stored in the XLDictionary.

QUESTION 11: *Does your tool provide analytical support from design documentation? For example, does it indicate the completeness of relevant documentation?*

Yes. While all analysis and design work can be done in Excelerator independent of a particular methodology, the product provides a comprehensive set of analysis tools that validate the design information according to widely accepted methodological practices. In addition to the standard XLDictionary reports and the product's ad hoc reporting capabilities, Excelerator includes seven major sets of reports: Graph Analysis, Record Content Analysis, Key Validation Analysis, Data Model Validation Analysis, Data Normalization Analysis, Screen/Report Data Usage Analysis, and Element Access and Derivation Analysis for a total of 37 standard reports and 25 matrix reports.

In addition, the documentation facility provides a means to track and control the completeness of deliverable documentation.

QUESTION 12: *Can your tool's design and development specification interface with particular DBMs and data dictionaries? For example, DATA MANAGER.*

Yes. Excelerator's Import/Export facility provides for a bidirectional transfer of any design data with any DBMS environment. The published specifications of the transfer file structure insure than any user can easily share data among tools and environments. Our present list of interfaces, which are available through our XL/User Group Library or Excelerator Services, includes links to:

- CDD/Plus from Digital Equipment Corporation
- Datamanager from Manager Software Products, Inc.
- DB2 from IBM

- dBASE III from Ashton-Tate
- IDD from Cullinet Software
- IMS from IBM
- Oracle from Oracle Corporation

Index Technology is also developing products targeted at specific DBMS environments.

QUESTION 13: *Can your tool be modified relative to an organization's existing design methodology? Please describe.*

Yes. The ability to customize our products to meet an organization's needs is an important element of Index Technology's product strategy. Customizer and Programmer Interface products allow users to modify or extend Excelerator to meet their specific development needs. Customizer enables users to easily define their own graph types, add new entities to the XLDictionary, create new menu structures, as well as modify existing, or develop new dictionary input forms. PR DEfine is the equivalent of Customizer for PC Prism.

Programmer Interface provides a set of "C" routines that enable developers to create seamless interfaces between existing products or specialized programs and Excelerator's XLDictionary. Together, these tools provide an organization with the means to develop an integrated workbench based on its own system design techniques.

QUESTION 14: *Describe your tool's ability to generate design, operations, and end-user documentation.*

Documentation is a byproduct of the planning, analysis, and design efforts accomplished with Index Technology products. The information recorded in Excelerator's dictionary can be output on-screen, to a file, or to a printer, using one of Excelerator's extensive reporting capabilities. These include canned XLDictionary reports, matrices and reports from Excelerator's structured and data analysis tools, user-defined reports from a flexible ad hoc report writing facility, or from the product's powerful Document Production Facility.

This last facility enables users to easily combine information from Excelerator's XLDictionary with information created/collected using other products, such as PC Prism, word processors, or spreadsheets. All output can then be moved to either Ventura, PageMaker, or Interleaf desktop publishing environments for final packaging.

QUESTION 15: *Describe your tool's ability to maintain design and system changes.*

Excelerator's XLDictionary provides analytical capabilities unmatched by many other CASE products. The entity relationships and the implications of proposed changes can be ascertained and evaluated with standard "where-used" and related reports, as well as the full functionality ad hoc Report Writer. The audit attributes within the Excelerator XLDictionary track: modified by, added by, last project, date added, date modified, number of changes, locked by, date locked, and lock status.

QUESTION 16: *Describe your tool's ability to generate programs for a range of platforms from design specifications. For example, COBOL programs for PC and mainframe.*

The Excelerator interface to MicroFocus COBOL Workbench supports COBOL development in both PC and mainframe environments, as do a number of other interfaces.

Index Technology has sold over 12,000 copies of Excelerator at over 1,000 different customer sites. These sites span a variety of environments including many different types of information systems and real-time, or embedded, systems including:

- a major information system for several AT&T groups
- the control system of the Bay Area Rapid Transit (BART)
- digital flight systems at Honeywell
- a personnel staff system at a California public utility
- the development environment for space flight programs
- the ordering system for a major financial institution.

QUESTION 1: *Is the underlying structure of your CASE tool a DBMS or data dictionary?*

Within the proposed environment, the structure of MSP's CASE tool is the Corporate Dictionary/Repository. Although managerView operates on personal computer Workstations, it is closely integrated with other MANAGER Products and their respective corporate dictionaries on the mainframe and is therefore considered dictionary driven. ManagerView also maintains its own local dictionary at the personal computer level representing work in process.

QUESTION 2:   *Does your CASE tool share or will it share, in the near future, file formats and specifications with other noncompeting CASE manufacturers? If yes, please explain.*

Within the proposed environment, the DICTIONARYMANAGER facility gives the user the ability to translate definitions from any MANAGER Products dictionary environment to the format of any chosen alien dictionary/directory. In a multidictionary environment, the strengths of each can be maximized for further control over automating the systems design process. Several vendors, competitive and otherwise, have written or plan to write interfaces to MSP's CASE tool environment. MSP feels it critically important to help ensure consistency of definitions across dictionaries/directories within a CASE environment.

QUESTION 3:   *Describe your CASE tool's ability to read procedure and source libraries and create CASE component specifications for existing systems.*

Within the proposed environment MSP does not provide a formal facility for what is commonly termed "reverse engineering," or the extraction of existing system components from source and procedural libraries for the purposes of re-engineering the systems. However, SOURCEMANAGER does make extensive use of reusable data descriptions and procedural routines (collectively termed reusable code) already in use at a given organization. SOURCEMANAGER can, therefore, identify and map reusable routines to both existing systems and systems currently in development. If the components of an existing system have already been documented on the Corporate Dictionary/Repository (DATAMANAGER), then the constituent system components can be downloaded to managerVIEW and re-engineered at the Intelligent Workstation. On completing the re-engineering process, the proposed system design can be uploaded to the Corporate Dictionary/Repository and incorporated into the organization's strategic information plan to identify missing components. After incorporation of the re-engineered system into the strategic information plan, the system is linked to a tactical implementation plan for each of the application development areas. SOURCEMANAGER can than be used to repaint and prototype the user interface dialogs and, on approval, regenerate the applications.

QUESTION 4: *Describe how your CASE tool interfaces with other CASE design tools.*

Within the proposed environment, although MSP's CASE tool does not overtly interface with other CASE design tools, the DICTIONARYMANAGER facility is a completely user-definable system that allows an organization to translate definitions from any MANAGER products dictionary to the format of any other chosen dictionary/directory. It helps keep definitions consistent, and it may also be used to generate database definition statements based on information contained in a MANAGER Products dictionary.

QUESTION 5: *Does the tool have graphical methodologies capable of exploding design diagrams and dictionary specifications to a reasonable depth? Please describe.*

Yes — in the proposed environment managerVIEW provides a flexible and tailorable graphical engineering methodology that facilitates the explosion of diagram components to further levels of detail. Logical and physical attributes of diagram objects can be defined locally [and subsequently uploaded to the Mainframe Corporate Dictionary/Repository (DATAMANAGER)] or automatically downloaded from the Corporate Dictionary/Repository. Diagram objects can be exploded to either like diagram-types (e.g., an object in a presentation diagram could be exploded to another presentation diagram) to show an additional level of detail, or, to a different diagram type (e.g., an object on an Entity-Relationship diagram could be exploded to a dataflow diagram) to provide additional semantic information. There is no limitation for leveling "depth." Supplied diagram types can be easily modified, or new diagram types introduced with ManagerView's Diagram Schema Editor.

QUESTION 6: *Is your tool capable of executing with window capabilities?*

Yes — managerVIEW operates in the Microsoft Windows (Presentation Manager) environment. The ergonomics of managerVIEW's Human/Computer Interface are directly derived from this environment. ManagerVIEW uses extensive multiwindow and "pop-up"/ "pull-down" menu capabilities.

QUESTION 7: *Describe the tool's ability to do strategic planning on a corporate or functional unit basis.*

In the proposed environment, METHODMANAGER's Strategic Information Planning (SIP) component enables the creation of a prioritized master plan for analyzing and satisfying an organization's information needs. The strategic information plan takes a wide view of an organization to ensure that the plan produced is comprehensive and does not omit significant interaction between different parts of the organization. METHODMANAGER is driven by a comprehensive and automated methodology — the MANAGER Method. The MANAGER Method divides strategic information planning into the following phases:

• Preparation
• Management Overview Study
• Full Strategic Information Plan

These phases identify and refine the organizational structure, the business processes and functions, and the data usage and dependencies. Automated checkpoints are positioned throughout the development process to ensure the completion of each phase before work can begin on the next. METHODMANAGER automatically utilizes Function Point and Affinity (cluster) analysis techniques to provide the planner with decision confirmation or mathematical backup for intuitive "hunches" about the overall information plan and the identification of potential subject databases. METHODMANAGER also automatically generates matrix diagrams showing relationships between many objects in terms of either the existence of a relationship or, if a relationship exists, the properties of it (e.g., inputs, outputs, assumed). Through the generation of matrices, the analysis and corporate rating of objectives, goals, requirements, and critical success factors, and the utilization of system priority tables, the Information Planner is able to produce accurate reports regarding the progress and completeness of the strategic information plan. Finally, the strategic information plan is linked to a tactical implementation plan for each application development project.

QUESTION 8: *Does your tool provide a thorough means of prototyping? Please describe.*

Within the proposed environment SOURCEMANAGER's Prototype Facility allows a proposed application(s) to be viewed as a cohesive unit before (or after) the generation of code or requirement specifications. Screens can be painted in either live or prototype mode, the former requires the input of requirement specifications for literal and variable fields. SOURCEMANAGER's Prototype Facility enables the developer to view these screens (live or prototype) either individually or as complete dialogs by gathering previously painted screens into prototype lists. In this way the developer can ensure the satisfaction of end-user requirements before the generation of code and/or the implementation of the application. Also, by presenting proposed applications to the end-user community as prototypes, end-users have an opportunity to become involved in the development of applications that they will be using on a day-to-day basis. Finally, on verification and approval of a proposed application, the application prototype can be easily reconciled with managerVIEW dialog-flow diagrams to ensure accurate and consistent documentation on the Intelligent Workstation.

QUESTION 9: *Describe the tool's ability to provide physical design specifications from logical design specifications.*

Within the proposed environment, for each application development project the relevant parts may be iteratively refined using the techniques of functional analysis/design and entity analysis. This process would take place within METHODMANAGER; Feasibility study, Business System Design, and User Interface Design. The result of this process is a functional model that consists of elementary functions with a corresponding entity model. Data accessed by elementary functions is represented in a Userview. The Userviews for a particular application are merged and input to a conceptual design process, which results in a conceptual schema. This schema (bottom-up) is then reconciled with the entity model (top-down) and, after any discrepancies have been resolved, a first-cut physical data design is produced.

QUESTION 10: *What design specification reports does your tool provide?*

Within the proposed environment, entity and userview models stored as entity association diagrams can be uploaded to a DESIGNMANAGER Workbench Design Area (WBDA). Models stored in the WBDA can then be normalized to first, second, or third normal forms. A variety of design specification reports can be generated from models having undergone the rigor of normalization.

Some of the more common reports include dependency, relation, and record lists; logical schema and network reports, cluster plots; IMS, and DL/1 physical design specification reports; DB2 and SQL/DS CREATE TABLE statement specifications; and intersecting data-element reports (for the identification of potential homonym/synonym situations). Workbench design areas can be easily stored on the MANAGER Products Administrative Information Dataset (MPAID) for later retrieval. All design specification reports are available from the Intelligent Workstation (managerVIEW). Normalized models can be subsequently downloaded to the Intelligent Workstation to ensure accurate and consistent documentation of proposed database designs.

QUESTION 11: *Does your tool provide analytical support from design documentation? For example, does it indicate the completeness of relevant documentation?*

Within the proposed environment, the METHODMANAGER facility automatically guides you through all phases of systems analysis, design and development. METHODMANAGER employs a set of methods (The MANAGER Method), which consists of four components: The Functional Model, Knowledge Base structure, Role Model, and A Set of Methods. The MANAGER Method will not only remind you of information you need to gather, but also verifies the completeness and consistency of data at every stage. It also generates reports and diagrams that can be easily reviewed by IS Professionals and End Users. For example, within the functional model there are relationships between functions. These are the tangible results of one function that feeds into other functions. These results may be represented in the form of a CID (Component Interface Diagram). The increasing degree of detail and the increasing rigor of the automated consistency and completeness checks ensure that the eventual design is correct and that the implementation phases may be reliably carried through.

QUESTION 12: *Can your tool's design and development specification interface with particular DBMs and data dictionaries? For example, DATA MANAGER.*

Within the proposed environment, managerVIEW, the intelligent workstation product, is architected to be DATAMANAGER dictionary driven. It is close-host connected to the mainframe Corporate Dictionary/Repository, and therefore a user may never need be concerned whether a command is for local (personal computer) or mainframe processing. ManagerVIEW routes all commands automatically within a design/development session. In addition, the DATAMANAGER facility directly interfaces with a number of DBMSs, including IMS/DLI, TOTAL, ADABAS, and System 2000/80. The DATAMANAGER facility in conjunction with DICTIONARYMANAGER offers support for interfacing with DB2 and SQL/DS. SQL CREATE statements can be generated for processing by the DBMS. The DICTIONARYMANAGER facility also provides support for IDMS/IDD and will allow users to define their own translation rules for converting MANAGER Products definitions to the syntax and format of any chosen dictionary/directory.

QUESTION 13: *Can your tool be modified relative to an organization's existing design methodology? Please describe.*

Yes — user definability is seen by MSP as key to the successful implementation of effective information resource management (IRM) in the CASE environment. Within the proposed environment MANAGER Products provide a comprehensive and flexible approach to the tailoring of diagram types and constituent objects and connectors on the Intelligent Workstation and member-type hierarchies and logical/physical attribute specifications on the Corporate Dictionary/Repository. MANAGER Products facilities such as User Defined Syntax, User Defined Commands, User defined Output, User Defined InfoSystem (on-line documentation), and the Diagram Schema Editor enable an organization to easily tailor the CASE environment to incorporate its terminology and Systems Development Methodology requirements. In an environment where Intelligent Workstations are closely connected to a mainframe-resident Corporate Dictionary/Repository, it is of paramount importance that these two components are compatible and synchronous (it is the only way that Close Host connectivity is possible). Within the proposed environment, Corporate Dictionary/Repository based member-type hierarchies, attributes, and connection rules can be automatically downloaded to the Intelligent Workstation tool (managerVIEW) in the form of a host dictionary schema that becomes the governing rules table for managerVIEW. In this way the mainframe and workstation environments are rendered consistent and compatible.

QUESTION 14: *Describe your tool's ability to generate design, operations, and end-user documentation.*

Within the proposed environment, the CONTROLMANAGER facility allows an organization to use the basic dictionary management software not only to model a complete system, but also to generate the appropriate descriptive documentation from it. There are multiple reporting functions within each MANAGER Products facility.

The DESIGNMANAGER facility, for example, provides an overall perspective of a logical design generated from its workbench, as well as a graphical overview of associations between records. There are multiple reporting functions within each MANAGER Product facility. Commands such as REPORT, LIST, PRINT, GLOSSARY are part of the basic dictionary management software and are not only tailorable, but flexible and powerful enough to provide instant where-used and impact-analysis reporting.

Complete on-line MANAGER Products documentation is provided via MSP's INFOBANK facility. Since every organization is unique, the user also has the ability to tailor MSP's documentation and/or append it with its own installation standard material. This documentation may be tailorable as appropriate for technical, operation, or end-user staff as necessary. In addition, the SOURCEMANAGER application generation facility provides extensive documentation, both embedded in the source code and printed separately. This will show the program's function as well as provide a graphic illustration of its structure.

QUESTION 15: *Describe your tool's ability to maintain design and system changes.*

Within the proposed environment, design and system elements may be maintained either at the local/Personal/Computer level, as in specific diagrams and/or held as members in various logical views on the Corporate Dictionary/Repository. System and design elements may then be tracked in various ways, for example, either by project or on a historical basis.

QUESTION 16: *Describe your tool's ability to generate programs for a range of platforms from design specifications. For example, COBOL programs for PC and mainframe.*

MSP has not as yet investigated the compatibility of SOURCE-MANAGER-generated COBOL code on platforms other than the IBM System 370 architecture. While OS/VS COBOL and COBOL II are fully supported, MSP cannot in good conscience state that other hardware platforms are supported at this time.

B.4 DESIGNAID'S RESPONSE TO QUESTIONNAIRE: SELECTION CRITERIA FOR CASE TOOLS

1. The underlying structure of DesignAid includes a DBMS for storing "design dictionary" data and DOS files containing the text and graphic documentation.
2. Dictionary data from DesignAid is accessible in a flat-file format. It can produce and accept through the load/unload facility its contents for use by other software products. There is also an Application Programmer Interface (API) that allows external

software to access DesignAid's dictionary data through a set of common calls.

3. There is a COBOL scanner in the DesignAid product that will scan code and populate the design dictionary with the referenced data elements.

4. DesignAid interfaces to other products as outlined in item 2 above for dictionary data. An example would be DesignAid's API interface to SAGE's APS (COBOL generator). In addition, there are utilities to allow DesignAid's files to be transported to such products as the Ventura Publishing System.

5. DesignAid has a feature referred to as file nesting that allows diagrams to be interconnected for decomposition purposes. There is no prescribed limit to the number of levels.

6. DesignAid has a split screen capability that allows the analyst to view two workspaces simultaneously.

7. DesignAid supports the graphical syntax for construction and maintenance of strategic models. If full methodology and analysis support of the methodology is required, we recommend the TIP Plan and/or TIP Define products marketed exclusively by Nastec.

8. DesignAid is used for screen and report mock-ups or user-view prototyping. This allows screens and reports to be easily created, and changes can be easily made. The tool has facilities for linking screens so screen sequence and interrelation can be demonstrated to the user.

9. The dictionary captures and reports considerable data that can assist in going from logical to physical design. In addition, if E-R modeling is done at the logical level, DESIGNAid can normalize the logical model, redraw the model, and create the input data needed for schema generation.

10. There are a variety of reports and outputs that represent and support the design specification.

11. The tool has complete analysis support for data modeling, process modeling, and real-time systems modeling.

12. The tool can interface with DBMs and DDs through the API or load/unload facility.

13. The tool can be modified and tailored in many areas to assist in deployment of an organization's standards.

14. DesignAid's unique integrated text and graphics editor allows for the creation and easy maintenance for any graphic and textual documentation.

15. There are extensive features in DesignAid to facilitate the changes to the systems documentation.

16. COBOL program generation is done by interfacing to TELON or APS. In addition, other code generators can be interfaced to, quickly and easily, due to Nastec's Application Programmer's Interface.

B.5 OPTIMA, INC — RESPONSE TO QUESTIONNAIRE: SELECTION CRITERIA FOR CASE TOOLS

General Notes

The questions supplied to vendors are meant to address the capabilities of a single CASE tool. Optima, Inc., in fact, supplies three separate tools that provide modular support of the development process and in combination cover the complete systems development life cycle. The tools, which run on standard PCs, are:

- DesignVision, a methodology-neutral interactive diagramming and documentation facility running under Microsoft Windows;
- DesignMachine, which provides comprehensive support for the Data Structured Systems Development (DSSD) methodology, from requirements definition through logical database design phases;
- Brackets, an interactive Warnier-Orr diagramming tool for building program structures, which includes COBOL code generation facilities.

Answers to the questionnaire will address Optima's complete product line. Where a special feature exists for a particular product within our offering, the product will be identified.

Additionally, all features described are as available in the current product release (version 1.1 for DesignVision, 2.0 from DesignMachine and Brackets). Any items under development or in design stages will be clearly identified as such.

QUESTION 1: *Is the underlying structure of your CASE tool a DBMS or data dictionary?*

Optima's philosophy is to segregate development efforts from production and operations. Therefore, one or more design dictionaries capture the status of development efforts and can be exported to the corporate data dictionary of choice on completion. PC DBMS technology is used to manage the information contained in the design dictionary and to facilitate querying and reporting.

QUESTION 2: *Does your CASE tool share or will it share, in the near future, file formats and specifications with other noncompeting CASE manufacturers? If yes, please explain.*

Optima not only provides this type of information to all registered customers, but also supplies query and reporting tools with DesignVision and DesignMachine to facilitate such access to design dictionaries. Additionally, Optima's experienced field consultants have provided direct support to clients wishing to develop product interfaces to support in-house development tools.

QUESTION 3: *Describe your CASE tool's ability to read procedure and source libraries and create CASE component specifications for existing systems.*

While reverse engineering features are not currently available in Optima's products, two approaches are under development, for release in 1989. The process-oriented approach will employ a code-structuring tool that will read in existing code and analyze its inherent structure. It will then reduce the structure to Warnier-Orr diagrams for subsequent modification and regeneration of source code.

A second, data-oriented approach will utilize the output specifications of an existing system (e.g., screens, reports, and files). After importing this information to a tool that will permit redesign of the output, the modified requirements can be distilled into the requisite database and process designs, and the code for the modified system can be regenerated.

QUESTION 4: *Describe how your CASE tool interfaces with other CASE design tools.*

DesignVision is supplied with an interface that permits exportation of data to DesignMachine. DesignMachine creates various Warnier-Orr diagrams, which can be stored or exported to Brackets for further development. Brackets can then import the diagrams as developed by DesignMachine.

Custom interfaces can be developed, as discussed in the reply to question 2. For example, one client uses Brackets to generate AD-ABAS database queries in the Natural fourth-generation language, and uses Brackets' export facilities to transfer the completed query to the mainframe for execution.

QUESTION 5: *Does the tool have graphical methodologies capable of exploding design diagrams and dictionary specifications to a reasonable depth? Please describe.*

All three products support this requirement. DesignVision permits the graphical decomposition of design diagrams, to a maximum depth of 1023 levels. Each step is automatically checked for balanced levels of inputs and outputs. Release 2.0, which is due for release in early 1989, will allow unlimited levels.

DesignMachine allows recursive definition of application designs through the establishment of subsystems. This means the depth of decomposition is theoretically unlimited.

Brackets allows the chaining of branches of a Warnier-Orr diagram to continue in separate files. Again, this approach permits unlimited number of levels of decomposition.

QUESTION 6: *Is your tool capable of executing with window capabilities?*

DesignVision was the first CASE tool available that provided full support for Microsoft's Windows environment. Windows has since evolved to become the industry standard, and has been endorsed by IBM for use as the OS2 Presentation Manager. It provides comprehensive hardware device support independent of application software packages, as well as the ability to share data between such applications and execute them simultaneously to maximize productivity.

Support of Presentation Manager is a key facet of Optima's strategic direction to be a full-service CASE vendor supporting IBM's Systems Application Architecture (SAA); DesignVision is the first step in the process. DesignMachine and Brackets currently can run as Windows Standard applications and will be released with full Windows/Presentation Manager support during 1989.

QUESTION 7: *Describe the tool's ability to do strategic planning on a corporate or functional unit basis.*

DesignVision would be the tool of choice for strategic planning. Its methodology-neutral approach can allow planners to choose from a variety of established techniques (e.g., entity-relationship modeling); or, through the extensive customization capabilities, planners can create their own diagram types, determine design dictionary attributes, and design reports and documentation for presentation.

QUESTION 8: *Does your tool provide a thorough means of prototyping? Please describe.*

Prototyping is not currently an integral part of Optima's tool set. To date, the approach has been to allow the developer to use one of many tools commonly available on site; once the prototype is finalized, it is brought into the DesignMachine to serve as the base for database design. As discussed in the reply to the third question, a prototyping tool is under development, which will permit not only the specification of new output designs, but the revision of existing system deliverables.

QUESTION 9: *Describe the tool's ability to provide physical design specifications from logical design specifications.*

The primary orientation of the current tool set is toward logical design, followed by code generation. A future release of DesignMachine will generate SQL DDL statements from its fifth normal form logical database designs.

QUESTION 10: *What design specification reports does your tool provide?*

DesignVision provides a standard set of report templates for the methodology models delivered with the product. As these models are changed by the user, or additional models are defined, the user has complete control over the appearance of the associated reports, through template control. These templates exist on up to three levels, so that alternative output definitions can be defined for the organization, specific methodologies, and/or individual projects. The interactive SQL query facility can also be used to generate custom reports from the design dictionary beyond those production reports defined with the product.

DesignMachine supplies the complete set of reports defined by the DSSD methodology from the data accumulated in the design dictionary. Examples are the output requirements form, output definition form, data requirements form, data definition form, logical output structures, and fully normalized database design.

QUESTION 11: *Does your tool provide analytical support from design documentation? For example, does it indicate the completeness of relevant documentation?*

DesignVision's interactive SQL facility permits project leaders to design their own queries to determine task completion. Frequently executed queries can be defined as one-word macros, which can be further augmented with SQL clauses at execution.

DesignMachine provides the most comprehensive support of completeness, predicated on the DSSD methodology. It maintains application facts in its design dictionary and guides analysts through the steps of DSSD, actually generating much of the work for the analyst from its inferential base at each step of the process. Completeness is documented by checklists and reinforced as each task is recommended for completion. Subsequent changes to earlier phases of the design will produce a ripple effect, identifying which areas of the project need to be reexamined in light of the changes. This ensures the referential integrity of the final design.

QUESTION 12: *Can your tool's design and development specification interface with particular DBMs and data dictionaries? For example, DATA MANAGER.*

Optima supports interfaces through both product features and the philosophy of an open data architecture. See answers to questions 2 and 9.

QUESTION 13: *Can your tool be modified relative to an organization's existing design methodology? Please describe*

DesignVision is extremely flexible in this respect. Through the use of pull-down menus and dialog boxes, users can create their own diagram symbols or choose from the library provided, and combine symbols into a diagram model for use with a specific methodology. For each graphical item, the client may specify what information is to be captured in the design dictionary, and how such information should be formatted on production reports. The ability to specify interactive syntactic and semantic validation rules (beyond the currently available edge balancing and SQL query features) is planned for a future release.

In DesignMachine, the rigorous support of the DSSD methodology allows for a lesser degree of flexibility. The trade-off is superior support and maintenance of design integrity, as well as the ability to predict and execute much of the work routinely performed by the analyst. The next release of the product will introduce "expert" modes of operation, which relax the application of methodology rules and afford greater flexibility in operation.

QUESTION 14: *Describe your tool's ability to generate design, operations, and end-user documentation.*

In addition to its flexible design dictionary specification and output formats, DesignVision is the perfect documentation tool by virtue of its support for the Windows environment. Using any Windows-compatible word processing package, or even desktop publishing software such as Aldus Pagemaker, it is possible to cut and paste information between these packages. This allows clients to choose the Windows product set they are most comfortable with, rather than requiring CASE vendors such as Optima to attempt to double as a word processing software supplier.

QUESTION 15: *Describe your tool's ability to maintain design and system changes.*

DesignMachine's abilities in this respect have already been discussed, in reply to question 11. By describing the changes in the requirements definition of an application, the areas where design modifications are necessary are automatically highlighted by the product. Such comprehensive support at a design level (as opposed to code-level modification) not only improves the quality of the finished product, but also results in accurate, updated documentation of the changes.

QUESTION 16: *Describe your tool's ability to generate programs for a range of platforms from design specifications. For example, COBOL programs for PC and mainframe.*

The DSSD development methodology applies equally well to all projects, regardless of their size. The effort required is proportional to the size of the task; there is no prohibitive overhead incurred up front for small systems, and the largest systems can utilize the same techniques without a geometric increase in complexity. Optima's tools work in concert with the methodology to provide support for a wide variety of environments.

Rather than using application generation techniques, which employ special development meta-languages to generate perhaps 80% of the boilerplate code for a system, Brackets works at a code generation level. This means the leverage factor in terms of inputs is not as high as an application generator, but the result is 100% of the application source code. Brackets is also not sensitive to particular physical implementation environments, as application generators typically are, which allows it to generate COBOL code for PCs and mainframes. Pascal and C language generation capabilities will be added in the next major release.

B.6 APS DEVELOPMENT CENTER — RESPONSE TO QUESTIONNAIRE: SELECTION CRITERIA FOR CASE TOOLS

QUESTION 1: *Is the underlying structure of your CASE tool a DBMS or data dictionary?*

The underlying structure of the APS Development Center is a "process" level dictionary. It contains information on each component of an application system (i.e., screens, report layouts, programs, data structures, etc.) and its relationship to any other component. It also stores process logic specifications, screen and report layouts, and database structure information. All of these specifications are used to generate one hundred percent (100%) of the code necessary to run a program.

QUESTION 2: *Does your CASE tool share or will it share, in the near future, file formats and specifications with other noncompeting CASE manufacturers? If yes, please explain.*

Yes. The APS Development Center offers an optional Excelerator Integrator. This component links the Excelerator project dictionary with the APS/PC subdictionary. It allows transfer of screen and report layout as well as data structure specifications transparently from Excelerator to the APS/PC workstation. Parameters are entered in a menu mode and the link is initiated by a mouse/window selection.

Sage is currently developing an interface to DesignAid and is a leading contributer in the EDIF CASE effort. The Electronic Data Interchange Format (EDIF) effort is attempting to define a standard interface to integrate any front-end tool with any back-end tool. Sage, and others, feel that this approach allows the customer to choose the best product in each class.

QUESTION 3: *Describe your CASE tool's ability to read procedure and source libraries and create CASE components specifications for existing systems.*

At this time, the APS Development Center can import existing BMS maps into its dictionary. Those maps can then be edited and modified using the APS Screen Painter. This is Sage's first release product in the area of reverse engineering.

QUESTION 4: *Describe how your CASE tool interfaces with other CASE design tools.*

See Question 2.

QUESTION 5: *Does the tool have graphical methodologies capable of exploding design diagrams and dictionary specifications to a reasonable depth? Please describe.*

No. Not applicable to code generators and the APS Development Center.

QUESTION 6: *Is your tool capable of executing with window capabilities?*

The only APS component that uses window technology is the APS/PC Link, Sage's micro-mainframe link. The APS Development Center can be used in a windowed environment, but the product itself (other than APS/PC Link) does not have windowing capabilities.

QUESTION 7: *Describe the tool's ability to do strategic planning on a corporate or functional unit basis.*

Not applicable to the APS Development Center and code generators.

QUESTION 8: *Does your tool provide a thorough means of prototyping? Please describe.*

The APS Scenario Prototype facility allows the user to display application screens in any desired sequence, enter data in those screens, and save that data for future sessions, create or change the screens, and pass data values to identically named fields on other screens. All of this can be done without generating COBOL code.

The conversion flow is determined by placing screen names in order in an ISPF environment. The list of screen names and their associated titles and descriptions can then be modified using ISPF editing commands.

QUESTION 9: *Describe the tool's ability to provide physical design specifications from logical design specifications.*

The APS Development Center does not translate diagrams into physical design specifications. However, the APS Logical View /DB/DC commands do provide a logical design approach to entering specifications.

QUESTION 10: *What design specification reports does your tool provide?*

The APS Development Center reports on entities in an application (programs, screens, reports, etc.) and their format/layout. Cross-reference reports are also available. Program reports show the scope of logical DB/DC commands used.

QUESTION 11: *Does your tool provide analytical support from design documentation? For example, does it indicate the completeness of relevant documentation?*

No. No.

QUESTION 12: *Can your tool's design and development specifications interface with particular DBMs and data dictionaries? For example, DATA MANAGER.*

Yes, the APS application dictionary can interface with most popular data dictionaries. Some customers have created links to Data Manager.

QUESTION 13: *Can your tool be modified relative to an organization's existing design methodology? Please describe.*

There is no need to modify the APS Development Center to fit an organization's development methodology. There is no enforced methodology inherent in the APS technology.

To tailor the technology to a specific DP shop, Sage offers an optional Customization Facility. This component allows you to create site-specific verb sets and routines. This magnifies your productivity gains by custom-coding macro type facilities unique to your organization.

QUESTION 14: *Describe your tool's ability to generate design, operations, and end-user documentation.*

The APS Development Center can generate application definition, scenario definition, data structure definition, program definition; report mock-up and screen hardcopy/field attribute reports can be produced.

For more information, see question 10.

QUESTION 15: *Describe your tool's ability to maintain design and system changes.*

Maintenance and enhancement changes are made at the specification level, not in native COBOL. This provides productivity gains to maintenance programmers as well as developers.

QUESTION 16: *Describe your tool's ability to generate programs for a range of platforms from design specifications. For example, COBOL programs for PC and mainframe.*

The APS Development Center is the only code generator available for OS/2 as well as MVS environments. The APS Development Center is also unique in its capability to generate to MVS or PC file structures. PC targets include MicroFocus CICS, IMS DB/DC, VSAM, and XBD System's SBD (PC-based SQL DBMS).

An application development can now reside entirely on a workstation (analysis through unit test). With a front-end design tool, APS/PC and Micro-Focus emulation environments developers can perform analysis, design, prototype, main build, and unit test functions without leaving the workstation. A developer would then regenerate for a mainframe target and upload compiler-ready source code.

B.7 MAESTRO'S RESPONSE TO QUESTIONNAIRE: SELECTION CRITERIA FOR CASE TOOLS

1. MAESTRO resides on a DBMS.
2. MAESTRO's open architecture allows interfacing to almost any other product on the market.
3. Using MAESTRO's procedural language, existing documents/programs can be scanned and data extracted into the various MAESTRO tools.
4. Data can be exported as a flat file from the other products and then read into MAESTRO.
5. Yes. There are no limits on the number of refinements within a graphic.
6. Yes — 12 Maximum
7. MAESTRO allows planning across an entire project, or local areas of a project. Planning information includes time estimates, elapsed time, resources, responsibilities, and task assignment.
8. Two types of prototyping are supported within MAESTRO:
   The first method used some procedural code and allows the user to toggle between screens developed in the analysis phase.
   The second method allows the user to input data into the above mentioned screens. This data is stored and can be replayed later within MAESTRO, or to the target machine for testing purposes.
9. Information can be extracted from graphics (for example, a data-flow diagram) and passed to a data dictionary.

For procedural design, a logical top-down process can be followed to produce the logical flow of an application. MAESTRO can take this pseudo-code and generate a skeleton program in the target language, which can then be further refined.

10. The type of reports are methodology dependent. Reports such as line attributes, relations, and "where used" are possible reports. The project Management System supports up to 2000 report output formats.

11. Time accounting for any document can be collected and reported against. It is up to the developer of that document to "flag" it as completed. MAESTRO's Project Management can monitor the status of all documents and tasks in the project.

12. MAESTRO can interface to all data dictionaries to a degree. In the case of Data Manager, extra routines have been built to ease queries, adds, updates, etc.

13. MAESTRO is not tied to any one methodology. The procedural language is supplemented by a powerful procedural/rule language on the PC that can enforce any standard. Currently, Yourdon and LSDM have been created and are supported as "shelf" products.

14. MAESTRO is a complete environment as well as a CASE tool. Documentation can be handled in a team approach through MAESTRO's extensive word processing capabilities. The documentation can be logically attached to a project and be stored on-line. Also the design specs, graphics, etc., can be routed to a laser printer for hard copy.

15. MAESTRO can handle many versions of an application. With this version control, it is possible to list or back out any changes made to the system.

MAESTRO also has a variety of tools to work on code not developed in MAESTRO. While this code cannot yet be returned to a graphic, tools for understanding and editing the logic exist today. All existing code can also be stored under the version control mentioned above.

16. MAESTRO is compiler independent. Any language can be used in all of MAESTRO's functions.

Generation of codes is table driven and can be completely modified for richness or even a new language.

MAESTRO will use any platform as a target machine. Multiple interactive and batch links to minis, mainframes, or PC's are supported.

B.8 RESPONSE FROM THE INFORMATION ENGINEERING FACILITY (IEF) TO QUESTIONNAIRE: SELECTION CRITERIA FOR CASE TOOLS

QUESTION 1: *Is the underlying structure of your CASE tool a DBMS or data dictionary?*

Yes, the Central Encyclopedia of the Information Engineering Facility is the cornerstone of the product. It is a DB2 application that stores all the information relevant to the business enterprise and its information systems. The Central Encyclopedia stores this information as a model and manages the relationships between the model data for each stage in the system life cycle.

The Local Encyclopedia is a logical duplicate of the Central Encyclopedia and stores the information relating to a model or model subset that has been downloaded to a professional workstation.

Model management activities occur on the Central Encyclopedia and include defining user access to models, copying, deleting, and renaming models. Model history-tracking provides a record of activities that change model contents.

The model merge feature allows multiple models to be merged into one model for further data sharing and control. The reverse capability is provided also on the Central Encyclopedia through model subsetting. The model subsetting feature allows multiple developers to work on the same analysis and design project simultaneously to facilitate large projects. Subsets are defined on the CENTRAL Encyclopedia and can then be downloaded to multiple workstations for parallel development. As each stage of the development process is finished, developers upload the subsets into the original model.

QUESTION 2: *Does your CASE tool share or will it share, in the near future, file formats and specifications with other noncompeting CASE manufacturers? If yes, please explain.*

Yes, file formats and specifications are currently shared via the IEF Public Interface. The bidirectional Public Interface allows import and export of information to and from the Central Encyclopedia. The Import facility creates an IEF model from files created outside the IEF, typically from data contained in some other data management product.

The Export facility provides a series of DB2 views and tables from the Central Encyclopedia from which information can be extracted. This information can be queried using any ad hoc reporting facility that supports DB2 databases, including IBM's QMF product, or formatted for transmission to another software tool (e.g., a data dictionary).

QUESTION 3: *Describe your CASE tool's ability to read procedure and source libraries and create CASE components specifications for existing systems.*

Re-engineering is a strategic direction for the IEF product, and is being investigated in detail within the research and development efforts established to support TI's CASE product. However, we are unable today to read existing source code or procedural languages and re-engineer it into Process and Procedure Action Diagrams for use with the IEF.

We have, however, written programs to read existing data sources (i.e., Data Manager, DL1 Databases, and DB2 Databases), format it into the IEF Public Interface Format, and load it into the Central Encyclopedia. The IEF then produces an entity-relationship diagram and entity hierarchy diagram (if appropriate) for analysis and design activities.

We have also imported data, process, and function information from the IEW product to the IEF Central Encyclopedia and thereby generated an entity-relationship diagram and a process hierarchy diagram for further analysis.

QUESTION 4: *Describe how your CASE tool interfaces with other CASE design tools.*

The IEF will interface with other CASE design tools through the Public Interface. For further details, please see answers to Questions 2 and 3 above.

QUESTION 5: *Does the tool have graphical methodologies capable of exploding design diagrams and dictionary specifications to a reasonable depth? Please describe.*

Yes, we support the Information Engineering Methodology. One of the benefits of this methodology is that there are deliverables from each stage, which feed the next development stage. For example, the entity-relationship diagram can be developed in the Information Strategic Planning stage and will then be utilized and further developed in the Business Area Analysis, the Business System Design, and the Technical Design stages. It will then be implemented physically through the 'Database Generation Toolset. The entity-relationship diagram could also be developed in the Business Area Analysis stage if no Strategic Plan is required. The same is true of business function/process information.

Within a given diagram there are many hierarchical levels that can be diagrammed as well. For example, in the entity-relationship diagram an entity type can be broken down into subtypes. Those subtypes (entity hierarchy diagram) can then be further decomposed to as many levels as necessary to define the business requirements. The business functions can also be decomposed multiple levels until an elementary process level is reached. There are no restrictions within the IEF toolsets on the number of levels within a given hierarchy.

QUESTION 6: *Is your tool capable of executing with window capabilities?*

Because Texas Instruments did not want to exceed a 640K memory requirement or significantly degrade the PC response time when using the IEF software, the IEF does not use windowing software in its execution. It does, however, provide similar functionality through the use of pop-up menus. At any point in the toolsets, if you need information that is provided within another diagram, it can be selected from a submenu and the information will be provided in textual format. With the advent of the Presentation Graphics in OS2, windowing will be provided.

QUESTION 7: *Describe the tool's ability to do strategic planning on a corporate or functional unit basis.*

The Information Engineering Methodology suggests beginning with an Information Strategic Plan when developing requirements for business automation. The IEF provides a Planning Toolset on the PC to automate portions of that stage. This toolset contains a Matrix Processor, an Indented List Editor, and Global Entity-Relationship and Function Hierarchy diagrams.

The Matrix Processor provides a set of predefined matrices used to analyze business needs and information requirements. It utilizes cluster analysis and affinity analysis techniques to identify the logical Business Areas, Natural Data Stores, and Natural Business Systems within the enterprise. The Indented List Editor provides a means to represent and manipulate organizational units and business functions. The Global Entity-Relationship Diagram is used to define the highest-level business entities and the relationships between the entities. The Function Hierarchy Diagram is used to define the major business functions.

The outcome of this strategic plan is an Information Architecture, a Business System Architecture, and a Technical Architecture on which the automation of that business can be supported.

QUESTION 8: *Does your tool provide a thorough means of prototyping? Please describe.*

Yes, once Business Area Analysis is complete and the Business System defined, the application can be generated to run under TSO for prototyping purposes. There is a TSO debugging facility for use that traces the business system activities back to the Action Diagram statements causing that action. In the event that processing changes need to be made, it is apparent to the Analyst/Designer what portion of the Action Diagram should be modified to trigger that change. Once the prototype is approved by the customer base, it is a short project to regenerate for an IMS-DC or CICS environment.

QUESTION 9: *Describe the tool's ability to provide physical design specifications from logical design specifications.*

The fourth stage of the methodology, Technical Design, addresses physical implementation of the data. At that time an automated transformation can be invoked to transform the entity-relationship diagram to a data structure diagram. The presence of this transformation means that an analyst does not have to be trained as a DBA in order to move from analysis to code generation. The DSD does allow those persons trained as DBAs to review and edit the "first-cut" design provided by the IEF.

The IEF will implement each entity type as a DB2 table, the relationships and partitionings as linkages, the identifiers as entry points, and the attributes as fields. The DBA can then specify additional indexes to improve performance. Within the DSD, additional specification takes place, such as the definition of the properties of the DB2 databases, tablespaces, indexspaces, and datasets.

QUESTION 10: *What design specification reports does your tool provide?*

All the graphic diagrams can be printed or plotted. Textual reports are also provided by the IEF.

The following reports are provided within Information Strategic Planning:

Business Function Indented List, Organizational Unit Indented List, Entity Type Object List, Business Function Object List, Business Area Object List, Current Business System Object List. Natural Business System Object List, Current Data Store Object List, Natural Data Store Object List, Information Need Object List, Organizational Unit Object List, Performance Measurements Object List

The following reports are provided within Business Area Analysis:

Entity Hierarchy, Entity Definition, Process Hierarchy, Process Definition, Attribute Cross Reference, Attribute Definition

The following reports are provided within Business System Design:

Procedure Definition, Procedure Step Definition, Commands List, Exit State List

The following reports are provided within Technical Design:

Field Definition, Implementation List, Data Definition Language

The following reports are provided within the Central Encyclopedia:

User Access, Model Access, Duplicate Object Name, Model Contents, Model Index, Entity Definition, Attribute Definition, Function Hierarchy, Function Definition, Elementary Process Information View Definition, Model Merge Conflict, Subset Expansion Conflict, Public Interface Import, Scoping Object Where Used, Function Point Calculation, Action Diagram, IEF KWIC Index

QUESTION 11: *Does your tool provide analytical support from design documentation? For example, does it indicate the completeness of relevant documentation?*

Yes, the IEF does provide analytical support within all stages of development. Since the model you build is the system documentation, it is important to check that model as it is being completed. An embedded consistency check implements the Information Engineering Methodology rule base. Models can be checked in full or part while working within a methodology stage. Furthermore, the portion of a model that has been scoped for use in the next methodology stage is automatically verified for consistency and completeness by the IEF.

QUESTION 12: *Can your tool's design and development specification interface with particular DBMs and data dictionaries? For example, DATA MANAGER.*

Yes, the IEF information captured during planning, analysis, and design can be exported from the Central Encyclopedia to products such as Data Manager. This has been done by an existing customer, as well as the information imported to the Central Encyclopedia from Data Manager. Ref. questions 2 and 4.

QUESTION 13: *Can your tool be modified relative to an organization's existing design methodology? Please describe.*

The IEF implements the Information Engineering Methodology. In order to provide the rigor and consistency required to generate error-free code and 100% application generation from diagrams, a methodology must be enforced. The Information Engineering Methodology is a proven methodology. It's a top-down, data-driven approach using both data and process modeling techniques. The IEM provides a framework of clearly defined stages, each with specific output deliverables. Within each stage, techniques are employed that lead to the development of high-quality, integrated information systems.

QUESTION 14: *Describe your tool's ability to generate design, operations, and end-user documentation.*

The models you generate using the IEF become the system and business documentation. All diagrams can be plotted or printed, with additional reports provided, as referenced earlier (See question 10). Much of what is generated can be used in User Documentation as well. An interface in the Ventura Desktop Publishing System can be used in conjunction with the IEF for publishing User Documentation.

QUESTION 15: *Describe your tool's ability to maintain design and system changes.*

Traditionally, design and system changes are made at the source-code level and then sometimes reflected in the system documentation. Within the IEF the changes are made with the graphic tools on the PC, so the model analysis and/or system design is changed there. Then the portion of the system affected is regenerated, compiled, linked, and placed in test/production. This ensures your documentation is always equal to the system in production, and it also ensures the changes are properly defined prior to implementation. This technique will save your corporation time and money in the maintenance cycle, as well as produce higher-quality systems.

QUESTION 16: *Describe your tool's ability to generate programs for a range of platforms from design specifications. For example, COBOL programs for PC and mainframe.*

Currently the IEF will generate applications to run in an MVS, IMS-DS, or CICS, DB2, VS Cobol-II environment. Work is underway to expand this environment further to include C language for PC and mainframe applications, and to move to a Unix-based platform with additional SQL-commpatible DBMS. Since the business area and system design are done independently of physical implementation considerations, they will remain valid for any platform we support in the future. Only the technical design and some construction parameters will differ by environment.

Bibliography

Atre, S., Data Base: Structured Techniques for Design, Performance, and Management, J. Wiley & Sons, 1988.

Brathwaite, K.S., Analysis, Design, and Implementation of Data Dictionaries, McGraw-Hill, 1988.

Brathwaite, K.S., Data Administration, J. Wiley & Sons, 1985.

Brathwaite, K.S., "Management Involvement in Data Security, Integrity, and Privacy," AGT Tech. Memo. No. 15, 1980.

Brathwaite, K.S., "A Study of Data Base Security, Integrity and Privacy in a Large Public Utility," AGT Tech. Memo, No. 20, 1980.

Brown, D., "RACF — A Program to Enhance Security and Control," EDPACS, Institute of Internal Auditors, Vol. 6, No. 12, June 1979.

Brown, P.S., "Computer Security — A Survey," NCC, AFIPS Press, 1976.

Brown, P.S., Security: Checklist for Computer Center Self-Audits, AFIPS Press, 1979.

Chen, P.P. (ed.), Proceedings of the International Conference on Entity-Relationship Approach to Systems Analysis and Design, North-Holland Publishing, 1979.

Chen, P.P. (ed.), Proceedings of the International Conference on Entity-Relationship Approach to Information Modeling and Analysis, North-Holland Publishing, 1981.

Courtney, R.H., "Security Risk Assessment in Electronic Data Processing Systems," AFIPS Conf. Proc. 46, 1977, NCC 97-104, AFIPS Press, 1977.

Davenport, R.A., "Data Analysis for Database Design," The Australian Computer Journal, Vol. 10, No. 4, 1979, pp. 122-137.

Dinardo, C.T., Computers and Security, AFIPS Press, 1978.

Durell, W.R., Data Administration, McGraw-Hill, 1985.

Engelman, C., "Audit and Surveillance of Multi-level Computing Systems," MTR-3207, The Mitre Corporation, June 1975.

Fernandez, E.B., Database Security and Integrity, Addison-Wesley, 1981.

Fosdick, H., Using IBM's ISPF Dialog Manager, Van Nostrand Reinhold, 1987.

Gillenson, M., Database: Step-by-step, J. Wiley & Sons, 1985.

Gillenson, M., & Goldberg, R., Strategic Planning Systems Analysis and Data Base Design, J. Wiley & Sons, 1984.

Hoffman, L.J., "The Formulary Model for Access Control and Privacy in Computer Systems," SCAC Report No. 119, May 1970.

Hsiao, D.K. Computer Security, Academic Press, Inc., 1979

Hubbard, G., Computer-Assisted Data Base Design, Van Nostrand Reinhold, 1981.

Kahn, B.K., "A Method for Describing the Information Required by the Data Base Design Process," Proc. Int. ACM/Sigmod Conf. Management of Data, 1976.

Katzan, H., Computer Data Security, Van Nostrand Reinhold, 1973.

Korth, H.F., and Silbershatz, R., Database System Concepts, McGraw-Hill, 1986.

Larson, B., The Database Expert's Guide to DB2, McGraw-Hill, 1988.

Lusardi, F., The Database Expert's Guide to SQL, McGraw-Hill, 1988.

Lusk, E.L., "A Practical Design Methodology for the Implementation of IMS Databases Using the E-R Model," ACM Vol. 4, 1980, pp. 9-21.

Martin, J., and McClure, C., Structured Techniques: The Basis for CASE, Prentice-Hall, 1988.

Novak, D., and Fry, J., "The State of the Art of Logical Database Design," Proc. 5th Texax Conf. Computing Systems (IEEE), Long Beach, Calif., 1976.

Statland, N., "Data Security and its Impact on EDP Auditing," EDPACS, Vol. 3, No. 4, Institute of Internal Auditors, Oct. 1979.

Weldon, J.L., Database Administration, Plenum Press, 1981.

Whitmore, J.C., "Design for Multics Security Enhancements," ESD-TR-74-176, Honeywell Info. Systems, 1974.

Yao, S.B., "An Integrated Approach to Logical Database Design," NYU Symposium on Database Design, May 18-19, 1978.

Index